Ineffability

AMS ARS POETICA, No. 2

ISSN 0734-7618

Also in this series:

No. 1. BRUCE BASSOFF. *The Secret Sharers: Studies in Contemporary Fictions.* 1983.

Ineffability

NAMING THE UNNAMABLE
FROM DANTE TO BECKETT

Edited by

PETER S. HAWKINS

&

ANNE HOWLAND SCHOTTER

AMS PRESS
NEW YORK

Library of Congress Cataloging in Publication Data

Main entry under title:

Ineffability, naming the unnamable.

  (AMS ars poetica; no. 2)
  1. Ineffable, The, in literature—Addresses,
essays, lectures. 2. English literature—
History and criticism—Addresses, essays, lectures.
I. Hawkins, Peter S. II. Schotter, Anne Howland.
III. Series: AMS ars poetica; 2.
PN56.I59I63 1983   809'.933   83-6013
ISBN 0-404-62502-9

Publication of this volume has been assisted by a grant
from the Andrew W. Mellon Foundation to The Graduate
School and University Center of The City University of
New York.

MANUFACTURED IN THE UNITED STATES OF AMERICA

Contents

Foreword

If, for Wordsworth, the "incompetence of human speech" is sad, others may see in that incompetence an extraordinary instigator of energetic *copia*, unwearying exuberance, synonymic reveling, the garrulous testing of limits. Still others may see mere non-sense in confronting, let alone trying to render, the ineffable. But even the latter must at times allow the fecundity of ineffability in urging us to metaphors and likenings—celebrating analogies even as we lament their inadequacies. To which the Tacitists might well reply: If language is man-made, then its celebrants may be no more than collective Narcissists, idolaters of self: the only All need not, cannot, ought never have been thought to be, consumable in words. And those with a yen for the poet Chlebnikov, who see each man as a new Adam, would herald the ineffable made effable in the new name newly given—the tiring-yet-invigorating task of endless creation by each after each—with intelligibility reduced to a needless, to-be-discarded, habit. Meanwhile, those content to see a Linnaeus as an Adam (or even a lexical Magellan) would see the folios on their shelves as impatient caravels that carry The Ineffable until that cargo leaves their hold and finds—once and for all—The Name That Can Be Told.

Each of the above stances and commitments, can lend itself to fanatic complacency, tepid espousal, or loud—or murmuring—uneasiness. Certainly the writers dealt with in this volume are not too given to Augustine's *pacem sabbati*—nor is Augustine himself, insofar as he is rhetor-writer. And the writers writing on those writers in this volume are often aware of and, fortunately, infected by the vexations inherent in verbal approaches to what is defined as untellable.

From the Introduction by Peter Hawkins and Anne Schotter to the Afterword by Bruce Kawin, the violence of silence is traced in many of its principal non-silent manifestations. For some, that violence comes to a head, in terms of formal poetics, in the Mallarméan emphasis on segmentation, *découpage,* the slash at the end of the line, the strophe, the poem, and the slash before the text embarks. But this volume as a whole would have us see that prosodic terminus as a late and limited symptom of a life-question: the mapping of experience in words written and spoken—and our vicissitudes, since Augustine, in casting some light on the boundaries of wording and on our struggle to articulate. If it does nothing else, the problem of ineffability spans the sacred and the secular—and reminds us how theology, that strange discipline of analysis around a center that is unanalyzable, not only engendered contemporary structures, but points to terrain we have yet to encounter.

This is a book that tries not to cross the *varco,* the pass, the straits—but to enlighten us about the nature(s) and configuration(s) of the *varco.* The world may not be made *"pour aboutir à un beau Livre"*; but concerns about the world and words have here, in collegial hands, indeed resulted in *"un beau Livre."*

—ALLEN MANDELBAUM

Notes on Contributors

ALFRED CORN is the author of three volumes of poetry, the most recent of which is *The Various Light* (Viking, 1980). His critical articles have appeared widely.

TIMOTHY CORRIGAN is an Associate Professor of English at Temple Univesity. He is author of *Coleridge, Language, and Criticism* and *The Displaced Image: Audience, Text, and Context in Contemporary German Cinema.* Currently, he is working on a study of visual technology in the Romantic period titled "The Poetic Spectacle."

MARJORIE GARBER, Professor of English at Harvard University, is the author of two books on Shakespeare, *Dream in Shakespeare: From Metaphor to Metamorphosis* (Yale, 1974) and *Coming of Age in Shakespeare* (Methuen, 1981). Professor Garber, who has also published articles on Shakespeare, Milton, and Marlowe, is currently at work on a study of the dramatic role of the audience in Shakespeare's plays.

PETER S. HAWKINS is associate professor of religion and literature at the Yale Divinity School, where he also has directed a program in religion and the arts. His published works include essays on Augustine, Dante, and Spenser in addition to a study of contemporary fiction, *The Language of Grace: Flannery O'Connor, Walker Percy, Iris Murdoch* (Cowley Press, 1983). In 1979-80, he was an Andrew Mellon Post-Doctoral Fellow at The City University of New York Graduate Center.

BRUCE KAWIN is Professor of English and Film at the University of Colorado at Boulder. His books include *Telling It Again and Again: Repetition in Literature and Film*; *Mindscreen: Bergman, Godard, and First-Person Film*; and *The Mind of the Novel: Reflexive Fiction and the Ineffable.* He has also published three books on Faulkner's screenplays and is a regular contributor to *Film Quarterly* and *Dreamworks.*

HEATHER MCCLAVE taught English and American literature at Harvard University before assuming her present faculty position at the Radcliffe Seminars. She has published various articles on American poets and women's prose, and has a book forthcoming on the sense of transcendence in Dickinson, Frost, Stevens, and Eliot.

STUART PETERFREUND, Associate Professor of English at Northeastern University, has written on all the major Romantics, and has published his work in such journals as *MLQ, SEL,* and *Genre.* A related essay concerning Shelley's idea of language has appeared in *Style,* and, along with the essay in this volume, comprises a part of the book on Shelley and language that Professor Peterfreund is in the process of completing. Peterfreund is also the editor of the journal *Romanticism Past and Present* and has published two volumes of poetry with Ithaca House. A third volume, *Mass Transit and Common Carriers,* is the winner of the first annual Curbstone Literary Award, and published by Curbstone Press in 1983.

MAUREEN QUILLIGAN is Associate Professor of English at Yale University. She is author of *The Language of Allegory: Defining the Genre* and of the forthcoming *Milton's Spenser: The Politics of Reading.* She is currently at work on a book about women in the sixteenth century.

ANNE HOWLAND SCHOTTER is an Assistant Professor at Wagner College, New York City. She has taught at Case Western Reserve, New York, and Temple Universities, and has held an Andrew Mellon post-doctoral fellowship at the Graduate Center of The City University of New York. She has published several articles on the *Pearl*-poet and the medieval Latin lyric.

ROBERT B. SHAW is an Associate Professor of English at Yale University. He is the author of a critical study, *The Call of God: The Theme of Vocation in the Poetry of Donne and Herbert* (Cowley), and of a book of poems, *Comforting the Wilderness* (Wesleyan). His articles and poems have appeared in many American and British periodicals.

WILLIAM SHULLENBERGER teaches literature at Sarah Lawrence College. Primarily interested in seventeenth-century literature and English Romanticism, he has published essays on Milton's poetics of faith and on *The Maid's Tragedy.*

LINDA CHING SLEDGE is the author of *Shivering Babe, Victorious Lord: The Nativity in Poetry and Art* (William B. Eerdmans, 1981) and articles on ethnic American literature. She has been a Mellon Fellow and a Rockefeller Fellow and is an Assistant Professor at Westchester Community College in Valhalla, New York.

KATHLEEN HENDERSON STAUDT was trained in Comparative Literature at Yale University and is now Assistant Professor of Humanities and Communications at Drexel University. She has written on conceptions of language and transcendence in the work of Blake, Shelley, Rimbaud, Mallarmé, and the contemporary British poet David Jones. She recently won a fellowship from the National Endowment for the Humanities for her work in progress on David Jones and modern poetics.

CHARLES WHITNEY is assistant professor of English at The Pennsylvania State University, Worthington Scranton Campus. He has held Mellon and NEH fellowships and has produced several articles on Bacon and a study of tradition and innovation, *Counterprophet: Bacon, Instauration, and Modernity.*

Introduction

What can anyone say about you, O Lord, and
yet woe to him who says nothing . . .

Augustine, *Confessions*, I.vi.

There is nothing to express, nothing with
which to express, nothing from which to
express, no power to express, no desire
to express, together with the obligation
to express.

Samuel Beckett, *Transition*, no. 5.

The essays collected in this volume are explorations of a problem as
difficult to articulate as it is to avoid: the struggle of language to speak about
dimensions of reality which are ineffable, that is, which lie "outside" the powers
of speech. The problem is one which is confronted throughout our normal
experience, as we daily discover our inability to express a thought or a feeling:
"I cannot tell you what this means to me"; "Words cannot convey our sympathy"; "I was speechless." But this confrontation of the limits of language has
also been the subject of the most sophisticated reflection, whether, as above,
it be the confession of St. Augustine that he can say nothing adequate about
God or Beckett's acknowledgement that there is, quite simply, nothing to
express. In either case, however, there remains an irrepressible "obligation to
express"—an obligation foreordained to failure, and yet one which even in
defeat presses hard against what cannot be said, perhaps even to the point of
enlarging our understanding of what the ineffable is.

Furthermore, if the juxtaposition of two figures as distant from one another as Augustine and Beckett indicates the abiding nature of the problem of
language and ineffability, it also demonstrates its persistence in the face of
vastly different assumptions about reality. If the ineffable is that about which
nothing truly can be said, perhaps (to borrow a line from Wallace Stevens's
"Snowman") we can differentiate between "the nothing that is not there and
the nothing that is"—between what we may call a "negative" ineffable and a
"positive" one. Although it has many secular manifestations, the latter is most
fundamentally a religious notion, one which acknowledges the great gulf fixed
between the divine and what human beings can think or say about divinity. In
our western, Judeo-Christian tradition we find manifestations of this both in the

1

taboo protecting the name of Yahweh—"I am that I am"—and in the rabbinic teaching that before God spoke the creation into being there was only the perfect silence of eternity. During the formative years of Christian theology the Fathers found a philosophic basis for received notions of God's transcendence in Plato's insistence that ultimate reality, because it is "colorless, formless, intangible essence, visible only to the mind" (to quote *Phaedrus* 247c), cannot be made manifest in the mutable, corporeal forms of diachronic speech. Thus Clement of Alexandria can write in the *Stromata* (chap. xii) a description of God's inexpressibility that gives evidence of a synthesis of Christianity and Platonism that will continue to be vital not only to Augustine and the Pseudo-Dionysius, but to Dante and Henry Vaughan as well:

> For how can that be expressed which is neither genus, nor difference, nor species, nor individual, nor number; nay more, is neither an event, nor that to which an event happens? No one can rightly express Him wholly . . . For the One is indivisible . . . And therefore it is without form and name. And if we name it . . . we speak not as supplying His name; but for want, we may use good names, in order that the mind may have these as points of support, so as not to err in other respects. For each one does not express God; but all together are indicative of the power of the Omnipotent.

If the rigor of Clement's Platonism stresses the inexpressibility of the "nothing that is," it must be remembered that Christianity on the whole emphasized the contrary mystery of God's communication. For not only did the unspeakable Word of God break the divine silence by speaking both creation and Scripture into being, but, more radically still, God spoke Himself into the body of our speech and into our mortal syntax: "The Word was made flesh and dwelt among us" (John i.1). Therefore any Christian notion of language and the ineffable must take into account not only the transcendence of God, but also the avenue of communication between our words and the divine Word which was opened up by the Incarnation—a route to be travelled by all practioners of what Marcia L. Colish has called "redeemed rhetoric."

In contrast to what we may speak of here as the positive ineffable there is the negative, the "nothing that is not"—not an overplus of being defying every category of speech, but a silence which is the absence of being. Out of this void our words call up everything that can be known, creating time and space and the only world any of us can ever experience. Rather than an all-expressive (and therefore inexpressible) Word—a Word which language can only fall short of—we have instead the linguistic equivalent of a "black hole." There may be, as Beckett said, "nothing to express," and yet the sheer fact of one's existence carries with it the "obligation to express." This is so because to fall silent is to disappear into the void from which we first spoke ourselves into existence "in the beginning." For this reason Mallarmé dreams of his Book and Stevens of his Supreme Fiction; for this reason Derrida proposes an infinitude of "writing," as if in the activity of language itself we might like Scheherazade keep the final night at perpetual bay. Thus the contemporary preoccupation with speech, and with the self-referentiality of texts, can be seen in part as a concern for human survival. To speak at all is to carry on an assault against silence; to express anything is to create something out of nothing.

The essays collected in this volume deal with works which range between these two poles of positive and negative ineffability; they also explore other aspects of the problem not easily classified into either category. We have chosen to emphasize the bipolarity, however, by beginning our literary investigation with Dante's *Paradiso,* certainly the fullest poetic flowering of the Christian Neo-Platonism of Augustine, and by ending with Beckett, perhaps the most striking spokesman of what we might call here the "negative way."

Between the extremes of Dante and Beckett is arranged a whole spectrum of authors and a variety of critical approaches. The collection makes no claim to be exhaustive, but seeks rather to offer the reader, in roughly chronological order, diverse conceptions of the ineffable and the literary tactics developed by them to carry on, in Eliot's phrase, their "raid on the inarticulate." With the major exceptions of Dante and Mallarmé, we have chosen to limit ourselves to works in English so as to make necessary linguistic analysis accessible to the reader. By and large we have also dealt with poetry, where the activities of language can be observed in their most concentrated form. Still, our essays also touch on drama and a variety of prose. While most of these essays are readings of particular authors, and in some cases of particular texts, we chose to open and close the collection with more general theoretical explorations of the subject. Our hope here is to ground our discussion of something as elusive as the ineffable in concrete literary example, while at the same time suggesting the extent to which language is always working against its own limitations.

The idea for this volume was first conceived in 1978–79 while the editors held Andrew W. Mellon post-doctoral fellowships at the City University of New York Graduate Center. For this opportunity, as well as for the subsidy for this collection, we would like to thank both the Mellon Foundation and Dr. Hans J. Hillerbrand, former Provost of the Graduate Center. During that year we were also encouraged by the late Professor Helaine Newstead, who invited us to present earlier versions of some of these essays to her medieval seminar, and by Professor Miriam Starkman, who chaired a special session at the 1979 meeting of the Modern Language Association at which later versions were read. We are grateful also to Mr. William Long of AMS Press for his editorial help.

For permission to use the copyrighted material included in this work, we make acknowledgement to the following publishers: to Grove Press for Samuel Beckett's *The Unnamable*; to Harcourt Brace Jovanovich, Inc. for T. S. Eliot's *Complete Poems and Plays, 1909–1950* and *Selected Essays*; to Editions Gallimard for Stéphane Mallarmé's *Oeuvres Complètes*; and to Alfred A. Knopf, Inc. for Wallace Stevens's *Collected Poems, Opus Posthumus,* and *The Necessary Angel.*

Portions of the material in the essay "On Not Having the Last Word: Beckett, Wittgenstein, and the Limits of Language" by Bruce Kawin have appeared in his book *The Mind of the Novel: Reflexive Fiction and the Ineffable,* published and copyrighted by Princeton University Press; reprinted by permission. A version of Alfred Corn's Essay, "Wallace Stevens and the Nothing that Is," appeared in the *Yale Review,* Spring 1982.

PETER S. HAWKINS

ANNE HOWLAND SCHOTTER

Dante's *Paradiso* and the Dialectic of Ineffability

Peter S. Hawkins

From the outset of the *Paradiso* Dante makes it clear that his pilgrim is modeled on St. Paul, that "man in Christ" who was "caught up into paradise, and heard such unspeakable words which it is not lawful for a man to utter" (II Cor. xii.4).[1] According to St. Augustine, the most influential interpreter of this rapture, Paul's experience of the ineffable was nothing less than unmediated contact with God: verbal beatitude.[2] For one extraordinary "moment" of eternity the Apostle was taken out of the diachronic body of our speech and thus enabled, along with the blessed, to understand God's language—a language so unutterably beyond our own that Augustine will refer to it paradoxically as silence.[3] It is this same translation into the divine ineffability that Dante claims for himself. But if St. Paul serves as the prototype for the voyager *in paradisum,* what then are we to make of the poet who writes thirty-three cantos of *terza rima* about an experience which is not only incapable of expression, but which is also unlawful for a man to utter? Perhaps this apparent divergence from the Pauline tradition accounts for the fact that the anxiety of the *Commedia,* which heretofore has been located in the pilgrim, shifts suddenly to the poet. Dante is openly aware that this "ultimo lavoro" travels uncharted territory— "L'acqua ch'io prende già mai non si corse" *(Par.* II.7)[4]—for while the Chosen Vessel made the same ultimate journey, *his* itinerary remained a closed book. Nor is the danger of the enterprise risked by the poet alone; the reader too is forewarned that the voyage "in pelago" *(Par.* II.5) is a perilous one and not to be undertaken lightly.

Certainly much of this uneasiness has to do with the fact that once the final apocalyptic cantos of the *Purgatorio* are behind us, Dante's mimesis of Scripture is complete. There remains only the ominous warning that ends the Book of Revelation, a warning understood to mark the definitive closing of the canon: "For I testify, unto every man that heareth the words of this book, If any man shall add unto these things, God shall add unto him the plagues of this book" (Rev. xxii.18). By beginning the *Paradiso* precisely where the Bible itself leaves off, Dante stands to "add" to a revelation that has already had its last word.

5

Thus, even though heaven has put its hand to the sacred poem, may not the poet's act be (to appropriate Adam's phrase for the original sin) a "trapassar del segno" (*Par.* XXVI.117), a trespass of the boundary set between human speech and the divine reality, the breaking of God's own taboo?

Dante defends himself against these charges at the opening of the *Paradiso* when essentially he states that what the poem will say is actually at several removes from the ineffable. For although the pilgrim saw God *in speciem,* that vision of beatitude can be represented to us only by the lightning flash (*fulgore*) that shatters the final canto and with it the entire poem:

> Nel ciel che più de la sua luce prende
>   fu' io, e vidi cose che ridire
>   né sa né può chi di là sù discende;
> perché appressando sé al suo disire,
>   nostro intelletto si profonda tanto,
>   che dietro la memoria non può ire.
>
>   (*Par.* I.4–9)

I have been in the heaven that most receives of His light, and have seen things which whoso descends from there has neither the knowledge nor power to relate, because, as it draws near to its desire, our intellect enters so deep that memory cannot go back upon the track.

What this journey "si profonda tanto" means for the *Paradiso,* as Dante's gloss in the letter to Can Grande further makes plain, is that the poem articulates the struggle of language to speak the little that memory can recall: it is the copy of a copy of an ineffable Original.[5] Therefore, when the pilgrim finally ends his journey in God, the poem has already, in fact, reached its end; the only way the poet can speak the ineffable words he once heard is in the silence that reigns once "alta fantasia" concedes its utter defeat.

Yet, if the silence of the poet's final poverty acknowledges the great gulf fixed between our words and the Word of God, the poem is nonetheless a *resonant* failure. It may well be (as Dante confesses in his ineffability *topoi*) only a shadow of the blessed kingdom (I.23), a little spark (I.34), the stuttering of a mute (X.25), not substantial enough even to be called "little" (XXXIII.123), but these disclaimers are all, in fact, claims of a relationship that obtains between human speech and God's full silence, between this poem and its ineffable subject.[6] Dante could do this without blasphemy because, having inherited a Christian notion of language which Marcia Colish has felicitously called "re-deemed rhetoric," he believed in the power of the divine Word to "dwell" in human speech, to reveal the inexpressible God through the finite medium of words in time and space.[7] This is not to say that the ineffable words were thought capable of any literal translation, but rather that mortal words may function as a call to vision, a preparation (as Augustine said of the writing of St. Ambrose) "to hear God's silent discourse and to see His invisible

face" ("ad audiendum silentium narrationis eius, et videndum invisibilem formam eius").[8]

While such claims were routinely made for Scripture, they might also be
extended to nonbiblical texts, as Augustine does for Ambrose. But what constitutes Dante's originality, not to mention his daring, is his appropriation of them
for his own poem.[9] Not only does the *Commedia* share with the Bible allegorical
and anagogical significance, it also claims to reveal the ineffable God in a similar
way. Thus in *Paradiso* IV, when Beatrice explains the appearance of the blessed
throughout the material spheres of the Ptolomeic universe, the poet is also
giving us a glimpse into the procedure of his fiction. For whether the heavenly
spirits show themselves to the pilgrim as lights, or the poem describes them to
us in words, configurations of any kind exist only provisionally, "per far
segno," to make signs for a reality which completely transcends our time and
spacebound *ingegno.*

> Per questo la Scrittura condescende
> a vostra facultate, e piedi e mano
> attribuisce a Dio e altro intende.
> (*Par.* IV.43–45)

> For this reason Scripture condescends to your capacity, and attributes hands and
> feet to God, having other meaning.

The primary analogy here is between the heavenly "script" which the pilgrim
sees as he ascends and the figurative language of the Bible, both of which are
accommodations of pure spirit to our "fleshly mind." But as John Freccero has
suggested, this analogy is relevant not only to what Dante saw then, but to what
he writes now: "that is, heaven's condescension to the pilgrim is matched by
the poet's condescension to us."[10]

If we push this kinship of accommodation further and say that Dante
intends us to read the *Paradiso* as if it were an extended Biblical anthropomor-
phism, then there are two conclusions which may be drawn. The first is that
the *cantica*'s claim to truth lies not in any supposed mimetic correspondence
between its language and the ineffable "other"; rather, the poem itself is a
metaphor whose meaning wholly transcends its literal terms. Secondly, it is a
metaphor of a certain kind, for when the Holy Spirit speaks in Scripture of
God's hands or feet—when, that is, He uses glaringly inappropriate language—
He does so precisely to remind us that there is no human speech adequate to
the divine reality. Thus for Augustine description of this sort is a sign that God
is more fully expressed in our awed silence than in anything which our voices
can sound; it is an inspired call to go beyond the letter of *every* text.[11] If read
aright, therefore, this kind of metaphor will introduce an analogy between our
speech and God's Word that will of necessity force the reader to see the
insufficiency of language; to see, that is, the fiction of metaphor. It will sabotage
its own literal meaning in order to draw attention to what cannot be spelled

in letters at all, but which words can nonetheless make the reader attend to and long for.

In *Paradiso* I Dante gives us a statement of the way the poem's metaphoric structure will function on behalf of the ineffable:

> Trasumanar significar *per verba*
> non si poria; però l'essemplo basti
> a cui esperïenza grazia serba.
>   (*Par.* I.70-72)

> The passing beyond humanity may not be set forth in words: therefore let the example suffice any for whom grace reserves the experience.

This *terzina* offers us one of the first of the poem's ineffability *topoi*, a straightfor-ward declaration that what the poet is about to tell us cannot, in fact, be put into words. Given this basic limit of language, the most he can do is bear witness with this, his mute *essemplo*, thereby pointing the reader to that beatitude which he can himself neither remember nor describe. If we look more closely at the line by line movement of the *terzina*, however, we may discover the peculiar tension of this poem, the poetic counterplot within Dante's visionary ortho-doxy. In the initial *trasumanare* he gives us a word of his own devising, a verb created to express the inexpressible transcendence of our life and language: "to pass beyond humanity." Juxtaposed to it at the end of l. 70 is a Latin phrase, *per verba*, which Denis Donoghue has I think rightly suggested to be an allusion both to St. Paul's rapture into the *arcana verba* of the third heaven (II Cor. xii.2-4) and to the "Latin" exegetical tradition of Augustine and Aquinas which grew up around it.[12] Placed between Dante's neologism (*trasumanare*) and this evocation of the language of heaven (*per verba*) is *significare*, literally "to mean" or "to describe," but at root denoting the semiotic activity of human language itself: the making of signs. As long as this line is read as a completed whole— "trasumanar significar *per verba*"—it offers us a dramatic display of verbal ingenuity and confidence, a variety of linguistic stops pulled to assert the transcendence of humanity in words: the sheer power of *significare*. And yet, of course, the line does *not* stand grammatically on its own, so that as the force of Dante's syntax pulls us on to what follows immediately upon it, the Prome-thean impulse within fallen language is brought up short by the stern reality of *non si poria*. What we see, then, in the assertion and negation of these two lines is a miniature of the poetic strategy of the entire *cantica*. For whatever the *Paradiso* offers with one hand, it resolutely withdraws with the other; what it speaks cannot be set forth in words.

But as we know from the third line, the *terzina* does not leave us at a stalemate, with the poem's self-contradiction rendering it meaningless and in vain. Although it abjures any claim to render the ineffable in its full silence, it nonetheless presents us not only with the *essemplo* of one who heard the unspeakable words, but also with the promise of the same beatitude "a cui esperïenza grazia serba," to any for whom grace reserves the experience. Viewed linguistically, this experience is nothing other than the eschatological end toward which the whole verbal creation groans in travail: the translation of our words into The Word. Thus, what the last line of the *terzina* brings us to is the possibility of *trasumanare* which we glimpsed in the first line and lost in the second—only now it is acknowledged as a reality *unsignified*, hidden in the implication of grace, a truth beheld between the lines until in eternity God's Word is "all in all." In this way, then, the *cantica*'s "passing beyond humanity" is a passage from the poet's language to his silence, but a silence far more eloquent than anything his words can say.

What we see in *Paradiso* I.70–72 is the process of a dialectic, a dialectic of ineffability, which moves from the claims of language, through a recognition of its limits, to the intimation of a transcendent, unrepresentable reality—a move that Dante describes in *Paradiso* XXIII.61–63 as a "jump" into silence:

> e così, figurando il paradiso,
> convien saltar lo sacrato poema,
> come chi trova suo cammin riciso.
>
> and so, depicting paradise, the sacred poem must needs make a leap, even as one who finds his way cut off.

Although this dialectic of ineffability is characteristic of all speech about the numinous, there are nonetheless some literary works in which it is focal. Stanley Fish has characterized these as "self-consuming artifacts," and traced their ancestry back to Plato and then through St. Augustine to the Christian West.[13] While he never once mentions Dante, his thesis is of great relevance to the *Paradiso*, certainly the most spectacular "self-consuming artifact" in literature. Fish shows how the dialectic arises out of a desire to communicate the ineffable, not for purposes of speculation, but rather to the end of conversion: to lead the reader-respondent into a direct experience of the ineffable. Although the dialectic uses "outer" words, they are considered to be only the instruments or vehicles of "inner" truth—a truth which Plotinus says in the *Enneads* is " 'Not to be told; not to be written': in our writing and telling we are but urging toward it; out of discussion we call to vision; to those desiring to see, we point the way; our teaching is of the road and of the travelling."[14] Because the ineffable is "not to be told; not to be written," the language of the dialectic must more or less openly disavow itself, forcing the reader to look not only beyond words, but beyond the diachronic world in which we (apparently) exist. Using the example of the *Phaedrus*, Fish describes the experience of reading such a work as a mimetic re-enactment of the Platonic ladder, with each successive "rung" rejected even as it is negotiated, until finally the whole structure is thrown over, leaving the reader with him- or herself—and with whatever enlightenment has grown within. Thus the strategy of the work is to emphasize the partitive, transitory, inadequate nature of language, and in so doing to call the reader to that higher ("intellectual") vision which can be realized only in silence. Therefore, language fulfills its purpose only by acknowledging its own inadequacy; or, as Fish puts it, "A self-consuming artifact signifies most successfully when it fails, when it points away from itself to something its forms cannot capture."[15]

Although Fish discusses St. Augustine, the great Christianizer of this Platonic tradition, he does not refer to the most remarkable example of the "anti-aesthetic" in the Augustinian corpus, the Ostia "vision" of *Confessions* IX.10.[16] We turn to it here because it provides us with an important precedent, if not with an actual model, for the dialectic of the *Paradiso*: a struggle to speak simultaneously about an experience of the ineffable and to dissolve that speech into silence. The episode, which virtually concludes the autobiographical portion of the work, opens on a day close to Monica's death, as she and Augustine find themselves discussing what the joy of the blessed will be.[17] Their conversation begins in the outer or corporeal words of normal discourse (what Augustine will speak of in *Confessions* XIII.15 as *syllabis temporum*), and proceeds by analogy to find some correlative on earth or in the material heavens by which to imagine the bliss which "eye has not seen, nor ear heard, nor mind conceived." When no such likeness can be found, they discover themselves undergoing a gradual interiorization of their speech—"interius cogitando et loquendo et mirando"—until they transcend even their inner selves and are translated into eternity, "the place of everlasting plenty, where you feed Israel forever with the food of truth." There, in the no place where God is "all in all," they are enabled to "speak" and "gasp after" the divine Word to such an extent that with the longing of their whole being they momentarily "reach out and touch" Him. That contact lasts only for the space of a heartbeat, however, before they once again fall back into their bodies, a re-entry which Augustine describes in linguistic terms as a fall from the infinite synchronicity of God's silence to the "noise" (*strepitus*) of our diachronic speech, "where each word has a beginning and an end—far, far different from your Word, O Lord, Who abides in Himself forever, yet never grows old and gives life to all things."

After an unspecified interval, the pair then attempts to reconstruct their experience of *trasumanare* in the outer words of mortality—a reconstruction which will first track the lost rapture in language and then try to erase its own traces:

> Dicebamus ergo: 'si cui sileat tumultus carnis, sileat phantasiae terrae et aquarum et aeris, sileant et poli et ipsa sibi anima sileat, et transeat se non se cogitando, sileant somnia et imaginariae revelationes, omnis lingua et omne signum et quidquid transeundo fit si cui sileat omnino—quoniam si quis audiat, dicunt haec omnia: Non ipsa nos fecimus, sed fecit nos qui manet in aeternum:—his dictis si iam taceant, quoniam erexerunt aurem in eum, qui fecit ea, et loquatur ipse solus non per ea, sed per se ipsum, ut audiamus verbum eius, non per linguam carnis

neque per vocem angeli nec per sonitum nubis nec per aenigma similitudinis, sed ipsum, quem in his amamus, ipsum sine his audiamus, sicut nunc extendimus nos et rapida cogitatione attingimus aeternam sapientiam super omnia manentem, si continuetur hoc et subtrahantur aliae visiones longe inparis generis, et haec una rapiat et absorbeat et recondat in interiora gaudia spectatorem suum, ut talis sit sempiterna vita, quale fuit hoc momentum intelligentiae, cui suspiravimus, nonne hoc est: Intra in gaudium domini tui? et istud quando? an cum omnes resurgimus, sed non omnes inmutabimur? (*Conf.* IX.10)

Therefore we said: If for anyone the tumult of the flesh fell silent, silent the images of the earth, and of the waters, and of the air; silent the heavens; silent the very soul itself; and if anyone should pass beyond the self by not thinking of the self, silent all dreams and imagined appearances, and every tongue, and every sign; and if all things that come to be through change should become wholly silent—for as anyone can hear, all these things say: 'We did not make ourselves, but He made us, Who endures forever'—if when they have said these words, they then become silent, for they have raised the ear to Him Who made them, and if God alone speaks, not through such things but through Himself, so that we hear His Word, not uttered by a tongue of flesh, nor an angel's voice, nor by the sound of thunder, nor by the riddle of a similitude, but by Himself Whom we love in all these things, Himself we hear without their aid—even as we then reached out and in swift thought attained to that eternal wisdom which abides over all things—if this could be prolonged, and other visions of a far inferior kind could be with-drawn, and this one alone ravish, and absorb, and hide away its beholder within its deepest joys, so that the sempiternal life might be such as was that moment of understanding for which we sighed, would it not be this: Enter into the joy of your Lord? and when shall this be? when we shall all rise again, but we shall not all be changed?

Most of the attention accorded this passage (and, indeed, the entire epi-sode) has to do with its mixture of Neo-Platonism and Christianity. More remarkable than the simultaneous presence of two "worlds of discourse," however, is the fact that discourse itself is under attack; that language is both the exorcist and the demon cast out. Given that the processes of writing and erasure are one process here, our response is unavoidably double. Is this a "self-consuming artifact" or witness to the same impulse that tried at Babel to take heaven by storm? For in this literary tour de force, remarkable in even so practiced a Ciceronian as Augustine, we are confronted by nothing less than a massive self-contradiction: a periodic sentence of 190 intricately woven words, whose express purpose is to dissolve language into the silence it repeatedly invokes. Furthermore, it is a sentence which, for all its density and weight, is given the most tentative rhetorical construction: launched by a surmise (*si cui*, 'if for anyone'), it continues in supposition until closing, most open-endedly, in a question. It is as if, despite its great verbal bulk, it were trying very hard not to be on the page at all. Thus, following closely upon the itinerary of the earlier conversation-vision, Augustine moves through the hierarchy of Creation, sum-moning forth each successive mode of revelation only to reduce each one to silence, even those which God has used to reveal Himself in a glass darkly:

"linguam carnis, vocem angeli, sonitum nubis, aenigma similitudinis." With its rejection of "every tongue and every sign," the sentence is ultimately bound to reject itself. This it does, but only in order to signal the unmediated experi-ence of the ineffable which Augustine and Monica "touched" in their transla-tion, "that He alone may speak Himself . . . through Himself, in order that we may hear His voice."

"In order that we may hear His voice": this ultimate experience of *tras-umanare,* situated at the central stillpoint of the sentence, is the final goal not only of this account, but of every verbal excursion into the *via negationis.* Moreover, by placing the beatific "sound" of God's "silent narration" at the center of a linear progression—a diachronic imitation of the eternal Now of God—Augustine also forces us to realize that this is not an end which the sentence can hope to attain in the "body" of our speech. All these words can do is reach after what they themselves cannot touch. And yet, as the continuing course of the sentence demonstrates, this acknowledgement of the limits of language can at the same time serve to point beyond them. For if we cannot now either hear or speak the Word in His ineffability, we can at least look forward, even as the sentence moves us forward in time and space, to the apocalyptic transformation of our speech; look forward, that is, to the moment and twinkling of an eye, when the divine Word "enraptures" and "absorbs" and "hides away" our mortal language in the resurrection of the flesh. Thus, by concluding the sentence with a citation of I Corinthians xv—St. Paul's great discourse on the *parousia*—Augustine leaves it open to its own future transfor-mation: the resurrection of human words into the eternity of God's "ineffabilia verba."

Augustine does not end the episode here, however, looking toward the eschatological experience which grace reserves for the blessed. Instead he goes on to announce that the text we have just read—and presumably not only this sentence, but the entire story of the rapture—is only a facsimile: "and thus I spoke, but not in this manner or in these words" ("dicebam talia, etsi non isto modo et his verbis"). In this sudden switch to the first person singular, our attention is moved from the visionary rapture of Augustine and Monica at Ostia ("dicebamus ergo") to the act of writing about it ten years later; to the *ego* who writes in this manner and in these words about an encounter with the ineffable which leaves all words and rhetoric behind. That we should be told at the end of the account that what we have read is a version or a paraphrase of the "vision," but not the actual journey *in id ipsum,* should come as no surprise. And yet, while we know that the "syllables inscribed in time" cannot speak God's eternal Word, the consummate skill of the rhetor is such that we are always in danger of forgetting it, in danger, that is, of mistaking the language of the episode for the truth that can only be heard when what is written or told passes away into silence. What Augustine's authorial "confession" at the end of the episode does, in effect, is prevent the reader's inevitable seduction by the pyrotechnics of his performance: he breaks his own spell. Instead of allowing us to marvel over his tour de force, let alone take it for an adequate description of the experience grace reserves for the silence of eternity, he forces us to take the story of his "vision" as only the next best thing—a consolation prize in the absence of the ineffable, pointing away from itself to "something" its forms cannot capture.

We have already seen how Dante makes this same discrediting gesture at the very beginning of the *Paradiso* when he says that his vision of beatitude can be neither recalled nor expressed as it actually was—hidden, "si profonda tanto," in God's ineffability—but can only be represented indirectly, in the condescension of intellectual vision to our senses, or, as he says of Plato in the letter to Can Grande, "per assumptionem metaphorismorum."[18] We have also characterized this metaphoric nature of the *cantica* as dialectical, moving through thirty-three cantos of assertion and negation, of writing and erasure, until the reader is left (like Augustine and Monica) with no mortal words to hold on to, but only the divine Word to reach out and long for. But if the inexpressible *fulgore* which concludes the *Commedia* is also the destruction of the poem's metaphor—the definitive rejection of the "ladder" which reader and poet have climbed in their ascent to the outer limits of language—it is a destruction for which the entire *cantica* has been in careful preparation. Like Augustine's periodic sentence in the Ostia episode, the language of the *Paradiso* is busy with its own elimination, with the conversion of speech into silence. In both instances we see the peculiar role which virtuosity plays in the dialectic of ineffability, for the highly self-conscious brilliance of these words demands to be used up in the act of reading. Their most spectacular effects are seen in their demise.

How the *Paradiso* gradually writes itself out of existence and into silence is suggested by a simile presented on the lowest "rung" of the visionary ascent, a metaphor which offers the first accommodation of the unrepresentable to representation. What the pilgrim sees in the sphere of the Moon are spirits who are but barely visible, who appear to him as imperceptibly as a pearl on a white forehead: *perla in bianca fronte* (*Par.* III.14).[19] While this sight initiates the pilgrim into the preliminary stages of the "vista nova," it also discloses to us the metaphoric action of the *cantica*. Just as pearl and forehead can be distinguished from one another only because they are off-white, so the poem "makes sense" to us precisely because it is *not* the ineffable, because the silence of God's infinite and eternal language has been shaded, differentiated, translated into the "syllables inscribed in time." Nonetheless, there is in this failure of pearl and brow to be absolutely pure the unmistakable evocation of utter whiteness—a whiteness which we cannot imagine, because to imagine it would of necessity be to introduce some coloration, some pearl or brow "in bianca," but which we can at least begin to abstract or intuit. It is on the verge of just this abstraction that the poet gives them to us here, as if poised on their departure, so faint and evanescent as almost to pass over before our eyes into undifferentiation: a partial likeness about to become full. What we are implicitly asked to do, even as we try to focus their imagery, is to follow pearl and brow entirely out of sight, into the silent invisibility from which the poet's metaphor has momentarily called them out. It is likewise with the spirits themselves who, having condescended "per far segno," suddenly vanish "as through deep water some heavy thing" ("come per acqua cupa cosa grave," *Par.* III.123)—vanish, that is, into a reality which is beyond signification, outside the possibilities of the poem itself.

This passing beyond signification is suggested most dramatically in the so-called "anti-images" of the *Paradiso,* such as the cross of Mars (*Par.*XIV) and the eagle of Jupiter (*Par.* XVIII–XX)—configurations of light which remain visible only long enough to be comprehended, and then fade indistinguishably into their meaning: paradigms of the "self-consuming artifact."[20] But if this is true of specific metaphors such as these, it is also true of the *cantica* itself, whose images and fictions constantly give way one after another, not in hopes of ever describing the ineffable, but rather to exhaust the possibility of expression. Following the dialectical movement suggested above, the poem can be seen everywhere to silence itself, but only after each negated assertion of likeness has enlarged our notion of what *cannot* be imagined, of what lies beyond the grasp of language.

In the sphere of the Sun, where the doctors of the Church appear as lights which sing and dance in two concentric circles, the poet bids the reader imagine what he saw by means of an extraordinarily extended analogy (*Par.* XIII.1–18):

> Imagini, chi bene intender cupe
>   quel ch' i' or vidi—e ritegna l'image,
>   mentre ch'io dico, come ferma rupe—,
> quindici stelle che 'n diverse plage
>   lo cielo avvivan di tanto sereno
>   che soperchia de l'aere ogne compage;
> imagini quel carro a cu' il seno
>   basta del nostro cielo e notte e giorno,
>   sì ch'al volger del temo non vien meno;
> imagini la bocca di quel corno
>   che si comincia in punta de lo stelo
>   a cui la prima rota va dintorno,
> aver fatto di sé due segni in cielo,
>   qual fece la figliuola di Minoi
>   allora che sentì di morte il gelo;
> e l'un ne l'altro aver li raggi suoi,
>   e amendue girarsi per maniera
>   che l'uno andasse al primo e l'altro al poi.

Let him imagine, who would rightly grasp what I now beheld (and, while I speak, let him hold the image firm as a rock), fifteen stars which in different regions vivify the heaven with such brightness that it overcomes every thickness of the air; let him imagine that Wain for which the bosom of our heaven suffices night and day

so that with the turning of the pole it does not disappear; let him imagine the
mouth of the Horn which begins at the end of the axle on which the first wheel
revolves—all to have made of themselves two signs in the heavens like that which
the daughter of Minos made when she felt the chill of death; and one to have its
rays within the other, and both to revolve in such manner that one should go first
and the other after.

The opening imperative, *imagini,* is repeated at the head of the three initial
terzine—an emphatic command not only to etch in mind "come ferma rupe"
the image inscribed on the page, but also to heighten our awareness of the
poet's activity: the making of metaphor "mentre ch'io dico." What he gives us
to retain is a totally fictional heaven in which several actual constellations are
selected and rearranged in the shape of a double Ariadne's crown: an astro-
nomical neologism! With the repetition of *imagini* and the painstakingly elaborate composition of the image, the passage once again all but coerces our
recognition of its tour de force: an eighteen-line demonstration of the poet's
ingenuity and of the power of verbal *trasumanare.* And yet, as soon as the
analogical picture is finished, the reader who was first told to hold on to it
(*ritegna l'image*) is now ordered to let it fall away. For what the reader has
obediently kept in mind is

> quasi l'ombra de la vera
> costellazione e de la doppia danza
> che circulava il punto dov' io era:
> poi ch'è tanto di là da nostra usanza,
> quanto di là dal mover de la Chiana
> si move il ciel che tutti li altri avanza.
> (vv. 19-24)

as it were a shadow of the true constellation, and of the double dance, which was
circling round the point where I was; for it is as far beyond our experience as the
motion of the heaven that outspeeds all the rest is beyond the motion of the
Chiana.

The effect of these lines is radically to undermine the preceding *imago*. And
yet, if the poet rejects his analogy as only a shadow of the truth, it is still a
shadow. Nor is the power of analogy itself entirely denied, for while the
dancing circles of light may be "tanto di là da nostra usanza," Dante conveys
this fact through another likeness, a comparison of the preternatural speed of
the Primum Mobile with the notoriously sluggish course of the river Chiana.
Although this comparison argues a dissimilitude between earth and heaven,
there is nonetheless the shadow of a likeness: the poet is not contrasting
movement with stasis, but two vastly different kinds of movement. But before
we can take this as an apparent (if tenuous) endorsement of the passing beyond
humanity in words, we must remember that Dante is not claiming to speak
directly of the ineffable here, but rather of different degrees of metaphor. He

is comparing heaven's "son et lumière" with his own imaginative fireworks; that is, he is comparing two accommodations to "nostra usanza." Therefore, no matter how remote from our experience the "vera costellazione" in the sphere of the Sun may be, no matter how far beyond even this dazzling demonstration of imaginative vision, it is still only a condescension, a translation of silence into sounds and shapes and shadows, a vision that will utterly dissolve once the pilgrim has assimilated its "point." What Dante gives us here and throughout the *cantica* is a palimpsest of images with no discernible Ur-text beneath them; an ineffable Source to be discovered by the poem only in its failure and dissolution, its passage from speech to silence.

There is nowhere in the *Paradiso* a more poignant presentation of this passing away of the text than in the first of the four ineffability *topoi* that punctuate the final canto:

> Da quinci innanzi il mio veder fu maggio
>   che 'l parlar mostra, ch'a tal vista cede,
>   e cede la memoria a tanto oltraggio.
> Qual è coliii che sognando vede,
>   che dopo 'l sogno la passione impressa
>   rimane, e l'altro a la mente non riede,
> cotal son io, ché quasi tutta cessa
>   mia visïone, e ancor mi distilla
>   nel core il dolce che nacque da essa.
> Così la neve al sol si disigilla;
>   così al vento ne le foglie levi
>   si perdea la sentenza di Sibilla.
>   (*Par.* XXXIII.55-66)

Thenceforward my vision was greater than speech can show, which fails at such a sight, and at such excess memory fails. As is he who dreaming sees, and after the dream the passion remains imprinted and the rest returns not to the mind; such am I, for my vision almost wholly fades away, yet does the sweetness that was born of it still drop within my heart. Thus is the snow unsealed by the sun; thus in the mind, on the light leaves, the Sibyl's oracle was lost.

The contrast Dante sets up at the beginning of the passage is between the growing perfection of the pilgrim's ability to see "face to face" (*veder*) and the proportional decline of the poet's speech (*parlar*), a decline accentuated by the rapid repetition of *cede . . . cede* in ll. 56–57. Charles Singleton has noted that this confession of failure at the end of the *cantica* returns us to the opening disclaimer of *Par.* I.4–9, where memory and language were first said to be overwhelmed by their "subject."[21] Between that threshold admission and this, the poem has almost completed its magnificent circle, and yet any notion of completion runs the risk of falsifying the particularity of this ending. Despite the perfection of its symmetry, the poem demands that we take it in some way as incomplete, stopped in its tracks from start to finish "a tanto oltraggio." The "outrage" here is God's infinite and eternal Light, "lo raggio/ de l'alta luce che da sé è vera" (ll. 53–54), which we have seen refracted throughout the *cantica* in myriad condescensions to our mortality, but which is now seen by the pilgrim "da sé," as it truly is. Consider that Light linguistically, however, and it is the silence of God's Word, defying the powers of all human speech but even now drawing the faltering words of the poet into its totality.

Be this as it may, it is the poet's renewed sense of separation from his experience, and of the profound distance of his words from *the* Word, that predominates in the three following *terzine*. He begins with the simile of a man who wakes from a dream to find that it has vanished, leaving only an emotional imprint behind: "la passione impressa." While the feeling testifies that "some-thing" has been seen, the dream itself—what is simply called here "l'altro"— does not return to mind. Dante then proceeds to apply this open simile (*Qual è colüi*) to himself (*cotal son io*). Just as the dream is almost entirely obliterated, so is the heavenly vision "quasi tutta cessa." What remains, like the inchoate recollection of emotion, is only a distillate: "e ancor mi distilla/ nel core il dolce che nacque da essa." At first glance the second of these two figures seems largely to repeat (if personalize) the first. And yet there is in the juxtaposition of these two "remnants" a movement from the palpable, direct "impressa" to the more subtle transformation of vapor and liquid; a movement, that is, toward dematerialization.

This process continues in the next and final *terzina*, where we turn from "impressa" and "distilla" to a still further stage of dematerialization: "Così la neve al sole si disigilla." For the first time in this short series the "original" departs without so much as a token of its reality or an intangible sweetness born in the heart: the snow simply evaporates into the sunshine without a trace. Like the word *impressa, disigilla* suggests the whole enterprise of artistic creation and signification—except, of course, that instead of conferring shape and form (cf. *sigillare, Par.* VII.69), *disigilla* points to its dissolution; points, that is, to the evaporation or un-signing of language, its imperceptible dissolve into the "ol-traggio" of God's ineffability.

The inherent melancholy of these metaphors about the loss of metaphor is accentuated by the *si perdea* of the final simile, an allusion to the Sibyl's oracular text scattered irretrievably in the wind: "così al vento ne le foglie levi/ si perdea la sentenza di Sibilla."[22] At the end of Vergil's account of this "decon-struction," we read that those who saw the inspired lines flutter word by word into oblivion walked away from the experience in disgust: "inconsulti abeunt sedemque odere Sibyllae" (*Aeneid* III.452). There is, however, no such rancor in Dante, and if in this eloquent declaration of defeat the poet foreshadows the death and dissolution of his own text, he does so only from the perspective of mortal language, knowing at once the desire to pass beyond humanity and the utter impossibility of doing so *per verba*. But once again, as with the terzina of *Par.* I.70–72, he does not leave us at a dead end. Rather, with a subtle allusion to the dispersal of the Sibyl's "sentenza," he points us beginning in l. 85. to the transcendent third term of the dialectic—a vision of the experience which grace alone reserves, when scattered "syllables inscribed in time" are gathered into one ineffable Word, bound by love into the silence of God's Book:

> Nel suo profondo vidi che s'interna,
>   legato con amore in un volume,
>   ciò che per l'universo si squaderna.
>   (*Par.* XXXIII.85–87)

> In its depth I saw ingathered, bound by love in one single volume, that which is dispersed in leaves throughout the universe.

By his own repeated witness, Dante can give us no selected readings from this divine Text. But what he can do is to heighten our longing for it so that no mortal words, not even those of the "sacrato poema," will satisfy. In thereby leaving the reader unfulfilled, this "self-consuming artifact" actually fulfills its destiny, leading us away from the sound of our own speech to a reality that escapes language entirely. In this way Dante's failure in fact makes good his promise to Can Grande, for as it scatters its words into the collection of the divine "volume," the work indeed ends in God Himself—"in ipso Deo terminatur tractatus"—and not in any human words about Him.

NOTES

1. "Scio hominem in Christo ante annos quatuordecim, sive in corpore nescio, sive extra corpus nescio. Deus scit, raptum huiusmodi usque ad tertium caelum. Et scio huiusmodi hominem sive in corpore, sive extra corpus nescio, Deus scit: quoniam raptus est in paradisum: et audivit arcana verba, quae non licet homini loqui." II Cor. xii.2–4. *Bible Sacra,* ed. Gianfranco Nolli (Milwaukee: Bruce, 1955). The English translation of Scripture used throughout this essay is the Authorized Version.

2. Augustine's major treatment of the rapture is found in *De Genesi ad litteram libri xii,* Bk. XII, *viz.* chs. xxvii–xxxvii. Cf. Thomas Aquinas, *Summa Theologica* II, II, 175, art. 3–6. For a survey of varying patristic and medieval interpretations of Paul's experience, see Joseph A. Mazzeo, *Structure and Thought in the 'Paradiso'* (1958; rpt. New York: Greenwood Press, 1968), pp. 84–110.

3. In *Confessions* XI.6, for instance, Augustine contrasts God's inner and silent Word with the "outer" words of His utterance: "Et haec ad tempus facta verba tua nuntiavit auris exterior menti prudenti, cuius auris interior posita est ad aeternum verbum tuum. At illa comparavit haec verba temporaliter sonantia cum aeterno in silentio verbo tuo et dixit: 'aliud est longe, longe aliud est. Haec longe infra me sunt nec sunt, quia fugiunt et praetereunt: verbum autem dei mei supra me manet in aeternum." (These words of yours, formed for a certain time, the outer ear reported to the understanding of the mind, whose interior ear was placed close to your eternal Word. Then the mind compared these words sounding in time with

your eternal Word in its silence, and said, 'It is far different, it is far different. These words are far beneath me. They do not exist, because they flee and pass away. The Word of God abides above me forever.') The Latin text of the *Confessions* cited throughout this essay is the 2 vol. Loeb Library edition (Cambridge, Mass.: Harvard Univ. Press, 1968); the English trans. based on John K. Ryan (Garden City: Image Books, 1960). Two relevant studies are Joseph A. Mazzeo, "St. Augustine and the Rhetoric of Silence," *Renaissance and Seventeenth Century Studies* (New York: Columbia Univ. Press, 1964), pp. 1–24, and Vladimir Lossky, "Les Éléments de 'Théologie négative' dans la pensée de saint Augustin," *Augustinus Magister,* Congrès International Augustinien (Paris: Études augustiniennes, 1954), II, 575–581.

4. All citations of the *Commedia* are from Charles S. Singleton's text and translation, Bollingen Series LXXX (Princeton: Princeton Univ. Press, 1970–75).

5. *Dantis Alagherii Epistolae,* ed. and trans. Paget Toynbee, 2nd ed. (Oxford: Clarendon Press, 1966), *Epistola* X.29: "Vidit ergo, ut dicit, aliqua 'que referre nescit et nequit rediens.' Diligenter quippe notandum est quod dicit 'nescit et nequit.' Nescit quia oblitus, nequit quia, si recordatur et contentum tenet, sermo tamen deficit. Multa namque per intellectum videmus, quibus signa vocalia desunt quod satis Plato insinuat in suis libris per assumptionem metaphorismorum; multa enim per lumen intellectuale vidit que sermone proprio nequivit exprimere." (He saw then, as he says, certain things 'which he who returns has neither the knowledge nor the power to relate.' Now it must be carefully noted that he says 'has neither knowledge nor power'—knowledge he has not, because he has forgotten; power he has not, because even if he remembers, and retains it thereafter, nevertheless speech fails him. For we perceive many things by the intellect for which language has no terms, a fact which Plato indicates plainly enough in his books by his employment of metaphors; for he perceived many things by the light of the intellect which everyday language was inadequate to express).

6. An important new study of the ineffability *topoi,* and an up-to-date bibliography of recent works on the subject, has been done by Robin Kirkpatrick, *Dante's 'Paradiso' and the Limitations of Modern Criticism* (Cambridge: Cambridge Univ. Press, 1978), pp. 36–43.

7. Marcia L. Colish, *The Mirror of Language: A Study in the Medieval Theory of Knowledge* (New Haven: Yale Univ. Press, 1964).

8. *Epistola ad Paulinam* (#147, 'Liber de videndo Deo'), 53 (*PL* XXXIII,671): "Haec verba sancti viri, quae non carnalia sed spiritualia sunt, in quantum intellegis, et vera esse, non quia ipse dixit, sed quia veritas sine strepitu clamat, agnoscis; in tantum intellegis unde adhaeras Domino, teque ipsum intrinsecus praeparas incorporalem locum mansionis eius ad audiendum silentium narrationis eius, et videndum invisibilem formam eius." (To the extent that you understand these words of the saintly man, which are not carnal but spiritual, and recognize that they are true, not because he said them, but because truth clamors in them without noise of words, to that extent you prepare yourself inwardly as the incorporeal place of His dwelling, to hear the silence of His discourse, and to see His invisible form.) English translation by Sr. Wilfred Parsons, *Letters of Saint Augustine* (New York: Fathers of the Church, 1953), III, 222.

9. For a thorough study of the originality of Dante's claims for the *Commedia,* with extensive bibliography, see Robert Hollander, "Dante Theologus-Poeta," *DSARDS* 94 (1976), 91–136. *Cf.* Mazzeo, *Structure and Thought in the 'Paradiso,'* pp. 25–49.

10. John Freccero, "*Paradiso* X: The Dance of the Stars," *DSARDS* 86 (1968), 85.

11. Augustine, *Contra Adimantum* (*PL* XLII, 142): "Sanctus enim Spiritus hoc ipsum

hominibus intelligentibus insinuans, quam sint ineffabilia summa divina, his etiam verbis voluit, quae apud homines in vitio poni solent; ut inde admonerentur, etiam illa quae cum aliqua dignitate Dei se putant homines dicere, indigna esse illius maiestate, cui honorificum potius silentium, quam ulla vox humana competeret." (Indeed the Holy Spirit, insinuating this very thing into a man's understanding, how the highest divine things are ineffable, chose even these words which are accustomed among men to be placed in vice, in order that thereafter they might be warned that even those things which men themselves think to say with some worthiness of God are unworthy with respect to His majesty, to whom an honorable silence would rather be fitting than any human voice [My translation]).

12. "On the Limits of Language," *SR*, 85 (Summer, 1977), 372–373.

13. Stanley E. Fish, *Self-Consuming Artifacts: The Experience of Seventeenth Century Literature* (Berkeley and Los Angeles: Univ. of California Press, 1974), pp. 1–43.

14. Plotinus, *The Enneads*, trans. Stephen MacKenna, 3rd ed., rev. B. S. Page (London: Faber and Faber, Ltd., 1962, 1963), VI.ix.4, pp. 617–618.

15. Fish, p. 4.

16. The only serious consideration of the Ostia episode in relation to the *Paradiso* that I have found is an aside by Kenelm Foster in his essay, "Dante's Vision of God," *IS*, 14 (1959), 34: "Clearly the pith of [the Ostia vision] is a longing to pass from relative being to absolute, from derived to Original, and the connexion of these terms is not only analysed but contemplated in a meditation moving around it from one pair of opposites to another—passing-away and stability, time and eternity, effects and their cause, signs and unsigned. In Dante too we find these contrasts, but in the *Commedia* especially the last one, the passage through signs or symbols to substance. And this was natural to a poet whose self-assumed task, *figurando il paradiso*, it was to make spiritual order imaginable. Images had to be Dante's starting point; a system of signs that both hid and half-revealed a reality 'chiuso e parvente del suo proprio riso'." Luigi Tonelli in *Dante e la poesia del ineffabile* (Firenze: G. Barbèra, 1934), pp. 207–214, includes the episode among the *Paradiso*'s "precedenti filosofici e letterari," though without specific literary analy-sis. Cf. Pietro Chioccioni, *L'Agostinismo nella 'Divina Commedia'* (Firenze: Leo S. Olschki, 1952), *passim*.

17. For the standard critical approaches to the Ostia episode, see Pierre Courcelle, *Recherches sur les 'Confessions' de saint Augustin*, 2nd ed. (Paris: Editions E. de Boccard, 1968), pp. 222–226, and the annotated bibliographical footnote in M. Pellegrino's *Le 'Confessioni' di sant' Agostino* (Roma: Editrice Studium, 1956), p. 199. For a brilliant study of inter-textuality in the passage, see André Mandouze, "L'extase d'Ostie: possibilités et limites de la méthode des parallèles textuels," *Augustinus Magister*, I, 67–84. Kenneth Burke also deals with the episode briefly (and with brilliance) in his *Rhetoric of Religion* (Berkeley and Los Angeles: Univ. of California Press, 1961; rpt. 1970), pp. 117–122.

18. *Epistola* X.29. See n. 5.

19. See John Freccero's introduction to John Ciardi's translation of the *Paradiso* (New York: New American Library, 1970), pp. ix–xxi, esp. pp. x–xi, for his analysis of *Par*. III.114. Two other excellent studies of the peculiar language of the *cantica* are Marguerite Mills Chiarenza, "The Imageless Vision and Dante's *Paradiso*," *DSARDS* 90 (1972), 109–124, and Daniel M. Murtaugh, "*Figurando il paradiso:* The Signs That Render Dante's Heaven," *PMLA* 90 (1975), 227–284.

20. Chiarenza, 85–86, writes perceptively about the "anti-images" of the *Paradiso*: "There are, then, stages in the development of Dante's imagery in the *Paradiso*.

Three of them are those already mentioned, in which we find, first, concrete shapes which can barely be perceived, then shapes in which symbolic meaning overshadows concrete form, and at last purely conceptual shape not found in the material universe. These stages lead the poet to the point at which he can go no further but must end his poem in order that it become fully imageless."

21. Charles S. Singleton, *Paradiso, 2. Commentary,* p. 571.
22. For some interesting analysis of the poet's allusion to "la sentenza di Sibilla," see Pier Boitani, "The Sibyl's Leaves: A Study of *Paradiso* XXXIII," *DSARDS* 106 (1978), 83–126.

Vernacular Style and the Word of God: The Incarnational Art of *Pearl*

Anne Howland Schotter

Any Christian visionary writer must confront the problem of how to convey the Divine in human terms. Throughout history theologians have spoken of two ways, the positive, which proposes analogies for God, and the negative, which denies that any analogies are valid. The two ways tend to work in a dialectical manner, the latter continually warning against the idolatry that the former might encourage.[1] The author of the fourteenth-century English *Pearl* confronts this traditional problem when he tries to convey the kingdom of heaven to his readers. His solution is to suggest it by various analogical devices, while at the same time using a naive dreamer as a warning against taking them literally. Among the devices that he chooses are parables (those of the vineyard and the pearl of great price), images (the paradisal garden, the Lamb, and the New Jerusalem), and an enigma (the Pearl maiden herself). It has often been pointed out that by using the maiden to criticize the dreamer's earthbound perception of these analogies, the poet makes the inadequacy of images in conveying the Divine an explicit theme of the poem.[2] I would like to argue that he makes the inadequacy of *language* in conveying the Divine an implicit theme as well. He uses the limitations of his specific poetic medium— the West Midland dialect of Middle English on which alliterative poetry was based—to explore the general problems of language in its attempt to express the ineffable. For at the same time that he exploits the most splendid resources of his medium, he includes some of its pedestrian characteristics as a warning against excessive trust in language. His rhetorical concerns thus take on a theological dimension as he uses human words to try to convey God's Word, while paradoxically insisting that it is impossible for them to do so.[3]

In this respect the poet follows Augustinian sign theory, which, although it is profoundly distrustful of signs of any kind, justifies the use of both words and visual images for Christian purposes. Saint Augustine frequently pointed out that words are inadequate to convey an ineffable Godhead, saying, for instance, in *De Doctrina Christiana,*

> God should not be said to be ineffable, for when this is said, something is said. And a contradiction in terms is created, since if that is ineffable which cannot be

spoken, that is not ineffable which can be called ineffable. This contradiction is
to be passed over in silence rather than resolved verbally.[4]

And yet, Augustine argued, if man could not use language to *express* God he
could nevertheless use it to *praise* Him, and the Christian preacher, moreover,
was obligated to spread God's Word with human words as best he could.[5] Since
language was a mediation made necessary by fallen understanding, rhetoric
was a weapon with which God's friends should be armed, despite the danger
that their hearers might enjoy beautiful language for its own sake. Such idolatry
could be prevented if language would warn against its own inadequacy—if the
signs would warn against being taken for the thing they signified.[6] The justification for using human language was to be found in an analogy with the Incarnation, for if language had fallen with Adam, it had been redeemed by Christ's
condescending to take on human flesh—and, therefore, human speech.[7]

Augustine held, furthermore, that a similar incarnational model justified
using a low style to express the Word of God: the gap between literary styles
was insignificant compared to that between human language and Divine. In
reformulating Ciceronian rhetoric, he abandoned the distinction between three
levels of style which was based on subject matter, arguing that no aspect of the
Christian story could be considered "low." Hence, as Erich Auerbach has
shown, he urged the Christian rhetorician to adopt a *sermo humilis*—a low style
for a lofty theme.[8] In this way Augustine was able to defend the style of the
Old Latin version of the Bible to the cultivated Romans who thought it barba-
rous, even while he continued to use elaborate figures of speech in his own
writing.

The *Pearl*-poet does not put forth his linguistic principles at all, let alone
do so with the explicitness of Augustine. But Augustinian sign theory persisted
in Europe through the fourteenth century, as can be seen in Dante's dependence on it to justify the use of the Italian vernacular for elevated literary
subjects.[9] It is likely, therefore, that our poet's thoughts on language were
informed by Augustine's. I would like to argue that he perceived the gap
between the high and low elements in his own alliterative poetic tradition in
the same way that Augustine perceived that which stood between the styles of
Ciceronian and biblical Latin. And furthermore, although in trying to convey
the heavenly vision he employed the high elements, he also used the low
elements of his tradition to warn against them. In this way he sought a *sermo
humilis* in which to achieve a poetic incarnation of the Word of God.

That certain elements of alliterative poetry can be considered low is a
reflection of the complex sociolinguistic situation of Middle English in the
fourteenth century: after three hundred years of domination by French, the
language was being used increasingly for imaginative literature, but because of
the great dialectal differences, those who used it had little sense of shared
literary values. Rather than one standard literary dialect, as South East Midland

was to become in the fifteenth century, there were several dialects, of which West Midland, with its traditional alliterative poetry, was just one.[10] All Middle English poetry was prone to infelicities of style, because of its dependence on conventional devices left over from an earlier, simpler age when performance, if not composition, was oral.[11]

Such devices, which might be called "low" elements, include both general topoi and more specific verbal formulas. While the topos I shall discuss in *Pearl* —that of "inexpressibility"—is part of the general European tradition which Middle English inherited, the formula, *se wyth sy3t,* is specific to alliterative poetry. Formulas developed largely out of the requirement that the poetry alliterate three words per line, a situation which led poets to choose stereotyped groups of words, such as *on erthe* or *sothly to say,* on purely phonetic grounds.[12] The resulting style, wordy and highly conventional, has not been well regarded by modern critics, one of whom objects that alliterative poets show an excessive tolerance to "pleonasm, and sometimes to sheer vacuity of expression."[13]

But while the style of alliterative poetry as a whole has been little es-teemed, that of the *Pearl* itself has been consistently praised, often for qualities which are just as characteristic of its tradition as the empty formulas: writers speak of a "high style" in which poets use words "as if they were jewels" and resort to "elaborate and colourful rhetoric for sheer pride of craftsmanship."[14] One characteristic of this style is the use of certain archaic adjectives, many of them "elevated" because they appear only in poetic contexts, to describe courtly and heroic subjects—adjectives such as *bry3t, clere, mery, ryche,* and *schene.*[15] In employing not only these words, but also such examples of the medieval rhetorician's "difficult ornament" as word-play, stanza-linking, and complex rhyme scheme, *Pearl* is acknowledged to be the most exquisite exam-ple of the alliterative high style that we have.

The poem has received praise not only for using the high elements, but also for transcending the low ones. But such a view overlooks the poet's intentional use of low formulas for a rhetorical purpose. For although he exploits all the resources of the alliterative high style at the supreme visionary moments—when the dreamer catches sight of the paradisal garden, the maiden, and the New Jerusalem—he also introduces at those moments certain low elements which work with the high in a dialectical fashion to warn against the distractions offered by beautiful language. By undercutting his own linguistic virtuosity, he demonstrates that language, for all its power, is inadequate to convey the Word of God. He thus uses the limitations of his own vernacular literary language to point out the limitations of human language in general.

In this process of undercutting, the *Pearl*-poet uses what J. A. Burrow considers the most common device with which Middle English poets dissociated themselves from their inherited literary medium: the naive narrator.[16] While the *Pearl* dreamer is apparently unaware of the conventional nature of his stylistic devices, the poet is extremely aware, and uses these elements to dramatize the limitations of human language. His strategy becomes especially clear in the debate section of the poem, where the poet has the maiden, as his spokesman, correct the dreamer's misconceptions.

The alliterative formula which the dreamer uses to describe his vision of heaven, *se wyth syȝt* (or *se wyth yȝe*), is one which points to the inadequacy of both words and images. Of all the formulas that have been criticized as being mere fillers to facilitate composition, this has been singled out as one of the most meaningless, something to be fitted in whenever a poet needed a second half-line alliterating on "S."[17] Marie Borroff, however, has justified its use in certain contexts where emphasis on vision is significant, notably in the work of the *Pearl*-poet himself. For she argues that when in *Sir Gawain* the members of King Arthur's court think that nothing so extraordinary as the Green Knight has ever been "sene in þat sale wyth syȝt er þat tyme, / wyth yȝe" (seen in that hall with sight before that time, with eye), the double pleonasm in the formula underscores the court's stupefaction, and slows down the action in a way appropriate to a mood of wonder.[18]

I believe that the poet uses *se wyth syȝt* self-consciously, fully aware of its limitations, both theological and rhetorical. The former lie in the faith which it implies in the ability of visual images to accurately convey the Divine. The dreamer in using the formula to describe his vision thereby expresses this faith; the poet, however, wants us to recognize that we see God through such images "through a glass darkly," rather than, as in heaven, "face to face" (I Cor. XIII.12). The theological limitations of the formula are further underscored by the fact that it is often used by the narrators of secular alliterative dream visions to express their astonishment at the splendor of earthly marvels. By putting the formula in the *Pearl* dreamer's mouth, the poet classes him with such dreamers as the narrator of *Wynnere and Wastoure,* to whom the king is one of the handsomest lords that anyone ever "sawe with his eghne," or that of "Summer Sunday," to whom Lady Fortune is such a woman as he never "sey . . . wiþ syȝth."[19]

The rhetorical limitation of *se wyth syȝt,* on the other hand, is simply that it is hackneyed. It is useful for pointing up the inadequacy of words for express-ing the Divine, for it allows the poet to undercut the effect of the language of the alliterative high style. Thus, in the midst of describing the maiden's dress with such elevated phrases as "beau biys" (fair linen), "al blysnande whyt" (all shining white), and "Wyth precios perleȝ al vmbepyȝte" (with precious pearls adorned all about), the poet inserts a "low" formula when he has the dreamer call her pearls the loveliest "þat euer I seȝ ȝet with myn ene" (that ever I saw yet with my eyes).[20]

That the poet is using *se wyth syȝt* pointedly in this case is suggested by the fact that the maiden soon repeats the formula when reproaching him for depending on the evidence of his eyes. She scolds him for believing that she is still alive, simply because he can "wyth yȝen [her] se" (l. 296), and goes on to say

I halde þat iueler lyttel to prayse
Þat leueȝ wel þat he seȝ wyth yȝe,
And much to blame and vncortayse
Þat leueȝ oure Lorde wolde make a lyȝe,
Þat lelly hyȝte your lyf to rayse,
Þaȝ fortune dyd your flesch to dyȝe.
Ȝe setten hys wordeȝ ful westernays
Þat leueȝ noþynk bot ȝe hit syȝe.

(ll. 301–308)

I hold that jeweler hardly worthy of praise
Who believes fully what he sees with eye,
And worthy of blame and lacking courtesy
Who believes our Lord would tell a lie,
He who faithfully promised to raise your life,
Though Fortune caused your flesh to die.
You take his words entirely amiss
You who believe nothing unless you see it.

The dreamer doubts the resurrection, she says, because he believes nothing unless "[he] hit syȝe," and believes everything that he can "seȝ wyth yȝe." By using a formula which the dreamer himself has used—one which has been tainted by having been used to describe too many secular marvels—the maiden points out at once the inadequacy of images and the inadequacy of words for conveying the Divine.

Later in the poem, when the dreamer has made some spiritual progress and is granted a vision of the Heavenly City, the same formula is used to emphasize his dependence on the book of Apocalypse, the source of his vision, and on St. John, its mediator. "As John þe apostel hit syȝ wyth syȝt,/ I syȝe þat cyty" (As John the apostle saw it with sight, I saw that city, ll. 985–986), says the dreamer, and his continued allusion to John's seeing the New Jerusalem (emphasized in the refrain of this stanza group) becomes almost iconographic, like the image of St. John peering through a door into heaven in the popular illuminated Apocalypse books.[21] But although the dreamer is using the formula to authenticate his vision, the poet is using it to point out the dreamer's too earthly perception. This is further suggested by the fact that in contemporary mystical writings St. John's vision is classified in Augustinian terms as a "spiritual" one, which, because reliant on figures and images, is inferior to an "intellectual" vision—presumably the Beatific Vision—involving the sight of God face to face.[22] The Beatific Vision is a major concern of the poet's in his biblical narrative *Purity,* where it is generally expressed by the formula *se wyth syȝt* or *se wyth yȝe.*[23] *Pearl,* however, must be characterized as a failed Beatific Vision to the extent that the dreamer never sees God's face. It is likely therefore that the poet, in having the dreamer use *se wyth syȝt* to describe what he *does* see, is pointing up the limited, mediated quality of the vision, as well as of the language with which he recounts it.

The second kind of conventional language which the poet uses to call attention to the inadequacy of words is a rhetorical commonplace—the "inex-pressibility topos."[24] This topos is not by any means limited to alliterative poetry, but is part of a larger literary inheritance. As a strategic device of self-deprecation for the purpose of winning the audience's approval, it was, indeed, traditional. But as Burrow has shown, this strategy became greatly intensified among fourteenth-century English poets who were trying to accom-modate themselves to their awkward medium.[25] In the *Pearl* the inexpressibility topos is used to suggest that the poet recognizes the limitations of the allitera-tive style—that he is deliberately using conventional apologies for the conven-tionality of his language. For while the dreamer uses these apologies conventionally, the poet expects us to recognize them as justified—expressions of the inadequacy of language not only on a rhetorical, but also on a theological level.

Here as elsewhere the poet uses the dreamer to exploit the ambiguity of the religious and secular connotations of words. In a Christian context, the inexpressibility topos was an important device of the negative way, part of the "rhetoric of ineffability" by which mystical poets sought to express the Divine.[26] Words which admitted their own inadequacy were held to be less likely to lead to idolatry than those which took themselves for granted, as Augustine, follow-ing Plato and Plotinus, had pointed out.[27] Dante of course makes the most notable use of the topos in such a context in the *Paradiso,* where he continually complains that language falls short of describing the Beatific Vision. It is possi-ble, as one critic has argued, that the *Pearl*-poet knew the *Divine Comedy,* and it is even more likely that he knew the anonymous Middle English mystical work *The Cloud of Unknowing,* which refers to mysteries "whiche man may not, ne kan not, speke."[28] Certainly he would have been aware of the mystical Latin hymns which assert, in paradoxical terms, God's ineffability.[29] The poet could thus measure the dreamer against writers whose linguistic doubts were pro-found and theological. But despite the frequent use of the topos in Christian contexts, it was originally classical, and it occurred throughout the Middle Ages in secular descriptions of any marvelous subject to which "words could not do justice."[30] It even had a form specific to alliterative poetry in the formula *it is to tor* [too difficult] *to telle,* which the *Pearl*-poet himself uses in *Sir Gawain* to describe indescribable luxury.[31]

Although this alliterative form of the topos is not used in *Pearl,* other forms are. The dreamer's mistake is to apply them in the conventional secular sense, without a true recognition of the inadequacy of human language. Thus, he paints a dazzling picture of the paradisal garden which foreshadows the New Jerusalem, drawing heavily on the language of the alliterative tradition:

Dubbed wern alle þo downeȝ sydeȝ
Wyth crystal klyffeȝ so cler of kynde.

Holtewodeȝ bryȝt aboute hem bydeȝ
Of bolleȝ as blwe as ble of Ynde;

As bornyst syluer þe lef on slydeȝ,
Þat þike con trylle on vch a tynde.
Quen glem of glodeȝ agaynȝ hem glydeȝ,
Wyth schymeryng schene ful schrylle þay schynde.

(ll. 73-80)

Adorned were all the slopes of the hills
With crystal cliffs of so clear a sort.
Woodlands bright were set about them
Whose trunks were blue as the color indigo;

As burnished silver the leaves swayed,
That trembled closely on each branch.
When a gleam of the sky fell against them,
They shone very brilliantly with a bright shimmering.

The dreamer devotes fifty-five lines to the garden, making it appear like a *locus amoenus* in a secular alliterative dream vision.[32] His understanding, if not his sincerity, is thus open to question when, in the midst of this description, he asserts that

Þe derþe þerof for to deuyse
Nis no wyȝ worþé þat tonge bereȝ.

(ll. 99-100)

To describe the splendor thereof
There is no one worthy who bears a tongue.

The poet puts this conventional disclaimer in the dreamer's mouth to warn against the beauty of the rest of the description, for he knows that the unworthiness of human speech is far greater than the dreamer realizes.

A similar strategy is used when the maiden appears to the dreamer in the garden. He takes her earthly guise for reality, describing her in the intensifying language of alliterative poetry, which is more appropriate to a romance heroine than to the beatified spirit of a child who died in infancy. As far as he is concerned, it is in keeping with this language that he claims inexpressibility when portraying the allegorical pearl on her breast:

A manneȝ dom moȝt dryȝly demme,
Er mynde moȝt malte in hit mesure.
I hope no tong moȝt endure
No sauerly saghe say of þat syȝt.

(ll. 223-226)

A man's judgment would be utterly baffled
Before his mind could comprehend its value.
I believe no tongue could endure
Nor say an adequate word of that sight.

But despite his assertion that human judgment and speech are inadequate, and despite his earlier claim to having been struck dumb when first seeing the maiden ("I stod ful stylle and dorste not calle; / Wyth yȝen open and mouth ful clos," ll. 182–183), the dreamer goes on to describe her with all the resources at an alliterative poet's disposal. He thus lacks the humility of the pilgrim Dante, who, when Beatrice appears to him in a similar situation near the end of the *Paradiso,* resolves to remain silent, his poetic abilities having been so overcome that he cannot describe her beauty.[33] The *Pearl*-poet, then, exploits the simultaneous secular and religious connotations of the inexpressibility topos in order to emphasize the split between the dreamer's and the reader's perception. And because this topos *is* a commonplace, a piece of "used" language, it paradoxically embodies in itself the very inadequacy of language to which it refers.

The likelihood that the poet is using these two types of conventional language—the formula and the topos—self-consciously in the visionary sections is strengthened by his discursive treatment of the limits of language in the debate section of the poem. The maiden, speaking for the poet, makes it clear that language is a much more fundamental issue than the dreamer, with his stock confessions of inexpressibility, perceives, as she touches, implicitly, on the Christian concept of the problematical relation between human words and the Divine Word discussed by Augustine. First, she points out that human language is a medium which encourages error; the dreamer does in fact "speke errour," as he puts it in a conventional apology to her (l. 422). While warning him against depending on the evidence of his eyes, the maiden says,

> Þre wordeȝ hatȝ þou spoken at ene:
> Vnavysed, for soþe, wern alle þre.
> Þou ne woste in worlde quat on dotȝ mene;
> Þy worde byfore þy wytte con fle.
> (ll. 291–294)

> Three words have you spoken at once:
> All ill-advised, indeed, were all three.
> You don't know what in the world one of them means;
> Your word has fled before your wit.

She characterizes the dreamer's three misconceptions (that she is in the paradise that he sees, that he can join her there, that he can cross the water) as three ill-advised "wordeȝ." And she points out that his "worde" fled before his "wytte"—that is, that he failed to achieve the embodiment of thought in language which Augustine considered a metaphor for the Incarnation.[34]

But despite the fact that the dreamer's language has failed, the maiden implies that human language *may* be used to bridge the gap between God and man. The early part of the debate deals with this problem, as can be seen from the prominence given to *deme,* the link-word in stanza-group 6 (ll. 301–360). In its ten occurrences in the stanza's refrain, the word ranges in meaning from "to judge" to "to speak," and it is applied in turn to God, the dreamer, and the maiden in a way that explicitly contrasts Divine and human speech as well as judgment. The maiden makes it clear, as Augustine had, that whatever the limitations of human language, man is entitled to use it to try to communicate with God ("þy prayer may hys pyté byte" [your prayer may move his pity], l. 355), and is in fact obligated to do so ("man to God wordeȝ schulde heue" [man should lift words to God], l. 314). She is recognizing here the Christian paradox that although God is ineffable, He has nevertheless, in Augustine's words, "accepted the tribute of the human voice, and wished us to take joy in praising Him with our words."[35] Human language, furthermore, is valid as a means of communication from God to man, as in His revelation in Scripture, but scriptural words are often misconstrued by fallen human beings. Thus the maiden, in a passage quoted earlier, scolds the dreamer for thinking that Christ would "make a lyȝe" about the resurrection (l. 304), and for taking Christ's words amiss ("ȝe setten hys wordeȝ ful westernays," l. 306). The dreamer continues his misunderstanding till near the end of the debate, when he complains that it would contradict Scripture if the maiden had indeed been made a queen in heaven—then "Holy Wryt" would be "bot a fable" (l. 592).

The maiden, then, implies that although man is obligated to try to communicate with God through language, his attempt will be doomed to failure—words are insufficient. More devastating in its consequences for the dreamer, however, is the suggestion that the ability to use language is *unnecessary* for salvation, since the maiden, who died while an inarticulate child, was saved. The dreamer's main objection to her high position in heaven is that she died too young to have earned that status. The linguistic implications of this point are brought forward when he argues that a child of two would have been unable to pray—to praise God with language:

> Þou lyfed not two ȝer in oure þede;
> Þou cowþeȝ neuer God nauþer plese ne pray,
> Ne neuer nawþer Pater ne Crede.
>
> (*ll.* 483–485)

> You lived not two years in our land;
> You never knew how to please God, nor pray to him,
> Nor knew either Paternoster or Creed.

The maiden answers him with the parable of the vineyard, whose moral is that earthly status is reversed in heaven ("þe laste schal be þe fyrst . . ./ And þe fyrst þe laste," ll. 507–571). She sharpens the moral with the standard medieval gloss that the "laste"—those who entered the vineyard late in the day—are the innocents, those who died in infancy (ll. 625–636). She further bolsters her argument by citing Christ's insistence that the Kingdom of Heaven is open to children ("let chylder vnto me tyȝt./ To suche is heuenryche arayed," ll. 718–719) and that one can enter it *only* if he becomes like a child ("hys ryche no wy3 my3t wynne/ Bot he com þyder ry3t as a chylde," ll. 722-723). In using these allusions to support her own position in heaven, the maiden is implicitly drawing on the Christian concept that the humility of the child is specifically linguistic. Augustine in particular was intrigued by the idea of the speechless (*infans*) or barely articulate child. In justifying the *sermo humilis* of the Bible, he frequently mentions its accessibility to children, saying for instance that Scrip-ture, while it "suits itself to babes," nevertheless lets our understanding rise to the sublime.[36] Again in the *Confessions* he tells of his initial contempt for scriptur-al Latin because its style was unworthy of Cicero: "as the child grows these books grow with him. But I was too proud to call myself a child. I was inflated with self-esteem, which made me think myself a great man."[37] The *Pearl*-dreamer, as he insists on the efficacy of language, is very like the young Augustine in rhetorical arrogance. The maiden's claim that she was elevated to the rank of queen in heaven is thus especially humiliating: she has shown that adult linguistic facility is insignificant from a Divine perspective.

Language, then, is a far more important theme of the *Pearl* than has generally been recognized. This theme has both rhetorical and theological implications, since the poet's sense of the inadequacy of his Middle English poetic style is sharpened by his recognition of the inadequacy of man's words *vis à vis* God's Word. The former he dramatizes by placing conventional and sometimes hackneyed language in the dreamer's mouth; the latter he treats discursively through the maiden's criticisms of the dreamer. By using language which warns against itself, the poet is able to achieve a poetic incarnation on the Augustinian model—to suggest the Divine Word through the limited medi-um of his own words.

NOTES

1.   For a succinct discussion, see John MacQuarrie, *God-Talk: An Examination of the Language and Logic of Religion* (New York: Harper and Row, 1967), pp. 25, 28-29.

2.   E.g., A. C. Spearing, *The Gawain-Poet: A Critical Study* (Cambridge, Eng.: Cambridge Univ. Press, 1970), pp. 155-56, 165, and Pamela Gradon, *Form and Style in Early English Literature* (London: Methuen, 1971), pp. 207-211.

3.   Two articles deal with the theme of language in *Pearl* in ways that differ from mine. James Milroy's "*Pearl*: The Verbal Texture and the Linguistic Theme" (*Neo-philologus*, 55 [1971], 195-208) discusses the dreamer's earthbound understanding of words, but in a context which is only implicitly theological; John M. Hill's "Middle English Poets and the Word: Notes toward an Appraisal of Linguistic Consciousness" (*Criticism*, 16 [1974], 153-169) is much closer to my work in treating the inadequacy of language in Augustinian terms, but, like Milroy's article, does not relate this inadequacy to the limitations of Middle English verse.

4. Trans. D. W. Robertson, Jr., *On Christian Doctrine* (Indianapolis: Bobbs-Merrill, 1958), I.vi.6; *PL* XXXIV, 21.

5. See, e.g., *Confessions* I.iv.4; *PL* XXXII, 622-623.

6. Augustine's statements about language are part of his larger concern that anything intended to move men toward blessedness not be enjoyed for its own sake. For Augustinian sign theory, see Stanley E. Fish, *Self-Consuming Artifacts: The Experience of Seventeenth-Century Literature* (1972; rpt. Berkeley: Univ. of California Press, 1974), pp. 21-43, and Joseph Anthony Mazzeo, "St. Augustine's Rhetoric of Silence: Truth vs. Eloquence and Things vs. Signs," *Renaissance and Seventeenth-Century Studies* (New York: Columbia Univ. Press, 1964), pp. 1-28.

7. See Marcia L. Colish, *The Mirror of Language: A Study in the Medieval Theory of Knowledge* (New Haven: Yale Univ. Press, 1968), pp. 22, 33-35, and more generally, the chapter "St. Augustine: the Experience of the Word," pp. 8-81.

8. "Sermo humilis," in *Literary Language and its Public in Late Latin Antiquity and in the Middle Ages,* trans. Ralph Manheim (Princeton: Princeton Univ. Press, 1965), pp. 27-52.

9. Especially in *De Vulgari Eloquentia*; on this point and on the general continuity of the theory, see Colish, pp. 264-265, 315-316. The case for the influence of Augustinian sign theory on two Middle English poems contemporary with *Pearl* is made by Mary Carruthers (*The Search for St. Truth: A Study of Meaning in Piers Plowman* [Evanston: Northwestern Univ. Press, 1973], esp. pp. 10-19), and Eugene Vance ("*Mervelous Signals*: Poetics, Sign Theory, and Politics in Chaucer's *Troilus,*" *NLH,* 10 [1979], 296). Robert O. Payne points out that the Augustinian concern that rhetoric would encourage idolatry continued through the fourteenth century ("Chaucer's Realization of Himself as Rhetor," in *Medieval Eloquence: Studies in the Theory and Practice of Medieval Rhetoric,* ed. James J. Murphy [Berkeley: Univ. of California Press, 1978], pp. 280-282).

10. See Albert C. Baugh, *A History of the English Language,* 2nd ed. (New York: Appleton-Century-Crofts, 1957), pp. 150-187, 227-237, and Basil Cottle, *The Triumph of English, 1350-1400* (New York: Barnes and Noble, 1969), pp. 15-50.

11. On the debasement of Middle English style, see J. A. Burrow, *Ricardian Poetry: Chaucer, Gower, Langland, and the Gawain-Poet* (New Haven: Yale Univ. Press, 1971), pp. 25-28. On oral performance in medieval literature, see Robert Kellogg, "Oral Literature," *NLH,* 5 (1973), 55-66.

12. For a brief account of the nature of the alliterative line, see Thorlac Turville-Petre, *The Alliterative Revival* (Totowa, N.J.: Rowman and Littlefield, 1977), pp. 51-56.

13. Burrow, p. 26. See also J. P. Oakden, *Alliterative Poetry in Middle English: A Survey of the Traditions,* II (Manchester: Manchester Univ. Press, 1935), 381-401.

14. Elizabeth Salter, *Piers Plowman: An Introduction* (Cambridge, Mass.: Harvard Univ. Press, 1961), p. 17. She refers to the "high rhetoric" and "formality" of many of the poets (pp. 15-17).

15. See especially Marie Borroff, *Sir Gawain and the Green Knight: A Stylistic and Metrical Study* (New Haven: Yale Univ. Press, 1962), pp. 52-90, and Larry D. Benson, *Art and Tradition in Sir Gawain and the Green Knight* (New Brunswick: Rutgers Univ. Press, 1965), pp. 126-143.

16. Burrow, pp. 39-40.

17. Burrow, p. 27.

18. Borroff, pp. 71-72; *Sir Gawain and the Green Knight,* ed. J. R. R. Tolkien and E. V. Gordon, 2nd ed. rev. Norman Davis (Oxford: Oxford Univ. Press, 1968), ll. 197-98. My translation.

19. *Wynnere and Wastoure,* ed. Sir Israel Gollancz (London: Oxford Univ. Press, 1930),

l. 89, and "Summer Sunday," in *Historical Poems of the Fourteenth and Fifteenth Centuries,* ed. Rossell Hope Robbins (New York: Columbia Univ. Press, 1959), p. 100, l. 64. Similarly, the dreamer in "The Crowned King" tells of the marvelous crowd of people which he "sawe in [his] sight" (in Robbins, p. 228, l. 33).

20. *Pearl,* ed. E. V. Gordon (1953; rpt. Oxford: Clarendon Press, 1966), ll. 197, 204, 200. This and subsequent translations of the poem are my own.

21. See George Henderson, *Gothic* (1967; rpt. Baltimore: Penguin, 1972), p. 149.

22. Edward Wilson, " 'Gostly Drem' in 'Pearl'," *NM,* 69 (1968), 90–101.

23. See C. G. Osgood, ed. *Pearl* (Boston: D. C. Heath, 1906), n. to l. 675, and Robert J. Menner, ed. *Purity* (New Haven: Yale Univ. Press, 1920), n. to l. 25.

24. So named by Ernst Robert Curtius, in *European Literature and the Latin Middle Ages,* trans. Willard R. Trask (1953; rpt. New York: Harper and Row, 1963), p. 159.

25. Burrow. pp. 39–42.

26. See Lowry Nelson, "The Rhetoric of Ineffability: Toward a Definition of Mystical Poetry," *CL,* 8 (1956), 323–336, Luigi Tonelli, *Dante e la poesia dell'ineffabile* (Florence: G. Barbèra, 1934), pp. 45–77, and Robin Kirkpatrick, *Dante's Paradiso and the Limitations of Modern Criticism* (Cambridge: Cambridge Univ. Press, 1978), pp. 36–50.

27. Peter S. Hawkins, "Saint Augustine and the Language of Ineffability," unpub. ms., pp. 8–11.

28. For the former point, see P. M. Kean, *Pearl: An Interpretation* (New York: Barnes and Noble, 1967), pp. 120–132; for the latter, *The Cloud of Unknowing and the Book of Privy Counselling,* ed. Phyllis Hodgson (London: EETS, 1944), p. 62.

29. See Nelson, p. 327, and Tonelli, pp. 70–75.

30. Curtius' examples are limited to secular ones (pp. 159–162). In Dante the secular topos coalesces with the Christian, and Tonelli has shown that the poet drew on its use by Provençal love poets as well as by the mystics (pp. 80, ff.).

31. He says that it is "to tor for to telle" of all the ornamental figures embroidered on the Green Knight's clothing (l. 165). See *OED,* Tor, a., for further examples in alliterative poetry. My interpretation of the formula as a use of the inexpressibility topos depends on a translation of *tor* as "difficult"; the more common translation, "tiresome, tedious," would make it an instance of *occupatio*—the announcement that the poet will curtail his description (see Benson, p. 172).

32. E.g., the landscapes in *Wynnere and Wastoure* (ll. 33–44) and the *Parlement of the Thre Ages* (ed. M.Y. Offord [London: EETS, 1959], ll. 1–20). On the conventionality of such landscapes, see Ralph W. V. Elliott, "Landscape and Rhetoric in Middle English Alliterative Poetry," *Melbourne Critical Review,* 4 (1961), 65–76.

33. *La Commedia seconda antica vulgata,* ed. Giorgio Petrocchi, IV (Rome: Arnoldo Mondadori, 1967), XXX.16–33.

34. *De Trinitate* XV.x. 19; *PL* XLII, 1071, and *De Doctrina Christiana* I. xiii; *PL* XXXIV, 24.

35. *On Christian Doctrine* I. vi. 6; *PL* XXXIV, 21.

36. *De Trinitate* I.2 (trans. Arthur West Haddan in *A Select Library of the Nicene and Post-Nicene Fathers of the Christian Church,* ed. Philip Schaff [Grand Rapids, Mich.: Wm. B. Eerdmans, 1956], III, 18; *PL* XLII, 820).

37. *Confessions* III.v (trans. R. S. Pine-Coffin [Harmondsworth: Penguin, 1961], p. 60); *PL* XXXII, 686.

"The Rest Is Silence": Ineffability and the "Unscene" in Shakespeare's Plays

Marjorie Garber

> "Whereof one cannot speak, thereof one must keep silent"—Wittgenstein

"Heard melodies are sweet, but those unheard / Are sweeter; therefore, ye soft pipes, play on." The paradox implicit in Keats's famous lines suggests the difficulties inherent in any approach to ineffability through the medium of language. The "unheard" melodies piped by figures on the Grecian urn are displaced and replaced by the melody of the poet who describes them. Although he calls the urn a "still unravished bride of quietness," in a sense he himself becomes the ravisher, by putting into words his response to the silent urn, and using the imagined songs of the "happy melodist" as a catalyst for his own poetic invention. "Ditties of no tone," rather like the harmony of the spheres, exist only in the words that describe them, since they cannot be heard by the human ear. But to leave the "unspeakable" literally unspoken is, for the poet, tantamount to deciding not to write a poem.

Poets from antiquity learned to deal with this problem rhetorically through strategic use of the "inexpressibility topos": "I cannot tell you how beautiful she was," "words cannot express my joy." Thus for example Virgil describes the horrors of the underworld by telling us that he cannot describe them: "non mihi si linguae centum sint oraque centum, / ferrae vox, omnis scelerum comprendere formas, / omnia poenarum percurrere nomina possim" (Nay, had I a hundred tongues, a hundred mouths, and voice of iron, I could not sum up all the forms of crime, or rehearse all the tale of torments").[1] The inexpressibility topos had the effect of aggrandizement through rhetoric, suggesting an immensity too great to be conveyed by words, while cleverly using words to convey it. Such strategies were necessary because otherwise the ineffable or unspeakable would have to be represented by silence, or rather by absence— since silence on the printed page becomes a spatial rather than an aural event.

In *Tristram Shandy* the reader is provided a blank page on which to write his own description of Uncle Toby's beloved, "For never did thy eyes behold, or thy concupiscence covet any thing in this world, more concupiscible than widow *Wadman*".[2] Wallace Stevens's poem "The Man on the Dump" ends virtually in midair, with "the the,"[3] as if inviting the reader to propose his own poem, and Robert Graves likewise teases the reader out of thought by titling the last poem in his book "Leaving the Rest Unsaid," and ending it in the middle of a sentence:

> Must the book end, as you would end it,
> With testamentary appendices
> And graveyard indices?
> But no, I will not lay me down
> To let your tearful music mar
> The decent mystery of my progress.
> So now, my solemn ones, leaving the rest unsaid,
> Rising in air as on a gander's wing
> At a careless comma,[4]

Such experiments create the visual equivalent of silence, by literally leaving unsaid what is alleged to be unsayable. But for lyric poets, novelists, and other monovocal writers the possibilities for representing ineffability directly are limited in both method and effect, because of the nature of the genres in which they work. When they are silent, no one speaks.

For the playwright, however, the possibilities are much more diverse. Since he is working with several characters at once, rather than with a single narrative or lyric voice, he can create dramatic opportunities for silence between them, either explicitly, through stage directions and clues in the text, or implicitly, by the nature of the theatrical encounters he designs for them. He can also make use of the inexpressibility topos, much in the manner of narrative writers, but with the addition of a wondering listener or audience on the stage. Moreover, as we will see, he can extend and reshape that topos into a more specifically dramatic mode by placing the inexpressible moment in a scene that takes place offstage, to be reported in retrospect by an onstage observer. In all of these cases, the playwright approaches the problem of ineffability in literature by exploiting the special nature of his medium.

As we should expect, most "ineffable" moments in Shakespeare come in the later plays, the final tragedies and the romances, where the content of the plays themselves seems frequently to demand a dramatic technique that goes beyond the limits of the quotidian and the expressible. Thus in several of the plays a character falls silent at a moment of strong emotion. When Macduff receives the news that his wife and children have been murdered, his shock and grief render him speechless, as Malcolm observes: "What, man! Ne'er pull your hat upon your brows. / Give sorrow words. The grief that does not speak / Whispers the o'erfraught heart, and bids it break" (*Macbeth* IV.iii.208–210).[5] Ineffability here is both a natural and a dangerous condition. Macduff must return to language in order to come to terms with his own unspeakable grief.

The question of ineffability is addressed even more directly in the opening scene of *King Lear*. When Lear asks his daughters which of them loves him most, he is asking for the inexpressibility topos, and from his two elder daughters that is what he gets. Goneril's reply is a classic example of the genre:

> Sir, I love you more than word can wield the matter;
> Dearer than eyesight, space, and liberty;
> Beyond what can be valued, rich or rare;
> No less than life, with grace, health, beauty, honor;
> As much as child e'er loved, or father found;
> A love that makes breath poor, and speech unable:
> Beyond all manner of so much I love you.
>   (I.i.55–61)

Regan, challenged to better this testament of incomparable affection, does so by overtopping. Her sister has "name[d her] very deed of love; / Only she comes too short" (71–72). Regan herself, she says, has no other joys: "I am alone felicitate / In your dear highness' love" (75–76). It is now Cordelia's turn, and although she has already warned the audience in an aside that she will "Love, and be silent" (62), her reply of "Nothing, my lord" nonetheless comes as a shock. "Nothing," of course, is not silence, but it is a signifier of silence, and in productions of the play it is almost invariably uttered after a protracted and anguished silence in which Cordelia struggles with herself. She knows what she must say. Just as Hamlet, listening to Claudius's unctuous words of pretended grief, realizes that he must abandon his inky cloak of mourning since the ritual of mourning has itself been sullied, so Cordelia sees the language of love sullied beyond retrieval by her sisters' "glib and oily" words. But one of the pitfalls of silence as a mode of communication is that it may be misinterpreted, as Lear misinterprets it here. Cordelia's scrupulous attempt to define her love by quality rather than by quantity fails, and the play moves inexorably toward tragedy. The truest definition of ineffability in the context of *King Lear* comes in fact not from any of Lear's daughters but from Edgar when he first beholds his blinded father: "the worst is not / So long as we can say, 'This is the worst.' " (IV.i.27–28).

A particularly compelling instance of a speaking silence on the stage occurs at the end of *Coriolanus,* when the hero capitulates to his mother's plea for him to spare Rome. In the course of the scene Volumnia speaks at length and without apparent result, repeatedly inviting Coriolanus's wife and child to add their voices: "Daughter, speak you." "Speak thou, boy" (V.iii.155, 156). Finally, in a rhetorical move calculated to provoke him, she turns to go, acknowledging the failure of her words: "Yet give us our dispatch. / I am hushed until our city be a-fire, / And then I'll speak a little" (180–182). Here the stage direction tells us Coriolanus "holds her by the hand, silent." Volumnia's silence has more effect than her words. On the stage the stony Coriolanus slowly relents, his impassivity turned to emotion, perhaps even to tears, since Aufidius will later taunt him by calling him "thou boy of tears" (V.vi.99). In taking her hand he reaffirms the filial bond, abandoning his intention to "stand / As if a man were author of himself / And knew no other kin" (V.iii.35–37). His gesture shifts the emotional center of the scene from mother to son, and when he finally speaks he is determined to yield to her wishes, although the consequences may be—as they become—"most mortal" to him.

This scene is a remarkable example of the rhetoric of silence, the ability of silence to convey an inexpressible emotion, here compounded at once of love, grief, and perhaps fear. The stage direction places emphasis not on the speeches of mother and son, but on the space, the silence, between them. In this case silence is a dramatic element as fundamental as speech, a theatrical means of expressing the inexpressible.

A slightly different attempt to use the rhetoric of silence occurs in *The Winter's Tale,* when Paulina decides to confront Leontes with his newborn daughter in the hope that he may alter his brutal behavior toward the impris-oned queen, Hermione. "We do not know," says Paulina, "How he may soften at the sight o' th' child; / The silence often of pure innocence / Persuades, when speaking fails" (II.ii.38–41). Perdita is an "infant," etymologically one who cannot speak. But Leontes will not listen, and there is no speaking silence of recognition between parent and child. When the recognition does come, six-teen years later, it will occur offstage rather than before our eyes, in a dramatic context which, as we will see, is significant for Shakespeare's treatment of ineffable emotion.

However, the true counterpart to the scene of Paulina and Perdita is not Leontes's rediscovery of his daughter, but rather his rediscovery of his wife, Hermione, who is likewise unable to speak since she is disguised as a statue. Paulina had described the infant Perdita as the image of her father, using metaphors from the art of printing: "Although the print be little, the whole matter / And copy of the father" (II.iii.98–99). The "awakening" of Hermione from statue to living woman is likewise achieved by a detailed scrutiny of a human being as a work of art. As the "statue" is unveiled, the repentant Leontes describes his lost wife as "tender / As infancy and grace" (V.iii.26–27), again reminding the audience of the earlier scene in which an actual infant appeared. And the unveiling is performed before a hushed onstage audience, as Paulina makes clear: "I like your silence; it the more shows off / Your wonder" (V.iii.21–22). "Wonder," the predominant emotion of Shakespearean romance, is also the emotion of ineffability, transcending verbal expression. Once again the playwright builds into his play a moment when no one on the stage speaks, and yet communication is achieved. In this scene the condition of wonder, the ineffable, seems particularly appropriate, since the setting is a chapel, the circumstances are highly staged and "dramatic," and the interaction occurs between human beings and a figure who appears to be other than human. When Hermione's identity is revealed she embraces her amazed husband, and Camillo seeks further confirmation of her nature: "If she pertain to life, let her speak too" (113). Here, as elsewhere in Shakespeare, language becomes an index of humanity, while silence demarcates emotions or experiences that transcend the human condition.

Modern English makes an interesting distinction between "ineffable," which means beyond expression, too great to be uttered, and "unspeakable," which means the same things, but can also mean inexpressibly vile. Shakespeare does not use the word "ineffable" in his plays, and he uses "unspeakable" as an intensifier, augmenting either felicitous or infelicitous events. Titus Andronicus is said to have suffered "wrongs, unspeakable, past patience" (V.iii.126), courtiers in *The Winter's Tale* allude to the "unspeakable comfort" brought to Sicilia by its young prince, Mamillius (I.i.36–37), and in the same play the shepherd who finds Perdita and the gold that was left with her is described as "a man, they say, that from very nothing, and beyond the imagination of his neighbors, is grown into an unspeakable estate" (IV.ii.39–41). As early as *The Comedy of Errors* Shakespeare uses "unspeakable" and the inexpressibility topos as a mode of exposition. At the beginning of the play the Syracusan merchant Egeon is asked by the Duke of Ephesus to explain "in brief" (I.i.28) his presence in an enemy town. Egeon replies that "A heavier task could not have been imposed/ Than I to speak my griefs unspeakable" (31–32) and then goes on to speak them for more than a hundred lines, pausing once as if to break off ("O, let me say no more!/ Gather the sequel by that went before" [94–95]) but is urged by the Duke to complete his tale of woe. Here, as in the other direct uses of "unspeakable" in Shakespeare, the events or persons described are pitiable or marvellous, but not really beyond expression. The word "unspeakable" becomes a manner of speaking, a shorthand term meaning something like "remarkable" or "immense."

None of these references touches upon a third possible meaning of "unspeakable" and "ineffable," that is, "something that may not be uttered," like the name of God. But it is that sense of the term which is perhaps the most interesting in view of the structure and function of the plays as a whole. Ineffability in this sense involves some kind of transgression of boundaries. A word or action becomes taboo because it is associated with gods or devils, with the sacred, or with forbidden knowledge. Thus when Macbeth salutes the witches with "How, now, you secret, black, and midnight hags! / What is 't you do?" he is told, "A deed without a name" (IV.i.48–49). It is this quest for forbidden knowledge that seals his doom. In this respect Macbeth is very like Marlowe's Doctor Faustus, another seeker after superhuman knowledge and power. Iago's abjuration of speech at the end of *Othello* is a related phenomenon, coming as it does immediately after Othello has called him a "demi-devil." "Demand me nothing," he replies. "What you know, you know. / From this time forth I never will speak word" (V.ii.302–303). In this case an unspeakable figure elects not to speak, and thereby allies himself even more closely with inhuman powers. Throughout the play Iago has manipulated language to gain his nefarious ends; now he wills himself to be anti-Logos, the uncreating Word.

More usually, however, these liminal encounters or boundary transgressions occur at the other end of the scale, in the realm of "wonder." We have seen the function of wonder as an aspect of the ineffable in *The Winter's Tale.* When Ferdinand first encounters Miranda in *The Tempest,* this quality becomes personified, as he addresses the unknown and unexpected figure as "you wonder!" (I.ii.429) and "the goddess / On whom these airs attend!" (424–425); she likewise imagines him to be "divine" (421). Significantly, Prospero has forbidden her to tell her name; it is literally taboo, ineffable, something not to be uttered. But she tells it nonetheless, and Ferdinand immediately deciphers the meaning:

> Ferdinand: What is your name?
> Miranda: Miranda. O my father,
> I have broke your hest to say so!
> Ferdinand: Admired Miranda!
> Indeed the top of admiration, worth
> What's dearest to the world!
>   (III.i.36–39)

In his eyes, as for a moment in the eyes of the audience, she becomes a living manifestation of ineffability.

Even in a play far removed from the genre of romance, "wonder" is connected with speechlessness and personal transformation. In *Much Ado About Nothing* the witty and voluble Benedick, described by Beatrice early in the play as "evermore tattling" (II.i.9), is reduced to uncharacteristic silence by Claudio's public accusation of Hero: "I am so attired in wonder," he declares, "I know not what to say" (IV.i.143–144). And it is here, in the realm of "wonder," that the inexpressibility topos in Shakespeare has its most powerful effect. Instead of eloquent silences at moments of great emotion, the audience is confronted by characters who try to express the inexpressible by acknowledging that they cannot do so. The fundamental use of this topos, as in antiquity, is for aggrandizement of the subject, whether it be a person, a feeling, or an event. There are numerous local examples in Shakespeare's plays, like Juliet's claim that "my true love is grown to such excess / I cannot sum up sum of half my wealth" (II.vi.33–34), but there are also larger instances that have a profound effect upon the shape and meaning of the plays that contain them.

The most strikingly dramatic use of the inexpressibility topos in the plays is that of the Prologues to *Henry V,* in which the Chorus repeatedly enjoins his audience to use its imagination: "Piece out our imperfections with your thoughts: / Into a thousand parts divide one man / And make imaginary puissance. / Think, when we talk of horses, that you see them / Printing their proud hoofs i' th' receiving earth; / For 'tis your thoughts that now must deck our kings"

(I.Prol.23–28). The audience's participation, its act of invention "In the quick forge and working house of thought" (V.Prol.23) is necessary here because of the inadequacy of Shakespeare's stage to portray accurately the great events of the play: "Can this cockpit hold / The vasty fields of France? Or may we cram / Within this wooden O the very casques / That did affright the air at Agincourt?" (I.Prol.11–14). The answer to these highly rhetorical questions is both yes and no. Literally, as the Prologue points out, such representation is impossible; what is required is not mimesis but identity—"A kingdom for a stage, princes to act, / And monarchs to behold the swelling scene!" (I.Prol.2–5). But having said that he cannot represent these things, the playwright proceeds to do so, just as Keats celebrates unheard melodies in a heard one. The phenomenological effect here is complex; paradoxically, what we are told is not real becomes real through the process of denying its reality. Throughout his plays— and not only in the histories—Shakespeare suggests that history is itself an artifact, continually recreated through reputation, memory, and retelling. In the great "Crispan Crispian" speech, King Harry envisages a man who fought at Agincourt retelling the history of that battle to his neighbors many years afterward: "Old men forget; yet all shall be forgot, / But he'll remember, with advantages, / What feats he did that day" (IV.iii.49–51). "With advantages"— that is, the old man will enhance his own contributions as he reports them in retrospect. If history is inevitably distorted in this way, the exact representation so despaired of by the Prologue is impossible; by acknowledging the inevitably fictive nature of retold events, Shakespeare gives to the dramatic action of his play an imagined reality which is truer than any historical fact. When Wallace Stevens writes that poetry is the only reality in this imagined world, he is speaking to the same apparent paradox.

In effect, then, by calling attention to the play as a play, a created artifact, the Prologue transforms the inexpressible grandeur of King, soldiers, and glorious victory into a mode of expression. The tension between prologue and play, artifice and action, works admirably to frame and deepen the dramatic events we see, by placing them in the context of those we can only imagine. The solution to the problem of inexpressibility here is that of art. Not surprisingly, this is also Bottom's answer, when he comes to describe his own ineffable experience in the Athenian wood—what he calls "Bottom's Dream." The "Dream" is Bottom's attempt to come to terms with his transformation into an ass, and his subsequent and bemusing amorous adventures with Titania, queen of the fairies. Here the events are ineffable or inexpressible not because of their immensity, as in *Henry V*, but because of their improbability—their "wonder" in another sense. Although the passage is familiar I will quote it here to clarify the dramatic point:

> I have had a most rare vision. I have had a dream, past the wit of man to say what dream it was. Man is but an ass, if he go about to expound this dream.

> Methought I was—there is no man can tell what. Methought I was—and me-
> thought I had—but man is but a patched fool if he will offer to say what me-
> thought I had. The eye of man hath not heard, the ear of man hath not seen,
> man's hand is not able to taste, his tongue to conceive, nor his heart to report,
> what my dream was.
>
> (*MND* IV.i.205-214)

This is a delightfully straightforward admission of the speaker's inability to say
what he has seen and known. The last line, a scrambled passage from First
Corinthians, is Bottom's attempt to compare his extraordinary experience with
a more orthodox Christian experience of ineffability: "Eye hath not seen,"
writes St. Paul, "nor ear heard, neither have entered into the heart of man, the
things which God hath prepared for them that love Him" (I.Cor.2:9). Bottom's
solution to this problem of communication is to have his indescribable adventures translated into a "ballet," or ballad, by Peter Quince. Again the unspeaking and unspeakable is to become a work of art. In a way this episode, or at
least the idea of making wonderful events into a ballad to testify to their truth,
anticipates an interesting piece of business in the sheep-shearing scene of *The
Winter's Tale,* in which Autolycus appears as a peddler selling broadside ballads.
The shepherdesses happily seize upon ballads describing such improbable events
as "how a usurer's wife was brought to bed of twenty moneybags at a burden"
(IV.iv.262-264), and how a woman "was turned into a cold fish for she would
not exchange flesh with one that loved her" (279-281). The veracity of these
tales is unquestionably accepted because they are written down; as Mopsa says,
"I love a ballad in print, a-life, for then we are sure they are true" (260-261).

Bottom's "dream" is called a dream because he cannot believe it actually
happened. Cleopatra also tells a "dream" which is closely related to the inexpressibility topos in both content and rhetorical effect, but her dream represents her imaginative vision of something only she and the offstage audience
believe was true. Her onstage audience is the deferent but politely disbelieving
Roman, Dolabella, who represents the limited perspective of literal reality, in
contrast to Cleopatra's magnificent tapestry of hyperboles. "I dreamt there was
an Emperor Antony," she begins. His "face was as the heav'ns," his eyes like
the sun and moon, "his legs bestrid the ocean," his voice to friends was like
the music of the spheres, but when he spoke to foes "he was as rattling
thunder." "In his livery / Walked crowns and crownets; realms and islands were
/ As plates dropped from his pocket" (V.ii.76-92). "Think you," she says to
Dolabella, "there was or might be such a man / As this I dreamt of?" and he
replies, "Gentle madam, no." Cleopatra's response, denying his denial, is perhaps as close as Shakespeare comes to defining the ineffable in language:

> You lie, up to the hearing of the gods.
> But if there be nor ever were one such,
> It's past the size of dreaming; nature wants stuff

> To vie strange forms with fancy, yet t'imagine
> An Antony were nature's piece 'gainst fancy,
> Condemning shadows quite.
>   (95–100)

"Past the size of dreaming" verbally condenses as it conceptually expands the idea of a man beyond description; even the aggrandizing "dream" comes too short in measuring the reality, the grandeur of Antony as he lived.

Structurally this speech is a proper pendant to Enobarbus's great praise of Cleopatra in Act II ("the barge she sat in, like a burnish'd throne, / Burned on the water . . ." [II.ii.193–242]), although Enobarbus uses paradox rather than hyperbole as the rhetorical basis of his description. Dolabella's "Gentle madam, no," is in part anticipated by the Roman sentiments of Enobarbus's audience, Agrippa and Maecenas, who despite their fascination think there are limits to Cleopatra's power. "Now Antony must leave her utterly," Maecenas concludes (II.ii.235). "Never, he will not," is Enobarbus's prompt—and accurate—reply. The *onstage* listeners are tempered in their response to this portrait of royal—and female—quintessence. But the *offstage* audience hears—and believes. We do not see the scene at Cydnus—the barge, the sails, the dimpled boys and bending gentlewomen—but we feel as if we have. The image is imprinted on our imaginations; and when, as she prepares for death, Cleopatra announces that she is "again for Cydnus" (V.ii.228), the vision of the incomparable queen on her barge comes vividly to mind. This is a spectacle that might perhaps be translated into theatrical action with the resources of a Cecil B. DeMille, but on the Elizabethan stage—and perhaps on any stage—to perform it would be to risk anticlimax, as spectacle competes with words. The scene gains in power precisely because of its displaced or deflected nature—the fact that we are told it, not shown it. This is what might be called "theatrical ineffability," a *coup de théâtre* on the level of text. And here we come to the third and perhaps the most remarkable of Shakespeare's dramatic expressions of the inexpressible, more innovative and in some ways more effective than either the actual silences on the stage or the skilled and evocative use of the topos of inexpressibility. I refer to what I would like to call "unscenes"—deflected or unseen scenes that take place offstage and are reported by an observer, usually an anonymous or disinterested "Gentleman," occasionally by a figure more centrally involved in the action.

Like Enobarbus's description of Cleopatra, these unscenes are in effect a translation of the inexpressibility topos into dramatic terms. Rather than declaring the events they describe to be indescribable, unscenes describe them at one remove, leaving the actual words and gestures of the participants to the audience's imagination, while vividly underscoring the emotional significance of what has taken place. In this way they are able to embody the central paradox of literary ineffability, by speaking about the unspeakable while leaving it literally unspoken. Significantly, the subjects of unscenes are almost without exception moments of extreme emotion, and frequently conflicted emotions: joy and fear, love and grief or anger. Their content, like their mode of expression, is ineffable.

One notable example of the unscene is Ophelia's description of Hamlet's distracted visit to her "closet," or bedroom, "his doublet all unbraced, / No hat upon his head, his stockings fouled, / Ungartered, and down-gyved to his ankle, / Pale as his shirt" (II.i.78–81). The scene as she reports it is so detailed that audiences may feel, once again, that they have seen it. She tells us that he took her by the wrist, perused her face, shook her arm and waved his head three times up and down, uttering a sigh "so piteous and profound / As it did seem to shatter all his bulk / And end his being" (94–96). At length he released her, and as he left the room looking behind him, "he seemed to find his way without his eyes," for he "to the last bended their light on [her]" (98; 100). These are very specific stage directions, and in fact many directors have yielded to tempta-tion and staged the scene, rather than leaving it to Ophelia's indirect narration. Yet there are cogent reasons why the indirect method of presentation is prefera-ble. The sigh that seemed to end his being, and the "look so piteous in purport, / As if he had been loosèd out of hell / To speak of horrors" (82–84)—these signs, as Ophelia describes them, betoken ineffable, unspeakable emotions, emotions that exist on the limits of human life and human possibility: "shatter all his bulk," "loosed out of hell." We may notice that in the course of this encounter Hamlet apparently says nothing at all, nor does the "affrighted" Ophelia. Moreover, the onstage witnesses, Claudius and Polonius, must inter-pret not what they see—since they do not see Hamlet—but rather what Ophe-lia reports, or what they would like to think her report signifies. "This is the very ecstasy of love," concludes Polonius (102), and Claudius is delighted to accept such an interpretation. We in the offstage audience do not know how to interpret the encounter, as we might if we had actually seen it; instead the moment itself remains unresolved in our minds, to be puzzled over in conjunc-tion with the later scene between Hamlet and Ophelia in III.i. Hamlet seems clearly to be gripped by some violent emotion—but is it love, grief, disgust at the frailty of woman, despair that his father's murder necessitates the end of his relationship with Ophelia? Because it is unseen, the unscene remains power-fully and teasingly ambiguous; by placing this episode offstage, Shakespeare ensures its ambiguity and maximizes its impact, while at the same time reserv-ing the high drama of confrontation for a point later in the play.

There are two memorable unscenes in King Lear, with some significant similarities between them. The first is the Gentleman's description of Cordelia as she hears of Lear's degradation, and the second is Edgar's account of the death of Gloucester. The Gentleman is a typical narrator for this kind of scene, since he has no "character," and exists only to tell his tale. He is in effect a transparent or translucent screen through which we can almost "see" the events he recounts:

Gentleman:
                      patience and sorrow strove
Who should express her goodliest. You have seen
Sunshine and rain at once: her smiles and tears
Were like a better way: those happy smilets
That played on her ripe lip seemed not to know
What guests were in her eyes, which parted thence
As pearls from diamonds dropped. In brief,
Sorrow would be a rarity most beloved,
If all could so become it.

Kent: Made she no verbal question?

Gentleman: Faith, once or twice she heaved the name of "father"
Pantingly forth as if it pressed her heart;
Cried, "Sisters! Sisters! Shame of ladies! Sisters!
Kent! Father! Sisters! What, i' th' storm? i' th' night?
Let pity not be believed!" There she shook
The holy water from her heavenly eyes,
And clamor moistened: then away she started
To deal with grief alone.
             (IV.iii.18–34)

Once again a moment of striking emotional and dramatic power takes place offstage. Cordelia's conflict between sorrow and patience, smiles and tears, is characteristic of Shakespearean unscenes, and represents an emotion which seems literally ineffable; it is very like the conflicting feelings that produce the telling silence between Coriolanus and Volumnia. Kent's question about whether she spoke is interesting, because up to this point the Gentleman has pictured Cordelia as a visual emblem, a silent spectacle, almost a work of art. The fact that we hear her words only through his recital distances them. The words are less important than the surrounding silence, the mortal woman less significant than the highly crafted description of her. The image of "sunshine and rain at once" ironically suggests a rainbow, God's promise to Noah that a flood would never again destroy the earth. But we should note that the pearls and diamonds, sunshine and rain, and implicit rainbow are all visual images evoked by Cordelia's absence. Were she present on the stage we would have a grieving daughter, not, as we do here, a vision of patience on a monument, smiling at grief.

The death of Gloucester likewise occurs offstage, and we may wonder why, in a play that seems to spare the audience no agony, this one catastrophe is not shown to us directly. We have seen the dismal spectacle of Gloucester's blinding, Lear's madness, and their heart-rending encounter on the fields near Dover. We are soon to see Lear enter carrying the dead body of Cordelia. But Gloucester's death is told to us indirectly, in Edgar's "brief tale" to Albany:

in this habit
Met I my father with his bleeding rings,
Their precious stones new lost; became his guide,
Led him, begg'd for him, sav'd him from despair;
Never—O fault!—revealed myself unto him,
Until some half-hour past, when I was armed,
Not sure, though hoping, of this good success,
I asked his blessing, and from first to last
Told him our pilgrimage. But his flawed heart—
Alack, too weak the conflict to support—
'Twixt two extremes of passion, joy and grief,
Burst smilingly.

(V.iii.190–201)

Some congruences with the Cordelia passage are immediately apparent: the eyes like jewels, the conflict between joy and grief, the image of a heart that "burst smilingly." Twice we have seen Edgar lead Gloucester from the edge of death, once at "Dover cliff" and a second time after the battle in which Lear's forces are defeated and Lear and Cordelia taken to prison. In both scenes Gloucester has sought death, and been protected and dissuaded from it by his disguised son. By placing the actual death scene offstage, Shakespeare avoids what would very likely be a repetitive and therefore anticlimactic confronta- tion. Moreover, the retelling aggrandizes through imagery. It does the one thing a direct observation of Gloucester's death could not do—it transforms him into a compelling image of ineffable paternal emotion, just as the Gentle- man's retelling made Cordelia into an image of ineffable filial emotion. Edgar, who would not "take" the desperate conditions of the mad King and blind Duke "from report" (IV.vi.141), here himself reports to the audience, and makes of Gloucester's absence a stunning portrait of human response to tragic knowledge. Both the Cordelia and the Gloucester unscenes, we should note, turn on the matter of *conflict*; it is this sundering of the passions, this tension between joy and grief, that creates—and to a certain extent, defines—the condition of ineffability.

The stylistic form of these episodes is in a way closer to the language of romance than to that of tragedy; they are more lyric than dramatic. Two other unscenes, both from *The Winter's Tale,* clearly demonstrate the appropriateness of such a technique to the dramatic strategies of a world so responsive to "wonder." In Act III, scene 1, we hear the testimony of the two messengers Leontes has sent to Delphos to consult with the oracle of Apollo on the question of Hermione's guilt or innocence. We do not see the scene at Delphos, but we hear about it from the messengers, Cleomenes and Dion, immediately upon their return to Sicilia. Although they have names, these characters are as unknown to us as the anonymous Gentleman in *Lear,* and likewise seem to exist only to give this one report.

Cleomenes: The climate's delicate, the air most sweet,
            Fertile the isle, the temple much surpassing
            The common praise it bears.

Dion: I shall report,
            For most it caught me, the celestial habits
            (Methinks I so should term them) and the reverence
            Of the grave wearers. O, the sacrifice,
            How ceremonious, solemn, and unearthly
            It was i' th' off'ring!

Cleomenes: But of all, the burst
            And the ear-deaf'ning voice o' th' oracle,
            Kin to Jove's thunder, so surprised my sense,
            That I was nothing.
                                    (III.i.1–11)

The unimaginable splendor of the temple and its occupants and the transcendent religious experience undergone by the messengers are here magnified,
rather than diminished, by their indirect presentation. The temple that surpass-
es common praise, the robes of the celebrants so extraordinary that the
speaker hardly knows what to call them, the "unearthly" sacrifice, the deafen-
ing voice of the oracle—all of these elements, unspeakably impressive, exist
for us only through the memories of the narrators in this scene. The effect is
once again closely akin to that of the inexpressibility topos, with the narrative
poet's "I cannot tell you" translated into the dramatic poet's "I cannot show
you." The obliquity of dramatic design, placing the events themselves at one
remove, sets those events apart from the familiar—and visible—norm of human
experience.

    Another scene from the same play similarly presents a "miraculous" event
by retelling, and with similar effect. The scene is that in which we hear of the
reunion between Leontes and Perdita, with the revelation of her identity. There
are many reasons why it is appropriate that this scene take place offstage. The
scene which is to follow is the great "statue" scene, which reunites wife with
husband, mother with daughter, and its dramatic effect might be dulled or
diminished if it were immediately preceded by another onstage recognition.
Since the audience does not yet know that Hermione is alive, the surprise effect
of the final scene would clearly give it primacy in dramatic design, and the
recognition of Perdita is properly subjugated to it.

    But there is another purpose served by placing the Perdita scene offstage,
one that has to do with the language spoken by those characters we actually
do see. The scene unfolds in a masterful, rapid-fire fashion, as one Gentleman
after another arrives with fragments of information which he offers to Autolycus—and, at the same time, to the listening audience. First comes the news that
Camillo and Leontes have recognized one another in a silent spectacle of
amazement:

> There was speech in their dumbness, language in their very gesture; they looked
> as they had heard of a world ransomed, or one destroyed. A notable passion of
> wonder appeared in them; but the wisest beholder that knew no more but seeing
> could not say if th' importance were joy, or sorrow—but in the extremity of the
> one it must needs be.
>
> (V.ii.14–21)

Again an apparent conflict in emotions accompanies a silent display of passion; no one could say whether they felt joy or sorrow. At this point a second Gentleman arrives, with the word that "the oracle is fulfilled; the king's daugh-ter is found; such a deal of wonder is broken out within this hour that ballad-makers cannot be able to express it" (24–27). "This news," he continues, "which is called true, is so like an old tale that the verity of it is in strong suspicion" (29–31). A third Gentleman confirms the report, and adds an account of the meeting of the two kings, a sight which "was to be seen," but "cannot be spoken of" (44–48). Sorrow and joy, once again, conflicted in them, "for their joy waded in tears." And the same conflict appeared in Paulina: "oh the noble combat, that 'twixt joy and sorrow was fought in Paulina! She had one eye declined for the loss of her husband, another elevated that the oracle was fulfilled" (74–77).

One further observation by the Third Gentleman is even more suggestive, since it points in so remarkably directive a way to the scene that is to follow. Speaking of Perdita he remarks that "she did, with an 'Alas,'—I would fain say—bleed tears; for I am sure my heart wept blood. Who was most marble there changed color; some swooned, all sorrowed" (90–93). The spectacle of one who seems to be marble changing color will be the main dramatic action of the "statue" scene, as, under Paulina's deft direction, Hermione "awakes" and reveals herself. In V.ii. the change is suggested in imagistic terms; in V.iii. it will appear to be literal, although both transformations, of course, are finally metaphors. The moment of "wonder" experienced by the hushed spectators in the chapel has been prepared for not only by Paulina's skill in staging, but also by the previous scene, in which the playwright uses all the resources at his command to describe an ineffable moment: the inexpressibility topos, the deflected scene or unscene, and the actual silence of characters gripped by strong and conflicting or transcendent emotions.

Shakespeare's middle and late plays are full of such moments of "woe or wonder," to use Horatio's suggestive phrase—moments of joy or grief, sorrow or awe, for which words are neither possible nor adequate. Because he is working with the medium of drama, he is able to represent such moments both directly and indirectly on the stage. Silence for Shakespeare is not a breaking of the frame, a violation of generic decorum, as it was in the case of Sterne's blank page or Graves's careless comma. Instead it is an integral part of his dramatic design, used in conjunction with other rhetorical and dramaturgical techniques to describe the indescribable. Edgar's agonized observation about "the worst" is a key to the playwright's own strategy; ineffable emotions, whether provoked by woe or wonder, cannot by their nature be spoken, but they may be circumscribed by speech and gesture. That Shakespeare knew this, and directed the dramatic energies of his most creative and innovative years to demonstrating it, can be seen in his approach to the most literally ineffable of all human experiences: death.

On the battlefield at Shrewsbury Hotspur dies in the middle of a sentence:

> O, I could prophesy,
> But that the earthy and cold hand of death
> Lies on my tongue. No, Percy, thou art dust,
> And food for—
> (*I Henry IV* V.iv.81–84)

Both his sentence and his "proud titles" are inherited by Prince Hal: "For worms, brave Percy" (85). A similar pattern develops at the end of *Hamlet*, where once again a noble man lies dying:

> Had I but time (as this fell sergeant, Death,
> Is strict in his arrest) O, I could tell you—
> But let it be.
> (V.ii.338–340)

The enigmatic silence of the grave displaces for the last time the language of the living. "The undiscover'd country, from whose bourn / No traveler returns" (III.i.79–80) is the site of the ultimate unscene, the transcendent offstage drama for which there is no reliable narrator. Death is the final and quintessential ineffability, its earthy and cold hand stilling the voice of the dying man as he faces the unutterable and unknown. The last words Hamlet speaks are not only his own epitaph but that of everyman, the playwright's eloquent acknowledgement of both the powers and the limits of language: "the rest is silence" (360).

NOTES

1. *Aeneid* VI, 625–627, trans. H. Rushton Fairclough, (Cambridge, Mass.: Harvard University Press [Loeb Classical Library], 1946). For a more extensive discussion of the inexpressibility topos in early literature, see Ernst Robert Curtius, *European Literature and the Latin Middle Ages,* trans. Willard R. Trask (1952; rpt. New York: Harper and Row, 1963), pp. 159–162.
2. Vol. VI. Ch. 38, in James A. Work, ed., Laurence Sterne, *Tristram Shandy* (New York: Odyssey Press, 1940), p. 471.
3. *Collected Poems of Wallace Stevens* (New York: Knopf, 1954), p. 203.

4. Lines 9–15, in Robert Graves, *The Poems of Robert Graves,* (Garden City: Doubleday Anchor, 1958), p. 289.

5. All citations from the plays are to *The Signet Classic Shakespeare,* ed. Sylvan Barnett (New York: Harcourt Brace Jovanovich, 1972).

Cupid Hatched by Night: The "Mysteries of Faith" and Bacon's Art of Discovery

Charles Whitney

Francis Bacon's *Of Principles and Origins According to the Fables of Cupid and Coelum* . . . is a hurried, sometimes brilliant fragment of a Latin polemic, about forty pages long.[1] Probably written during the productive five years between Bacon's political ruin and his death in 1626, the piece appears to be the only result of his stated intention to expand his popular mythography, *The Wisdom of the Ancients*. Bacon, called by D. C. Allen "the best English allegorizer of mythology,"[2] in *Cupid and Coelum* does something that we usually associate with allegorical poets rather than with mythographers: he attempts to think through philosophical problems by using the images and icons of religious myth. He derives theories about the nature of matter and scientific method from ancient accounts of the Creation that he considers to embody genuine wisdom, and he criticizes other philosophies on the grounds that they depart from the mythological wisdom he has uncovered.

The most surprising aspect of Bacon's allegory is that he finds a significant parallel between his pragmatic scientific method and negative theology. Although in many works he suggests that the goals of his scientific enterprise include fulfillment of man's spiritual nature through "instauration" of his Edenic condition, a basic purpose of *Cupid and Coelum* and of Bacon's other philosophical works is, after all, to demonstrate the fruitlessness of metaphysical inquiry and the fundamental necessity of protecting the working scientist from the demands and distractions of religious dogma. Yet in *Cupid and Coelum* Bacon proposes that even if the subject matter of science must remain strictly natural, the actual method for grasping scientific truth is itself to be modeled on the theological inquiry into God's ineffable nature.

In his scientific enterprise in *Cupid and Coelum,* Bacon explicitly aims at harmonizing pagan mysteries with Christian truths, drawing on a long tradition of such synthesis and addressing himself to a sophisticated audience familiar with and sympathetic to this hybrid tradition. Sometimes, as with our present subject, Bacon's Christian reading of a pagan allegory even becomes an important step in establishing the allegory's scientific meaning.

The Christian theological context is most evident in Bacon's interpretation of a single motif, the hatching by the primal goddess Night of an egg containing Cupid. Although the motif may seem outlandish at first, it comes to us from Aristophanes's *Birds* and is a variant (probably Orphic) of the standard Hesiodic creation story, a story that actually does have some historical connection with Semitic accounts of the Beginning, including Babylonian and Phoenician as well as Mosaic.[3] Bacon's two-fold interpretation of Night, which comprises an imaginative but confused contribution to the iconography of the beyond, leads to his comparison between devotional and scientific methodology. Bacon first suggests that Night stands for an object: God's primal unknowable plan for the universe. Then, drawing on the analogy between God's creation of the world and the scientist's creation of an explanation of the world, Bacon construes this primal nocturnal creative power as a kind of scientific Muse: he makes Night stand for the scientific method of "induction by negation," the only scientific way of explaining, even in part, the created world. Negative theology, Bacon thus suggests, parallels negative induction, for man must learn to know the universe through negatives just as he "knows" God through negatives.

Although Bacon's treatment of the Cupid-hatched-by-Night motif draws on traditional Christian symbolism, it in fact radically modifies it to the extent that Bacon puts this tradition in the service of his revolutionary program for discovery of scientific truths which are as yet ineffable. It must be recognized nevertheless that even by attempting to make such a paradoxical combination plausible Bacon anticipates a distinctively modern attitude toward man's free and anxiously isolated relation to an unknowable deity.

Bacon's account of Cupid, taken from among the many stories in Natale Conti's article on Cupid in his *Mythologiae* (IV, 14),[4] is as follows. In the beginning of all things, when there were only Chaos and Night, Night hatched an egg from which "Cupid, or Love" (the Greek god Eros) emerged, and Cupid then united with Chaos to beget most of the gods and the entire natural universe. As Conti's quotation from the *Symposium* explains, Cupid, the goddess Venus, and their Greek counterparts have both a celestial and an earthly identity. Our Cupid is Bacon's higher and "elder" one, not the son of the Celestial Venus—"in whose presence Cupid's work is done" (*Symposium* 180e)—but simply an alternative allegorical representation of the idea of love.

For Bacon, Chaos represents "the disordered mass or congregation of matter"; Cupid stands for the ultimate object of scientific inquiry, "the highest law of being and nature, which portions out and runs through the vicissitudes of things . . . the virtue of the primary particles conferred by God from the multiplication of which the variety of all matter emerges and is blown forth" (III, 80–81). The primary particles or atoms move and interact according to the amorous "appetites" placed in them; their invisible motions produce all the sensible world of objects, motion, and desire. Cupid thus represents the first cause of nature, "except for God," who lies beyond nature and natural knowledge. Bacon identifies Cupid's mother, on the other hand, as at once God and Night:

> Cupid is elegantly feigned to have hatched from an egg that was incubated by Night. Certainly the divine philosopher [Solomon] declares that "God hath made everything beautiful in its season, also he hath given the world to their disputes; yet so that man cannot find out the work that God worketh from the beginning to the end" (III, 81).

This, the first stage of Bacon's interpretation of Night, focuses on the hidden divine source prior to nature: Night represents God's unknowable plan, the heavenly cause of the first natural cause, Cupid.

The pairing of Chaos and Cupid as Platonic principles of matter and form or as Empedoclean principles of strife and harmony suggests the traditional context from which Bacon's interpretation, guided by his mythographic source, arises. Bacon's prospective readers might have thought of Spenser's Garden of Adonis, where Venus retrieves new material for her continual creation of life from the accommodating god Chaos, waiting nearby. The frontispiece of Sandys's translation of Ovid's *Metamorphoses,* depicting the once-warring elements united by Love, would also have seemed appropriate to Bacon's interpretation when the translation later appeared. Bacon's general sympathy for Lucretius in *Cupid and Coelum* entitles us to say, however, that for him the governing idea of this tradition of Cupid and Chaos lies not in the Platonism prominent in Conti's account but in the Epicurean association of Venus with the spirit of universal harmony operating through *atoms* that we find in the invocation of *De Rerum Natura.* Where Conti in his closing remarks on Cupid speaks of him as "the divine force of reciprocal desires inducing things to join and coalesce, or I will say more, the divine mind of Nature which induces these same motions by itself,"[5] Bacon speaks of Cupid as representing the laws of motion "conferred by God" but for all practical purposes describable purely in the terms of materialistic atomism. Bacon thus narrows the philosophic resonance of Conti's Neoplatonic notion of the *anima mundi* in order to make it suitable for a philosophy that considers the scientist's proper study to be the essentially mechanical motion of tiny particles, rather than a divine mind operating in nature itself.[6]

Precisely as a consequence of this narrowing of Cupid's significance, however, Bacon confers a deep meaning upon Night: as we have seen, it is she, not Cupid, who now represents the divine agency itself. Bacon further suggests that religious context of his Night when in the course of his argument he twice asserts the equivalence of his Hesiodic story to the account of Creation in sacred writ (III, 86, 110–111). Cupid is "the heaven and the earth" (Gen. 1:1) created by God, and hence God presumably is represented in the Greek myth by Night; later, Bacon associates Cupid more specifically with the universal order of things that began with the creation of light, and there Night, apparently, corresponds either to "the word of omnipotence" that preceded the creation of light or to the Spirit of God that moved over the deep. In a more explicit connection of Night with the concept of a hidden God, Bacon in the "Nemesis" article in the *Wisdom of the Ancients* finds that Nemesis's mother, Night, represents the secret providence of God working in the world.

Bacon's association of Night with God as the divine and unfathomable source of nature's order has no counterpart in Conti, or in the treatments of Night in Boccaccio, Gyraldo, or Cartari, other mythographic sources Bacon was likely to have consulted.[7] The Night of the mythographers, despite her great antiquity, more often than not stands for ignorance, sloth, death, confusion, and the forces of evil in general. True, her huge black wings, star-studded blue cape, peacefulness, and promise of astrological wisdom are often celebrated. However, the gruesome couple encouraging Satan in *Paradise Lost,* Chaos and his consort Night, "eldest of things" (II, 962), and Milton's first Prolusion, "Whether Day or Night is the More Excellent," stem from the more dominant negative view.

Bacon's promotion of Night, on the other hand, recalls a somewhat different set of theological contexts. In the first place, Bacon may have connected Aristophanes's primal, birdlike goddess with the Creator God of Genesis because he was familiar with the common translation of Genesis 1:2 as "the Spirit of God brooded over the abyss." While the Vulgate, Tyndale, Geneva, and King James versions all render the passage as a variation on "the Spirit of God moved upon the face of the waters," the assertion that the original Hebrew verb suggests "brooding"—that is, a bird's incubation and hatching of its eggs—was widely known and discussed in Bacon's time. For instance, Timothy Bright in his often-reissued *A Treatise of Melancholy* (1586) says that "the Spirit of the Lord did as it were hatch, and brood out all living thinges, out of the Chaos [abyss] mentioned in Genesis."[8] Bacon's erstwhile court associate Sir Walter Raleigh, whose *History of the World* Bacon may well have read, offers St. Basil's two suggestions for the passage in Genesis: "brood" and "flutter."[9] The most famous literary use of the "brood" translation is Milton's invocation to his primordial, brooding, winged, pregnant heavenly muse (*Paradise Lost* I, 19–22); but Milton, needless to say, makes no mention of the goddess Night here.

How, indeed, can the God of Light be likened to Hesiod's murky grotesques? Educated readers of Bacon's *Cupid and Coelum* might well have considered, for one thing, the theology of "invisible" and "uncreated" light. In commentaries on Genesis Augustine had distinguished between the light created on the first day and the invisible intellectual light that preceded it; Donne in a sermon of 1621 refers to the primal *"luce inaccessibili,* the light that none can attain to." Raleigh's *History* likewise speaks of "a light by abundant clarity invisible"; the Hermeticist and Neoplatonist Francesco Patrizi, whom Bacon along with many of his contemporaries is known to have read, extends the same idea when he maintains that the "uncreated light" existing before the Creation's visible light contains the ordering principles of the universe. Patrizi in his *New Philosophy of the Universe* derives an entire natural philosophy on the basis of this axiom.[10] All of these writers probably have in mind the heavenly *lux inaccessibilis* of Timothy 6:16, as well as the "thick darkness" from which the Old Testament God sometimes speaks and acts. The English translation (authorized by Bacon himself) of the Cupid article in the *Wisdom of the Ancients* shows that the religious paradox of invisible light might well occur to contemporary readers: for the translator Sir Arthur Gorges, Night's effect is to "dazzle the eies of mans understanding" with divine revelation.[11] Ironically, it seems that Bacon's Night is somewhat like the "bright essence increate" Milton hails after finishing his unpleasant task of describing the essence's antithesis, the mythographic Night (III, 6).

But invisible—or blinding—light is hardly identical with the utter darkness of night itself, and the religious context of Bacon's first interpretation of Night holds still further implications. The *Kabbalah*[12] recounts that in the Beginning,

> Within the most hidden recess a dark flame issued from the mystery of *eyn-sof,* the Infinite, like a fog forming in the unformed—enclosed in the ring of that sphere, neither white nor black, neither red nor green, of no color whatever.

God's light later appeared, but then was "put away and hidden" until some future time.[13] The unorthodox attempt actually to represent (as Bacon does) God's presence or activity before the creation by using the murky figures of Hesiod's *Theogony* is limited to the kind of Neoplatonic syncretism that finds Christian theology hidden behind diverse representations of God.[14] George Chapman's *Hymnus ad Noctem* (1594) makes such an attempt to identify God and Night, and this poem is based on an Orphic hymn, just as Aristophanes's own story probably is. Day for Chapman serves the lust of the eye and stands for the fallen world; Night is the condition of oneness and repose before the creation of the world. Chapman—who along with Raleigh belonged to the so-called "School of Night"—seems to be glossing the second of the three phrases in Genesis 1:2, "darkness was on the face of the deep," when he addresses Night this way:

> Sorrowes deare soveraigne, and the queene of rest,
> That when unlightsome, vast, and indigest
> The formelesse matter of this world did lye,
> Fildst every place with thy Divinitie,
> Why did thy absolute and endlesse sway,
> Licence heavens torch, the scepter of the Day,
> Distinguisht intercession to thy throne,
> That long before, all matchlesse rulde alone?[15]

Bacon's first interpretation of Night, then, can be viewed as one possible product of the following combination: Aristophanes's Night, the brooding creature in Genesis 1:2, the theological and philosophical tradition of invisible light, and mystical Neoplatonic, syncretic representations of God's nature such as the *Kabbalah* or, more likely, Chapman's *Hymnus.* By attributing aspects of genuine divinity to Night rather than to Cupid, Bacon thus appeals to, combines, and extends several venerable Judeo-Christian and Neoplatonic ideas.

Yet here too, as in his interpretation of Cupid, Bacon adapts these traditional ideas to his own untraditional uses. For he has in effect kicked the nocturnal deity upstairs in order to give the scientist a free hand in investigating the facts of nature without concerning himself about theological mysteries. The misguided efforts of scientists to find natural truths in theology are an affront to God; on the other hand, the ways of a dark and unknowable God need not concern data-gatherers: "indeed nothing corrupts philosophy as much as seeking the parents of Cupid" (III, 81). Bacon's use of Night as a way to free the scientist to investigate nature without being troubled by metaphysical speculation exemplifies a modern and pragmatic concern for epistemology, for the problems of what can be known and of how truth can be discovered. One can be fairly sure that Bacon himself has only a mild interest in the theological implications of his first interpretation of Night, even though he, like the followers of late medieval *devotio moderna,* stresses the emptiness of rational accounts of God's nature.[16]

But Bacon's scientific appropriation of Night by no means removes religion from the picture. By suggesting the divine stature of Night Bacon is, as he develops his own explanation, able to present his art of discovery as the scientific version of negative theology. Although Night is impenetrable in herself, for Bacon she "refers most aptly to the demonstrations through which Cupid is brought to light" (III, 81), that is, to the one true scientific method ("induction by negation") by which the laws of nature can be established:

> Therefore this Cupid [i.e. the universal laws of nature] truly is an egg hatched by Night; for the conception of him which can wholly be had advances through exclusions and negations (III, 81-82).

That is, because the scientist employing exclusions remains "in the dark" about the solution to his problem till the very end of his inquiry, Night's hatching of Cupid is an appropriate representation of his activity ("Probatio autem per exclusionem facta, quaedam ignoratio est, et tamquam nox, quoad id quod includitur" [III, 82]).

On the strength of his previous interpretation of Night as the divine cause of the natural world, Bacon goes on to compare negative theology to negative induction: "It is the prerogative of God alone, that when his nature is inquired of by the sense, exclusions shall not end in affirmations" (III, 83).[17] Cupid, in contrast, the "emanation" (III,111) of the divine Night, *can* be brought to light by the right method of "exclusions." Just as Milton later identified his Muse as the brooding Holy Spirit who gave birth to the universe, so Bacon character-izes his art of discovery by reference to the nocturnal universal mother. This epistemological significance defines Bacon's main interest in Night, who be-comes the hidden, brooding Muse of the scientist.

Bacon conceived his fundamental contribution to the modern world to be his method of understanding through obscurity, or, as he called it, induction by negation or by exclusion. This method is essentially an attempt to minimize the role of the intellect, imagination, received opinion, and vanity in science, and to discover general laws of nature by relying as much as possible on direct and thorough observations and experiment. Bacon takes to heart the attack of Renaissance skeptics on man's capacity for knowledge, but preserves an indom-itable and pragmatic optimism about the possibilities of human knowledge when man's faculties are properly governed. After systematically collecting all pertinent facts in the investigation of any problem, Bacon explains in Book II of the *Novum Organum,* the scientist must not construct a speculative theory on the basis of his facts, but must, by an elaborate system of cross-references, eliminate all possible wrong answers until he is left with only one possible solution. Thus in inquiring about the nature of heat, for instance, Bacon com-piles three tables of observations of instances in which heat is present, absent, and either increasing or decreasing. He then eliminates all qualities of nature which can be shown to be only occasionally associated with heat, in order to find the one quality which is always present if and only if heat is: a particular kind of rapid motion of the particles or atoms. In the terms of Cupid and Coelum, this negative process will supposedly lead to discovery of the Erotic laws governing all the motions of primary particles, and hence will lead to the relief and restoration of man through science. By protecting the scientist's disinterest and objectivity, this method avoids the system-building vanity, spec-ulative confusion, and slavish adherence to tradition endemic to the class of learned men.

> These things which are determined through affirmatives [i.e. through authority, speculation, "revelation," deduction, "naive" induction, etc.] are like the offspring of light; but those which are determined through negatives and exclusions are as if molded and reared up by darkness and night (III, 81).

With this second significance of Night as a negative method for under-standing the natural world, then, Bacon seems to be implying that the essential feature of his empirical scientific vision, induction by negation, is in some sense the fulfillment or at least the parallel of religious notions of understanding through obscurity, of advancing through a series of inadequate representations of God (unknowable in himself) in order to achieve at least a negative under-standing of what Sir Thomas Browne at the end of *Hydriotaphia* calls the "divine shadow." Bacon's striking interpretation shows that religion provides not just a new Edenic goal for the scientist to work for, but that the notion of God's ineffability helps Bacon to articulate his method and provides authority for it.

Specifically, Bacon arrives at the identification of Night, negative theology, and negative induction by combining the Orphic conception of Night as the source of divine wisdom with Christian negative theology. A glance at Conti, Bacon's main source, reveals the Orphic connection. Conti recounts the Orphic creation myth, in which Night plays a major role as the *offspring* of Phanes, whom Conti rightly identifies with Eros and Cupid. (The Aristophanic version of this myth also adopted by Bacon from Conti may originally have been parodying the Orphic genealogy by reversing the roles of parent and offspring). Conti does not discuss Night's significance in Orphic religion, but Bacon and many of his readers would probably have known that the so-called "Counsels of Night" are the primary sources of Orphic wisdom: since Night was present at the Creation, she was supposedly able to deliver her special knowledge of the world's construction to Orpheus. The Orphic fragments themselves were available in a number of editions in Bacon's time.[18] Perhaps Bacon also knew of Giovanni Pico della Mirandola's attempt to connect pagan and Christian notions of ineffable knowledge by conflating the Orphic Counsels of Night with the divine word of God's creation. As Edgar Wind tells us, Pico noticed that both Plato and the Old Testament referred to the true God as "counsel"; pseudo-Dionysius calls Christ "the angel of Counsel"; Avicenna calls the first cause of the universe the "counselling cause"; this cause is for Pico identical with the hidden supreme deities of both the Kabbalists (*eyn-sof,* "Ensoph") and the Orphics (Night).[19]

By saying "It is the prerogative of God alone, that when his nature is inquired of by the sense, exclusions shall not end in affirmations," Bacon refers to the negative theology originally associated with pseudo-Dionysius. His use of the Orphic Night thus finally blends with a Christian devotional method to form a model for science. Dionysius's "method," the general outlines of which Bacon seems to know, bears several interesting similarities to Bacon's own. (Bacon briefly discusses Dionysius's ideas concerning angels in *The Advancement of Learning* [III, 296].) In the first place, Dionysius has a daemonic fixation on the magical oxymoron of light from night with which Bacon plays. In *Mystical Theology* he repeats at length his praises of the "superessentialem divinarum tenebrarum radium," the "transcendent ray of divine darkness." Like Bacon's, Dionysius's method prescribes important empirical and inductive phases. Bacon's unusual method depends upon an initial thorough collection of all facts bearing in any way on a given problem, and ends with an elimination of possible answers until only one answer remains. Dionysius calls for compiling a thor-ough list of all the names that have been applied to God in the Bible and all aspects of him that are described there. Then the process of elimination begins, until all characteristics attributed to God are seen to be unworthy of Him and

He can be experienced as an infinitely rich darkness filled with invisible light.[20] The significant parallel is that in both cases the process of elimination takes place because, as Bacon says in the *Instauratio Magna,* "the testimony . . . of the sense has reference always to man, not to the universe [for Dionysius, read "not to God"]; and it is a great error to assert that the sense is the measure of things" (IV, 26).

Bacon's nocturnal method is designed to preserve the irreducible other-ness of nature's harmonies from the restless dissonances of the mind. Likewise, the search for God can preserve a sense of otherness through a kind of induc-tion by negation. The Baconian scientist must sacrifice the ordinary uses of his sense, intellect, and imagination in order to remain open to as-yet-unknown insights. In the *Instauratio Magna* Bacon says of the insight his method produces, "being gathered here and there from very various and widely dispersed facts, [they] cannot suddenly strike the understanding; and therefore they must needs, in respect of the opinions of the time, seem harsh and out of tune, much as the mysteries of faith" (IV, 52). Bacon stresses the impotence of all mere analogies and devices of the wit for revealing genuinely new natural truths:

> If, for instance, before the invention of ordnance [artillery], a man had described the thing by its effects, and said that there was a new invention, by means of which the strongest towers and walls could be shaken and thrown down at a great distance; men would doubtless have begun to think over all the ways of multiply-ing the force of catapults and mechanical engines by weights and wheels and such machinery for ramming and projecting; but the notion of a fiery blast suddenly and violently expanding and exploding would hardly have entered into any man's imagination or fancy; being a thing to which nothing immediately analo-gous had been seen . . . (IV, 99).

If we consider this last passage in the context of *Cupid and Coelum,* it becomes a critique of the theological dialectic that is complementary to Dionysi-us's *via negationis*: the *via causalitatis.* Unlike the former, which moves from the negation of all sensible attributes to spiritual illumination, the *via causalitatis* moves from effects to causes that have the same natures, though infinite, as the finite effects one perceives.[21] The way therefore depends on finite analogies for the infinite. Raleigh grandly illustrates the *via causalitatis* when he reverses the night-light progression and says, "in the glorious lights of heaven, we perceive a shadow of his divine countenance."[22] Ascending through nature to nature's God, as Pope says, roughly characterizes what many allegorical poets as well as scientists do when they consider the theological implications of their materi-al.[23] Nature, Bacon himself declares, constitutes the "footsteps of the Creator imprinted upon his creatures" (IV, 33). But for Bacon, as we have seen, the right scientific *method* must be negative, because the vision of nature must be purified of the misleading analogies bred by man's corrupt sense and understanding, not fed by those analogies.

While the Neoplatonism of pseudo-Dionysius and of the Orphic fragments is an important context for understanding the mythography of *Cupid and Coelum,* Bacon's Puritan sympathies suggest another important context for considering the religious dimensions of Bacon's method. Calvin's uncompro-misingly negative instincts compel him to limit sharply the value of the *via causalitatis* in the following passage:

> It is therefore in vain that so many burning lamps shine for us in the workmanship of the universe to show forth the glory of its Author. Although they bathe us wholly in their radiance, yet they can of themselves in no way lead us into the right path. Surely they strike some sparks, but before their fuller light shines forth they are smothered. For this reason, the apostle, in that very passage where he calls the worlds the images of things invisible, adds that through faith we under-stand that they have been fashioned by God's word (Heb. 11:3). He means by this that the invisible divinity is made manifest in such spectacles, but that we have not the eyes to see this unless they be illumined by the inner revelation of God through faith. And where Paul teaches that what is to be known of God is made plain from the creation of the universe (Rom. 1:19), he does not signify such a manifestation as men's discernment can comprehend; but, rather, shows it not to go farther than to render them inexcusable.[24]

For Calvin's purely subjective "inner revelation of God through faith" we must substitute Bacon's antithetical—but complementary—purely objective percep-tion of particular facts. For all of Calvin's religious pessimism and Bacon's secular optimism, both formulations represent extreme reactions to the weak-ness of man's faculties and moral resolve and to the related problem of finding an adequate criterion for absolute truth.

The Cupid-hatched-by-Night motif suggests that Bacon's view of scientific method supplies a link between notions of the ineffable religious experience and the modern literary and scientific goal of remaining open to the "revela-tions" of nature. For Bacon this openness to the experience which is as yet ineffable extends to interpretations not only of nature but also of texts. Bacon leaves his corpus of scientific writings substantially incomplete or, rather, he proposes his scientific works and asks others to write them. The nature of the truth Bacon seeks is ineffable in the sense that, as he says in the *Instauratio Magna,* it cannot even be conceived or imagined beforehand. Bacon projects the idea of divine ineffability into the future as the hope and expectation of wondrous and totally novel discovery.

But finally, it must be stressed that despite the similarities between Bacon's science and religious experience there is an important contrast—that between knowing and being. Bacon's negative way limits human reason in order to achieve greater disinterest and objectivity; that of the religious visionary does so in order to achieve a union with God that goes beyond the limits of knowl-edge. To the religious visionary, night can represent a method but it is also a goal, because God dwells in darkness, "in the dim silence where lovers lose themselves," as Ruysbroeck sings;[25] for Bacon, however, Night represents a method and a *limit,* a space that if approached appears to be only nothingness. Although the scientist imitates Night's engendering of the world by his use of negative induction, the world he explains is purely material, and his findings are precise and certain: Night herself remains a presence closed off to him. Just so, the Kantian "thing-in-itself" is meaningless to the scientist because it lies beyond phenomena.

It might be said, then, that while the night of the Greek mythmakers, the Neoplatonists, and the religious visionaries is a night of plenitude, filled with a presence that is unknown but overpowering and sustaining, the ineffable night of the Baconian scientist is one of absence and emptiness. As the Orphic Night hatched Phanes, the universal god of light, Bacon's Night helped to hatch the European Enlightenment. But in his interpretation of myth, Bacon has identified his basic contribution to the Enlightenment as the transformation of the ancient goddess Night into the infinite, empty night of the Newtonian universe. Bacon's Night also finds a parallel in the relentless "darkness" of doubt that Descartes employs to reduce the given world to the isolated residuum of the *cogito.*[26]

At the midpoint of the rapidly changing seventeenth century, Henry Vaughan's great Hermetic poem, "The Night," presents what is in many respects the old Night: in the line "God's silent, searching flight" Vaughan suggests Chapman's, if not Bacon's, conflation of Hesiodic and Mosaic accounts of the Creation. But in his *Pensées,* Pascal will respond to a different aspect of Night's legacy:

> When I see the blindness and misery of man, when I consider the muteness of all the universe, and man with no light, adrift by himself as if he had strayed into this corner of the universe, without knowing who put him here, what he has come to do, what will happen when he dies, incapable of any knowledge, I am filled with terror. . . .[27]

NOTES

1. *The Works of Francis Bacon,* ed. and tr. James Spedding, Robert L. Ellis, and Douglas D. Heath, 7 vols., 2nd ed. (London: Longmans et al., 1870), III, 79–118 (Latin), V, 459–500 (English). The translations from *Cupid and Coelum* in this paper are my own; in quoting passages from Bacon's other works, I have used Spedding and Ellis's translations.

2. *Mysteriously Meant: The Rediscovery of Pagan Symbolism and Allegorical Interpretation in the Renaissance* (Baltimore: Johns Hopkins Univ. Press, 1970), p. 244.

3.   Ellis identifies the source of the motif in his introduction to *Cupid and Coelum* (*Works*, III, 66); for the motif in Greek mythology see *The Presocratic Philosophers*, ed. G. S. Kirk and J. E. Raven (Cambridge: Cambridge Univ. Press, 1957), pp. 21–24, 38–48. On possible connections between Greek, Hittite, and Semitic accounts see Kirk and Raven, pp. 31, 33–37.

4.   On Bacon's extensive use of Conti in *Cupid and Coelum* see B. C. Garner, "Francis Bacon, Natalis Comes and the Mythographical Tradition," *Journal of the Warburg and Courtauld Institute*, 33 (1970), 264–291.

5.   Natalis Comitis, *Mythologiae* (1567; rpt. New York: Garland, 1976), p. 128ʳ. Conti expands on this idea in his 1581 Venice edition (pp. 272–273).

6.   On Bacon's incomplete shift from a "dynamic" to a "mechanist" philosophy see Paolo Rossi, *Francis Bacon: From Magic to Science*, tr. Sacha Rabinowitz (Chicago: Univ. of Chicago Press, 1968), p. 126, and Garner, "Francis Bacon, Natalis Comes and the Mythological Tradition," p. 273.

7.   On Bacon's mythographic sources see C. W. Lemmi, *The Classic Deities in Bacon* (Baltimore: Johns Hopkins Univ. Press, 1933). Articles on Night can be found in Giovanni Boccaccio, *De Genealogia Deorum Gentilium Libri*, ed. Vincenzo Romaro (Bari: Gius, Laterza, 1951), I, 34–36 (Book I, ch. 9), and in Natalis Comitis, *Mythologiae* (1567), pp. 72ʳ–73ʳ (Book III, ch. 12), Lilio Gyraldo, *De Deis Gentium* (1548), pp. 83ʳ–83ᵛ (Syntagma I), Vincenzo Cartari *Imagines Degli Dei Antichi . . .* (1571), pp. 330–333 (all rpt. New York: Garland, 1976). The mythography of Night can occasionally be found combined with serious religious consideration of Night. Ruben's 1614 wood panel, *The Flight Into Egypt* (Kassel, Gemäldegalerie) may offer a suggestive parallel to Bacon's interpretation. As she had done in medieval depictions of the crossing of the Red Sea, Night in her mythographic gear serves as a guide for the holy refugees in Rubens's painting. Interestingly, the mother/son pair Mary and Jesus is complemented here by Night and the figure of Cupid hovering over her and extending a wand. For other religious representations of Night see *Lexikon der Christlichen Ikonographie*, ed. Engelbert Kirschbaum, S. J., et al. (Freiburg: Herder, 1971), and below.

8.   Quoted in H. F. Fletcher, *Milton's Rabbinical Readings* (rpt. New York: Archon, 1967), p. 125.

9.   *A History of the World*, ed. C. A. Patrides (Philadelphia: Temple Univ. Press, 1971), p. 93. Luther supplies a barnyard flavor for Genesis 1:2 in his *Commentary*; in *Religio Medici*, xxiii, Sir Thomas Browne speaks of "that gentle heat that brooded on the waters, and in six days hatched the world." See F. T. Prince, ed., *Paradise Lost, I, II* (London: Oxford Univ. Press, 1962), p. 107.

     Alchemists from Roger Bacon to Paracelsus to John Dee speak of the philosopher's stone as the "philosopher's egg," which "represented the primordial chaos out of which the ordered world had emerged" according to J. P. Zetterberg, "Hermetic Geocentricity: John Dee's Celestial Egg," *Isis*, 70 (1979), 291. Piero della Francesca's *Pala di Brera* (*Madonna with Child, Six Saints, Four Angels, and Duke Frederick II of Montefeltro*) strikingly displays the primorial egg motif by depicting an egg suspended from a golden chain above the Madonna's head. On the symbolism of creation involved, see *L'opera completa di Piero della Francesca*, Oreste del Buono and Pierluigi de Vecchi, eds. (Milano: Rizzoli, 1967), p. 106.

10. See especially *De Genesi Contra Manichi*, 1.3.6, ed. J. P. Migne (Paris, 1845), 34, 177, where Augustine says the light of God before the creation would appear as darkness to "carnal eyes"; John Donne, *Sermons on the Psalms and Gospels*, ed. Evelyn M. Simpson (Berkeley: Univ. of California Press, 1963, no. 6, p. 143; Raleigh, *A History of the World*, p. 87. Patrizi, *Nova de Universis Philosophia* (Venice, 1593), speaks

of the light of God that surrounds, illuminates, permeates, makes firm, and unites the universe (*Panaugia*, p. 1^v). He considers in detail the supercelestial light (*Panaugia*, Book 8, pp. 18^{r}f.) and its inaccessibility (p. 74^r). As his subtitle suggests, Patrizi seems to follow what Vasco Ronchi calls the tradition of the "metaphysics of light" (*perspectiva*), deriving the principles of the universe from study of the nature of light. See Ronchi, *The Nature of Light: An Historical Survey*, tr. V. Barocas (Cambridge: Harvard Univ. Press, 1970), pp. 61–64.

11. *The Wisedome of the Ancients*, tr. Sir Arthur Gorges (1619; rpt. New York: Da Capo Press, 1968), p. 79. Bacon used the following apothegm, which he ascribed to the Neoplatonist Philo Judaeus, in *The Advancement of Learning*: "the sense is like the sun; For the sun seals up the globe of heaven, and opens the globe of earth; so the sense doth obscure heavenly things, and reveal earthly things" (*Apothegms, New and Old*, no. 120, in *Works*, VII, 146).

12. Bacon knew something of the *Kabbalah* through Agrippa's *On the Vanity and Uncertainty of the Sciences*, and probably also through Giovanni Pico della Mirandola, Patrizi, Giordano Bruno, and others.

13. *Zohar: The Book of Splendor*, sel. and ed. Gershom Scholem (New York: Schocken, 1963), pp. 27, 30.

14. The "abyss" of Chaos or Tartarus is typically identified with the earth "without form and void" by contemporary biblical commentators (see, for instance, Raleigh's *History*, 1.1.5, pp. 90f.). But the influential ancient apologist Eusebius, who attempts to reconcile Moses's account of the creation with the *Timaeus*, specifically says that the divine light before the creation is distinct from both day and night. See *Preparatio Evangelica*, 11.23, in *Patrologiae, Series Graeca*, ed. J. P. Migne (Paris, 1857), 21,909. For Giovanni Pico della Mirandola's radical attempt to combine the two accounts see below, p. 58.

15. *The Shadow of Night* in *The Poems of George Chapman*, ed. P. B. Bartlett (1941; rpt. New York: Russell and Russell, 1962), p. 20. The influence of Chapman is even more likely in that he was part of the Northumberland Circle (the so-called "School of Night"), which included Bacon's court associate Raleigh as well as the English atomists who influenced Bacon and whose scientific aid he sought. This circle blended "the thought of the atomists, Aristotle, Nicholas of Cusa, the fabled Hermes Trismegistus, Bruno, Gilbert, and Copernicus," according to R. H. Kargon, *Atomism in England from Hariot to Newton* (Oxford: Clarendon Press, 1966), p. 15.

16. On the relationship of mystical theology, nominalism, and the *devotio moderna* see "Nicholas Cusanus" in Ernst Cassirer, *The Individual and the Cosmos in Renaissance Philosophy*, tr. Mario Domandi (Philadelphia: Univ. of Pennsylvania Press, 1963), pp. 7–45.

17. Paolo Rossi, *Francis Bacon*, p. 122, suggests a possible alchemical context for Bacon's nocturnal method. It might be added that the alchemical process of *nigredo* (blackness) or *melanosis* (blackening) was allegorized by the famous Simeon ben Cantara: the process of burning and disintegration thus stood for the return of a given substance to the condition it had in the original Chaos of the world, so that the substance might undergo a "divine birth" of its essential nature (Joseph Campbell, *The Masks of God: Creative Mythology* [New York: Viking, 1968], pp. 278–279. For Bacon's analogy between his method and the alchemical process see *Novum Organum*, II, 16. Rossi, however, entirely overlooks the religious context of Bacon's interpretation of Night, as have other commentators.

18. D. P. Walker, *The Ancient Theology: Studies in Christian Platonism From the Fifteenth to the Eighteenth Century* (Ithaca: Cornell Univ. Press, 1972).

19. *Conclusiones de Modo Intelligendi Hymnos Orphei*, quoted in Edgar Wind, *Pagan Mysteries in the Renaissance*, 2nd ed. (New York: Norton, 1968), pp. 276–282.

20. *Mystica Theologia,* tr. Johannes Scotus Erigena in *Patrologia Latina,* ed. J. P. Migne (Paris, 1853), 122, 1171–1176.

21. "Analogy" in *The Catholic Encyclopedia* (New York: Robert Appleton, 1907); see Thomas Aquinas, *Summa Theologica,* I, Q.3, a. 3 and I, QQ. 3–13, a. 1.

22. *History of the World,* p. 85.

23. On the idea of the *speculum creaturarum* see R. S. Westfall, *Science and Religion in Seventeenth-Century England* (New Haven: Yale Univ. Press, 1958), p. 27, and Ian T. Ramsey, *Models and Mystery* (London: Oxford Univ. Press, 1964), which compares scientific and theological methods.

24. *Institutes of the Christian Religion,* I.5, tr. F. L. Battles, 2nd ed. (Philadelphia: Westminster, 1960), I, 68.

25. Quoted in Evelyn Underhill, *Mysticism: A Study in the Nature and Development of Man's Spiritual Consciousness* (New York: Noonday, 1955), p. 346.

26. Descartes' doubting is "like a man who walks alone in the darkness," he says in *Discourse on Method,* tr. Laurence J. Lafleur (Indianapolis: Bobbs Merrill, 1950), p. 11.

27. *Penseés,* no. 198.

Milton's Spenser:
The Inheritance of Ineffability

Maureen Quilligan

When Milton first thought of writing a drama of the Fall, he posed himself a difficult—some might say insuperable—problem: how to present events which happened before the Fall which the audience would not be able to understand by virtue of their "sinful state." Adam and Eve's initial nakedness would have presented an immediate impasse to the stagecraft of the 1640s (and to later times), and from the blatant physical difficulties of this fact we may perhaps sense some of the impact of more subtle ineffabilities confronting Milton as well. The successive drafts of the projected play contained in the Trinity MS all answer the question by dodging it; the third draft, first to be titled "Paradise Lost," sketches a play in which Moses, acting as prologue, describes not only his own miraculous state of "corporeal incorruption," but also explains to the audience that "they cannot see Adam in this state of innocence by reason of their sin."[1] Instead of an unpresentable Edenic interlude, Milton planned the first two acts as a traditional debate between three of the four allegorical "daughters of God"—Justice, Mercy, and Wisdom—on what "should become of man if he fall," plus a celebration of the first nuptials by "Heavenly Love" and "Evening Star." We do not meet any of the principals familiar from the epic account until Act III, which would have presented "Lucifer contriving Adam's ruin," nor would we glimpse Adam and Eve directly until Act IV when we could see them already "fallen." Milton's reluctance to risk confronting his postlapsarian audience with a prelapsarian experience is maintained through the fourth and last manuscript draft of "Adam Unparadized," which also delays introducing the original couple until after they have fallen (and can be presented clothed).

Milton appears in these early drafts to have taken into account at least some of the more particular difficulties posed by the story he chose to tell, which Dr. Johnson named as central to the imperfections of the epic Milton eventually wrote:

> The plan of *Paradise Lost* has this inconvenience, that it comprises neither human actions nor human manners. The man and woman who act and suffer are in a state which no other man or woman can ever know. Their reader finds no

transaction in which he can by any effort of the imagination place himself; he has
therefore, little natural curiosity or sympathy.[2]

For Dr. Johnson, as for Milton at least initially, prelapsarian innocence is utterly
inconceivable for fallen mankind—virtually unimaginable and unknowable.
Milton's solution in the Trinity MS—to substitute allegorical characters for a
direct presentation of the happy couple—serves only to emphasize the problem. Fallen mankind can appreciate the situation only mediately, through
animated language, or through the darkened glass of figuration (personification), not directly and "face to face." It is perhaps all the more startling,
then, that *Paradise Lost* in its ultimate manifestation presents not only prelapsarian Adam and Eve at great length (provoking Johnson's complaint), but other
celestial characters as well—not to mention God the Father Himself. In the light
of Milton's first reservations, the audacity of the ultimate attempt is brilliantly
bold.

We may well wonder what allowed Milton to shed his hesitancy about
presenting the unpresentable, about saying the ineffable. Fundamental to the
transformations involved in the leap Milton took is the switch in genres. What
becomes immediately interesting in the change from drama to epic is that
potential in the tradition of epic which might provide a bridge between the
sinful limits of the audience's understanding and the unspeakable bliss of
prelapsarian union. In this context, the most striking difference between manuscript play and final epic is the loss of allegorical characters, a loss especially
intriguing because those numerous characters had in part answered the problems of the story's very ineffability. It is as if the choice of epic, a more mediate
narrative form, allowed the loss of the allegory. Yet this loss is something of
a paradox in the light of Milton's immediate precursor in the tradition of
English epic. In the Trinity MS Milton had also jotted down ideas for an heroic
poem, elsewhere discussed along the lines of Tasso and Spenser, to be built
upon Arthurian material or the story of some renowned knight or biblical
character.[3] In effect, then, by substituting the matter of the Adamic drama for
the British epic material, Milton reveals another decision similar to his dismissal
of the allegorical characters from his *dramatis personae*: to drop both the idea of
a British, national epic and the use of allegorical characters from his treatment
of the Fall, is to deny at once the paradigmatic status of Spenser's *Faerie Queene*
to his own epic. Similarly, both rejections come connected to Milton's having
taken upon himself the stature of the Mosaic bard, effected when he substitutes
his own epic voice for the dismissed dramatic prologue of the manuscript drafts.
Thus all three choices are intricately connected to his new understanding that
it would be possible, in fact, to celebrate in an enduring effort of human art
the ineffable beauty of prelapsarian unions, both between God and man, and
man and woman.

To consider Milton's stance toward Spenser as a necessary part of his grappling with the fundamental ineffability of the story he has to tell is not merely to make an already complicated question more difficult. It will help, I think, to shed some light on the remarkable burden of originality Milton shouldered when he undertook, in essence, to rewrite Genesis as a Renaissance epic. Much of Milton's originality lies in the audacious, unallegorical literalness of his account which is, at the same time, organized by an all pervasive self-consciousness about the mediated "literariness" of his undertaking. As the poem most immediately preceding Milton's in the literary tradition of its genre (other hexameral poems were not shaped as Vergilian epics[4]), the *Faerie Queene* with its self-reflexive language becomes a useful context for Milton's shaping of his own self-reflexive concerns about his poem's potentially presumptuous artistry. Spenser's demarcation of the ineffability of Milton's material offers a usefully self-effacing foundation for the poetry of *Paradise Lost,* specifically as Milton's poem makes a rhetorical appeal to the reader to leap beyond the limits of the poem's speaking into ineffable understanding. Paradoxically, the more Milton incorporates references to the self-conscious mediateness of Spenser's sort of allegory in *Paradise Lost,* the more he is able to suggest an opposite potential in his own epic. By referring to the *Faerie Queene* and its self-conscious limits, Milton may safely open up his poem to the experience of divine, unmediated presence. In his insistence on the paradigmatic nature of the fallen language of the *Faerie Queene,* Milton marks the interfaces of his own fiction's limits. The ways in which the seams of his text fold in upon themselves reveal that if the stitchery is Milton's, nonetheless the fabric is God's.

Concrete examples are absolutely necessary in undertakings such as these— the more concrete and obvious, the better. The most obvious Spenserian precursor text underlying the moment of greatest ineffability in *Paradise Lost* —the blind poet's invocation to Light in Book III—is the vision offered the Redcrosse Knight by Contemplation in the "allegorical core" of the Legend of Holiness, *Faerie Queene* I.x. By scrutinizing the similarities and differences between these two moments of prophetic inspiration, we can appreciate the difficulties confronting any singer of eternal stillness and the ways by which Milton's song inherited some of its possibilities from Spenser's.

Spenser's vision looks out from the pinnacle of the "highest Mount" that has a number of complexly interconnected analogues; it is "Such one" as that from which Moses received "writ in stone / With bloudy letters by the hand of God" the prophecy of his own death; "Or" it is "like that sacred hill," which was this first mount's antitype, or the fulfillment of its *figura,* that is, the Mount of Olives, where Christ often walked—He who redeemed the kind of death deemed needful on Sinai. The third analogue is more surprising: "Or like that pleasaunt Mount, that is for ay / Through famous Poets verse each where renownd." Parnassus has no inevitable, sacred link to the other two, which are, at least to typological ways of thinking, substantially the same mountain. There are a number of ways to accommodate what seems to be Spenser's astoundingly blithe suggestion of equality between the three moun-tains, implied by the three connecting, parallel "or's."[5] Surely one part of Spenser's purpose in making this surprising comparison is to insist on the very mediateness of his own, that is, of Mount Contemplation's association with the first two mountains. To find Parnassus at the end of the list is both to celebrate it and to recognize the limits of the power it evokes by metonymy. The Muses with their "heavenly" notes and lovely lays, allow poets to envision mounts which are only analogues to the mountains of Scripture. Spenser does not equate Parnassus with Sinai or mere poetry with sacred prophecy. The *Faerie Queene* is *not* writ in stone by the hand of God, and it is important for Spenser's purposes of vision that the reader remember this fact. With the mention of Parnassus, Spenser indicates his own saving awareness that Mount Contempla-tion is merely *like* the other three mountains and reminds the reader that his stanza had begun "Such as." Poetry, by offering analogous vision and language parallel to God's is heaven*ly—like* to God's Word, but not that ineffable lan-guage itself. While Spenser grants to the language of his poem great power, he denies to it the ultimate potency of divine origin.

Still, from this carefully defined spot, Spenser can glimpse, if he cannot sing about, the beauty of the eternal city:

> Whose wals and towres were builded high and strong
> Of perle and precious stone, that earthly tong
> Cannot describe, nor wit of man can tell;
> Too high a ditty for my simple song;
> The Citie of the great king hight it well,
> Wherein eternall peace and happinesse doth dwell.
>
> (I.x.55)[6]

The song Spenser does sing, in being lower, may yet suggest by analogy the song which is too high for him. Blind Contemplation is able to describe what the Redcrosse Knight in peering, sees: the new Hierusalem, home of saints, future home of the future St. George who does not yet, however, know who he is. The vision is also prophecy when Contemplation, foreseeing, foretells the knight's victory: "though Saint *George* shalt called bee,/ Saint *George* of mery England, the signe of victoree" (I.x.61). Yet this "George" must be further read back into his origins: if the new Jerusalem glimpsed from the mountaintop is to be his future home in the time after the Apocalyptic end of time, he must learn of his first home: an "heaped furrow," smallest of lowly declivities, "Where thee a Ploughman all vnweeting fond,/ As he his toylesome teme that way did guyde,/ And brought thee vp in ploughmans state to byde." St. George than is *ge-orgos* (γη̇·ὄργοσ), "worker of earth," who must learn to return from the height of vision to the level plain on which his journey beings, and ends.

O holy Sire (quoth he) how shall I quight
  The many fauours I with thee haue found,
That hast my name and nation red aright,
  And taught the way that does to heauen bound?
This said, adowne he looked to the ground,
  To haue returnd, but dazed were his eyne,
Through passing brightnesse, which did quite confound
  His feeble sence, and too exceeding shyne.
So darke are earthly things compard to things diuine.
                               (I.x.67)

With the figure of blind Contemplation, Spenser reads the Redcrosse Knight's name and nation right, and in doing so reads out the significance of his name and his earthly (as opposed to "faerie") Englishness.

In the moment of vision the usual relations between sign and signified, between read text and its significance, seem reversed, as in this episode the procedures of the allegory are made a part of the literal action of the poem. The *Faerie Queene* is in its normal methods allegory, a *dark* conceit, by which we usually understand that the significance is hard to see, though the phenomena of the text are clear enough. In the moment of vision, when the Redcrosse Knight is allowed to read, and be read into, pure significance, he turns back to the phenomena of this world and *they* seem dark. On the mountaintop he, like Contemplation, is blind to signs. "So dark are earthly things compard to things diuine." It is out of this kind of moment, merely glimpsed, that he must learn to read the world; yet Spenser makes Contemplation read his very name, George, to insist upon the usual disjunction that exists between our normal experience, lost in the earthly darkness of signs, and the meaning of this episode which, by a densely self-reflexive reference back to the experience of reading, seems to negate itself and offer pure, blinding light.

It is the merest glimpse, however, and although the vision is rapturous, the place—even though it is itself only an analogue to other sacred places—not a place where earthly man may stay. The Redcrosse Knight must go back down the mountainside and work the significance of the vision in the world. If the episode of Contemplation offers an anatomy of the reading experience in terms of our interpretation of St. George, Spenser does so as well in terms of the figure of Contemplation. The blind seer, rather than Mercy, "reads" the way to heaven for us because Spenser may, by his blindness, by his fasting, by his spare thinness, indicate with transparent clarity the skeletal structure of significance which his story attempts to incarnate: "Each bone might through his body well be red." Even pure significance is something which may only be appreciated by the mediated act of reading. Spenser's epic begins, after all, with the *Legend* of Holiness which is essentially and only a text to be *read.*[7]

If the splendid joys of the citizenry of heaven prove "too high a ditty" for Spenser's song, then Milton's largest difference from his precursor spans the leap his poem makes to partake of the choiring of that citizenry:

> Hail, Son of God, saviour of men, thy name
> Shall be the copious matter of my song
> Henceforth, and never shall my harp thy praise
> Forget, nor from thy Father's praise disjoin.
>   Thus they in heaven, above the starry sphere,
> Their happy hours in joy and hymning spent.
>   (III.412–417)

The probable qualification of Milton's implicit claim that his song joins the heavenly choir's is that the poem merely reports what is, or could have been, heard. The angels' song is given in direct discourse; it is not until the epic voice turns to describe their singing, however, that the possessive pronoun belongs to them, not him. Yet even in this directness of discourse, Milton's muse functions differently (if also still mediately) from Spenser's, for Spenser's lan-guage is never heard, or even overheard; words are always *read*. Spenser implies the potent danger of Archimago's evil words by the images they silently create, able to lure the Redcrosse Knight astray, and by the injunction to the reader "let none them read." Conversely, Milton lets the reader first hear the full power of Satan's seductive speech. Contemplation, in physical appearance and in the service he performs for the Redcrosse Knight, is in the realm of reading: a nearly silent, unvoiced action of the *eye*, while the blind bard of *Paradise Lost* is rightly called by convention, "the epic *voice*."

All of the titular heroes of the various legends of the *Faerie Queene* are, in fact, readers of one sort or another; Faerieland is a bookish place. There are, by contrast, no readers in *Paradise Lost* and if anyone can be said to do anything so mediate as read, what is read is not sign but phenomenal signified—as in Adam's naming of the animals. In the context of these two distinctly different presentations of the text, Spenser's in an unvoiced (if not exactly silent) realm of reading, and Milton's in the auditory, dramatic conflict of heard "voices," Harold Bloom has made a provocative suggestion about Milton's relation to Spenser.

> Influence-anxieties of all kinds, with all their afflictions of secondariness . . . inhibit *writing*, but not nearly so much the oral, logocentric tradition of prophetic speech. Insofar as Spenser . . . truly was Milton's Great Original, then even Milton was inhibited, for Spenserian vision became an attribute of Milton's id-component. But Milton's prophetic, oral original was Moses, who became an attribute of the Miltonic superego, and thus stimulated the largest power of *Paradise Lost*, which is its marvelous freedom in expanding Scripture to its own purposes.[8]

As we have seen, Milton appropriates Mosaic stature to himself by becoming the epic voice inspired by Moses's muse, at the same time he dismisses mediat-ing Spenserian allegory by electing to write the story he had first conceived as drama in epic form. The epic voice of the narrative poem substitutes for Moses as prologue to the play. With his second choice, Milton makes a decision to elect what Bloom would call the prior mode of prophetic speech. Milton, of course, would have read Moses's account just as he read Spenser's poem, but the frame of Moses's account is oral while Spenser's text, as we have seen, everywhere calls attention to its own readable textuality. Bloom's distinction is coherent with the pivotal difference between Milton's dramatic, prophetic immediacy in Book III and Spenser's mediated *reading* of the distance between human song and divine agency in Book I.

While the dialogue in heaven prophesies all human history, Contemplation's prophecy to the Redcrosse Knight gives a lesson in interpretation—that is, in reading the text of the poem within its apocalyptic context. Milton's text of the voice, so to speak, is also apocalyptic, typologically acknowledging ends in beginnings, but the immediacy of the experience insists on the permeability of the boundary between the human and the divine. The seeing we get in Book III of *Paradise Lost* is in the direction from which Spenser's Redcrosse Knight looks only to discover that he is blinded: we look down from Milton's heaven, not upward at it.

Similarly, while Milton's invocation in Book III is to light, what he "sees" when that light is granted is not anything to be seen in heaven, though it is something to be heard, and is very much bound up with our new opening perspectives in the poem. One new aspect is surely the extremely personal anguish of the invocation, which involves the fact of John Milton's own historical, physical blindness, something which is a fact in itself and no mere poetic figure, though poetry can transform its mere literalness. If Contemplation's blindness was a conventional sign of his "higher thoughts," his blindness to the things of this world, and the Redcrosse Knight's dazed eyes evidence of the height of his unwonted vision, Milton's blindness is and remains in the poem a literal, historical fact, however much Milton places it within its proper, literary context:

> Those other two equalled with me in fate,
> So were I equalled with them in renown,
> Blind Thamyris, and blind Maeonidies,
> And Tiresias and Phineus prophets old.
> (III.33-36)

Though very different from these pagan precursors, not only in the lagging fame but in the truth of his vision, Milton in the brief list outlines the forbidden sacred and sexual knowledge that will be the matter of his song. The historical actuality of his blindness, framed in this specifically pagan literary context, still reinforces its literal difference, and insists (as the dismissal of the allegory had also implied) that there is the potential in this poem for literally imaging the truth.

If the invocation to Book III radically differs from the invocation to Book I by reason of its particular, personal note, it also differs in the amount of choice

Milton allows himself. In Book III, Milton himself chooses which of the mounts he prefers to haunt, whereas in the opening to Book I he offered the three mounts for the Muse's preference. The poet chooses Sion in the invocation to III:

> Yet not the more
> Cease I to wander where the Muses haunt
> Clear spring, or shady grove, or sunny hill,
> Smit with the love of sacred song; but chief
> Thee Sion and the flowery brooks beneath
> That wash thy hallowed feet, and warbling flow,
> Nightly I visit.
> (III.26–32)[9]

Alastair Fowler helpfully glosses this passage as meaning that Milton "loves Hebrew poetry best." Immediately thereafter, of course, Milton lists the blind pagan poets and prophets who share "sometimes" in his nocturnal musings, as he allows to the generic tradition of recompensing vision in blindness a capacity to shape his love of Sion's song: he reframes Moses's book, rewriting it in terms not only of Revelation (that final book of the Bible corresponding to Moses's first), but in the form of classical epic. In such a way Milton turns his affliction into poetic election, and if he nowhere hints that the fact of his blindness is God's visible sign of his vocation, it is perhaps because he intended that only the poem should be.

Only the poem, in its audaciously ineffable subject, can acquit Milton of the presumption in the claim that his blindness is recompensed in vision. The invocation requests it in terms of the poet's relation to his audience:

> So much the rather thou celestial Light
> Shine inward, and the mind through all her powers
> Irradiate, there plant eyes, all mist from thence
> Purge and disperse, that I may see and tell
> Of things invisible to mortal sight.
> (III.51–55)

The sight we get, again paradoxically, is not of the things invisible, how they might look were we able to see them, but of how those invisible entitites *see,* how, in fact, they can be said to see us. It is not a question of seeing God face to face, but of seeing ourselves as God sees us. We share God's perspective, which may seem a more audacious thing for Milton to offer the reader, though in fact it is not: we simply see what we always see, God's created universe, His creatures, only this time we see them in a new light.

> Now had the almighty Father from above,
> From the pure empyrean where he sits

High enthroned above all highth, bent down his eye,
His own works and their works at once to view:
(III.56–59)

We also "see" the sanctities of heaven receiving from "his sight" (their seeing him? or their being seen by him? or both?) "beatitude past utterance," as Milton assigns ineffability to those who might actually be able to see God. Not seeing God, but following His glance, we focus on the creature we have watched throughout the first two books in nearly grotesque, Brobdingnagian wide-screen close-up, now in God's perspective a mere creature crossing a boundary:

> Satan there
> Coasting the wall of heaven on this side night
> In the dun air sublime,
>   *   *   *
> Him God beholding from his prospect high,
> Wherein past, present, future he beholds,
> Thus to his only Son foreseeing spake.
> (III.70–79)

The dialogue we overhear in Book III had, no doubt, its origins in the debate between Justice, Mercy, and Wisdom which Milton cancelled when he turned from drama to epic; God takes the part of Justice and the Son that of Mercy as they discuss what "will happen should man fall." With its laying bare the theological, dogmatic bones of the narrative as God looks backward, forward, omnipresent in time as well as space, the opening speech in the dialogue is notable for the efficiency with which it demonstrates what has happened to human understanding "by reason of their sin." The light in which we see ourselves is undeniably harsh, our position with respect to the fiction distinctly uncomfortable. More than most others, it is a moment which immediately approaches the pinnacle of inspiration figured in the character of the prophet Moses; the blind bard, blessed with prophetic insight, can repeat the voices heard, and if not overcome the audience's incapacity, then, at least, confront the audience with the fact of their sinful capacities.[10]

The bard's blindness not only avails Milton of Contemplation's perspective, it controls the dynamic of seeing and hearing which so marks the dialogue in which silence is for a moment utterly deadly and in which the Logos "silent yet spake." The blindness may also control the irony involved in letting the last words of the book take place on another mountaintop, with another kind of inspiration, in a graver kind of light. So at the very end of Book III, Satan—

> Down from the ecliptic, sped with hoped success,
> Throws his steep flight in many an airy wheel,
> Nor stayed, till on Niphates' top he lights.
> (III.740–742)

As this last example illustrates, Milton's vision of the ineffable being of God is organized, not as Spenser's was, in terms of a slow and arduous ascent, but from the top down. Nowhere is the difference between the two visions more apparent than in the way the downward spiraling exit from the height of Milton's vision in Book III retraces the steps of the Redcrosse Knight's laborious ascent in Book I of the *Faerie Queene*. I do not mean to suggest that Milton, in overgoing Spenser, rewrote Contemplation's vision to specification but that both poets, working in a cohesive tradition, necessarily use the same tools (Dante had also used them). Milton uses these same instruments, however, very differently.

Immediately after Milton ambiguously takes up his harp in the choiring of angels' praise, the epic voice moves to Satan's progress:

> Thus they in heaven, above the starry sphere,
> Their happy hours in joy and hymning spent.
> Mean while upon the firm opacous globe
> Of this round world, whose first convex divides
> The luminous inferior orbs, enclosed
> From Chaos and the inroad of darkness old,
> Satan alighted walks:
>
> (III.416–422)

The troublesome verb, "alighted," again twists the radical opposition between lightness and darkness, blindness and insight, into the downward torque of gravity (here, for the moment, under Satan's control). The mention of Satan lets the whole dialogue in heaven be bracketed by a saving sort of self-consciousness that is, if not exactly Spenser's, then Spenserian. The foregoing part of the bracket (the left side, so to speak) is Satan's flight through Chaos when he takes off from the most Spenserian threshold in the poem—hell gate—at which Sin, replica of Spenser's first threshold marker, Errour, had sat.[11] At the end of Book II, Chaos was a space in the process of being "allegorized," as Sin and Death can there labor and create. The closing, or "right side" of the bracket is Satan's making his way through another "allegorical" landscape, the Paradise of Fools, with its monastic trash flying in the wind, literalizing life's *vanitas*. The brackets can be seen to act as a neatly allegorical envelope for the most literally rendered scene in the poem, the dialogue in heaven (which was, oddly enough, that which was originally to have been allegorical).

The allegory is, as usual, associated with Satan, and his perspective— always mediate—signals the need for ever greater self-consciousness; in the Paradise of Fools those who have sought their "reward on earth, the fruits/ Of painful superstition and blind zeal,/ Nought seeking but the praise of men," find their fit retribution alongside all the "unaccomplished works of natures hand." This place of punished presumption is imprecisely located in the general scheme, but precisely in one particular: after walking there and from there "far distant," Satan sees the magnificent sparkling structure of Jacob's ladder:

The work as of a kingly palace gate
With frontispiece of diamond and gold
Embellished, thick with sparkling orient gems
The portal shone, inimitable on earth
By model, or by shading pencil drawn.
The stairs were such as whereon Jacob saw
Angels ascending and descending, bands
Of guardians bright

                              (III.505–512)

The beauty of the stairs, though distinctly inimitable by other than verbal human arts, is strikingly enough *not* ineffable: Milton's song describes it, assigning limits to the plastic arts. While they have to be described by analogy, "as of a kingly palace," "such as" Jacob saw, the stairs are approachable by Milton's muse:

Each stair mysteriously was meant, nor stood
There always, but drawn up to heaven sometimes
Viewless, and underneath a bright sea flowed
Of jasper, or of liquid pearl, whereon
Who after came, sailing arrived,
Wafted by angels, or flew o'er the lake
Rapt in a chariot drawn by fiery steeds.

                              (III.515–522)

The vision offered here is meant to be understood as prior to any biblical or postbiblical revelation; it has no "models." And yet for Milton, of course, the image of the stairs has a venerable history: it is the symbol of contemplation embroidered on Lady Philosophy's gown in Boethius's *Consolation*[12] and the central figure of Dante's sphere of Saturn in *Paradiso* XXI–XXII. From Dante also Milton no doubt took his image of sailing, as in *Purgatorio* II where the souls of the penitent are wafted to shore by angels' wings. What Spenser's Contemplation offers is, to be sure, no specific vision of stairs or ladders; nonetheless, what he sees insists most naturally upon ascent and descent:

As he thereon stood gazing, he might see
  The blessed Angels to and fro descend
  From highest heaven, in gladsome companee,
  And with great joy into that Citie wend,
  As commonly as friend does with his frend.

                              (I.x.56)

If Spenser turns our vision upward to outstrip our sense of wonder, seeing for a moment beyond his poem's usual ken, then Milton works his way slowly downward. The Redcrosse Knight sees in a moment the whole city of Hierusalem; Satan from the bottom step

Looks down with wonder at the sudden view
Of all this world at once.
                              (III.542–543)

The Redcrosse Knight had seen nothing when he looked downward, being
momentarily blind. If there is but a little narrow path "that was both steepe
and long/ Which to a goodly Citty led his view" in Book I of the *Faerie Queene,*
this passage is imagined in *Paradise Lost* as:

A passage down to earth, a passage wide,
Wider by far than that of after-times
Over Mount Sion, and, though that were large,
Over the Promised Land to God so dear,
By which, to visit oft those happy tribes,
On high behests his angels to and fro
Passed frequent, and his eye with choice regard
From *Paneas* the fount of Jordan's flood
To *Beersaba,* where the Holy Land
Borders on *Egypt* and the Arabian shore;
So wide the opening seemed, where bounds were set
To darkness, such as bound the ocean wave.
                              (III.528–539)

The fact that this point of rest for Satan is also the passage taken by Milton's
muse, down over Sion in this more direct, wider, and less constructed influence
of power than Spenser had allowed in his upward glimpse, begins to explain,
I think, the huge expansiveness and freedom associated with Satan's flight
across the buoyant voids of Milton's created cosmos. If the dialogue in heaven
was audacious, the poetry of Satan's flight is true epic and a fictive analogue
to the bard's flights beyond the Aonian mount, above previous attempts at
heroic quest, those quests to which Milton alludes in the simile for Satan's
vision: as of a scout seeing new land or some shining metropolis. This is the
kind of language to which Edward Said must be referring when he says that
"Milton's verse seems to have overpowered the void within his epic"[13]:

                              then from pole to pole
He views in breadth, and without longer pause
Down right into the world's first region throws
His flight precipitant, and winds with ease
Through the pure marble air his oblique way
Amongst innumerable stars, that shone
Stars distant, but nigh hand seemed other worlds,
Or other worlds they seemed, or happy isles,
Like those Hesperian gardens famed of old,
Fortunate fields, and groves and flowery vales,
Thrice happy isles, but who dwelt happy there
He stayed not to inquire;
                              (III.561–571)

Milton's description of the sun whose rivers "run potable gold" is aureate style straining the limits of the word's ability to answer the child-like question of wonder, "what if—." So of Satan Milton remarks, "The place he found beyond expression bright." If Satan, no mean orator himself, finds the light of the sun beyond expression, Milton does not; rather, he again assigns the sense of ineffability elsewhere.

Of course description would not be possible without all the analogues, the "if's" and the "as's" of the offered comparisons, as in the famous reference to the sun spot through the "optic tube" which Galileo "yet never saw." So, whether Satan flew "by Centre or eccentric," it is "hard to tell." The mere fact that we follow Satan's flight at all introduces a bit of necessary indeterminacy as well, for it is in itself a parody of an epic quest, the full heroism of which will be, in due time, denied. But Satan, insofar as he stands looking down on earth from the lower stair, stands at a very privileged spot for Milton. It is a "passage" which allows God to bend His "eye with choice regard" downward on His creatures. Close to Sion, it must be the same "place" from which Milton invokes his Muse: the passage is, in fact, the *way* of Milton's Muse.

The opening itself "so wide" is like the bracketed vision of the ineffable godhead presented in Book III, bracketed as Milton explains "where bounds were set to darkness." The boundaries of the central vision of "voice" itself are those two moments of a very Spenserian kind of allegory, through whose mediate landscapes (Chaos, the Paradise of Fools) Satan's parodic flight of heroism moves. Together, these brackets limn the necessary self-consciousness Milton has of the limits of his fiction. The bounds set to darkness, if they may be sensed as boundaries to the quite personal conduit of Milton's voluntary numbers, are also limits "such as bound the ocean wave." This must be a reference to the miraculous binding back of the Red Sea waters when Moses led the chosen people across to freedom out of bondage, to a wilderness in which they would wander before finally gaining the Promised Land—across that border between Egypt and the Holy Land which God eyes with "choice regard" in the immediately preceding lines—a wide and momentous passageway. Moses's passage was, of course, the same one traversed by Dante's souls when they are ferried across the wide water in *Purgatorio* II, for their Psalm recalls the typological moment in the Old Testament which exactly prefigures their entrance into Purgatory.[14] If this analogy is to be read—and it is analogy ("such as")—then the passage of Milton's Muse may function just as Moses's did, to lead his faithful readers finally to the Promised Land within. How close the analogue is may be measured by the exactness of the parallel between the poem's end and Moses's pilgrimage. *Paradise Lost* leaves off with the Edenic couple "hand in hand with wandering steps and slow," making their way out of paradise.

The world was all before them, where to choose
Their place of rest, and Providence their guide:
(XII.646–647)

Moses's guidance had left off historically at just such a spot, and so Milton's
appropriation of Mosaic stature for the epic voice reinforces the persuasive
humility of his stance. He leaves his reader a truly vast freedom of choice. That
the *Faerie Queene* had begun in just such a landscape, with the same movement
of wayward progress by a solitary couple on their way back to a fallen Eden,
reveals how much Milton's reading of Spenser has informed his following of
Moses's word. Milton locates what had been the fictive area of choice for
Spenser's reader (the difference between letter and spirit) within a literal, historical time continuum, specifically that of Scripture. *Paradise Lost* is not another
book of sacred scripture, but it does function in ways analogous to that text.
Divinely inspired, it still allows its reader the fictive choice of freedom to
choose. Like the historical people in the desert, like Adam and Eve at the end
of *Paradise Lost,* the reader has only Providence for guide in the most crucial
moment of choice. Milton has withdrawn his own human claims for being the
agent of that choice.

By offering back to God of the darkness of his fiction, its framing limits,
as well as the truth and light it aims to contain, Milton arrogates to himself a
remarkable humility. An age too late, or too cold a climate, might damp "his
intended wing . . . if all be mine/ Not hers who brings it nightly to my ear."
The longer one ponders that proposition, the more one sees that Milton claims
less and less of the poem for himself. In a sense the easiest way around the
problem of ineffability is to let divine agency take over one's language: if one's
own words will never be able to reach up to God, then God—the Logos
Himself—will surely come down to redeem the very limitations of that verbal
struggle. Insofar as he claims in the poem to have been directly and literally
inspired by Christ, Milton need not apologize for, or even alert the reader to,
the mediacy of his Muse. His claims for direct, literal inspiration—as if the
poem were some kind of automatic writing—are everywhere in the text and
transform much of the self-conscious references to his own artistry, as in his
description on the passageway of the Muse, into a signal to the reader to
consider the option that Christ literally works within its fiction. In a very
economical way, Milton was able to dismiss the need for allegory in his approach to the ineffable being of God because, with what appears to be absolute
certainty about his own inspiration, he did not need a language in which the
divine presence was other, or *allos.* If at the end of the published *Faerie Queene*
Spenser prays for the ultimate vision, "O that great Sabbaoth God, graunt me
that Sabaoths sight," Milton in *Paradise Lost* has given us what that seeing sounds
like, the poem itself his record of the answered prayer.

NOTES

1. *Poetical Works of John Milton, Facsimile Edition,* ed. Harris Francis Fletcher (Urbana: Univ. of Illinois Press, 1945), II, 16; cited hereafter as *"Facsimile,* ed. Fletcher."
2. Samuel Johnson, *Lives of the English Poets,* ed. Warren L. Fleischauer (Chicago: Henry Regnery Co., 1964), p. 36.
3. *Facsimile,* ed. Fletcher, pp. 20–22; "A Heroicall Poem may be founded somewhere in Alfreds reigne. especially at his issuing out of Edelingsey on the Danes. whose actions are well like those of Ulysses" (p. 22). Milton mentions Arthur in particular in "Mansus," ll. 80–84: "revocabo in carmine reges,/ Arthurumque etiam sub terris bella moventem."
4. Burton O. Kurth, *Milton and Christian Heroism: Biblical Epic Themes and Forms in Seventeenth-Century England* (1959; rpt. Hamden, Ct.: Archon Books, 1966), pp. 33–52; "The fact that DuBartas had adopted a strictly classical form modeled on Vergil's for his *Judith* (1565) before he began work on the *Divine Weeks* indicates that his choice of the discursive form for the hexameral subjects was deliberate" (p. 43).
5. Isabel G. MacCaffrey, *Spenser's Allegory: The Anatomy of Imagination* (Princeton: Princeton Univ. Press, 1976), pp. 76–78.
6. All quotations of *The Faerie Queene* are from *Spenser's Faerie Queene,* ed. J. C. Smith (1909; rpt. Oxford: Clarendon Press, 1964), 2 vols; hereafter cited in the text.
7. For further discussion of the significance of reading to the poem, see my *Language of Allegory: Defining the Genre* (Ithaca: Cornell Univ. Press, 1979), pp. 227–238, 254–260.
8. Harold Bloom, *A Map of Misreading* (New York: Oxford Univ. Press, 1975), p. 50.
9. All quotations of *Paradise Lost* are from the Alastair Fowler edition (London: Longman, 1968); hereafter cited in the text.
10. For Milton's general program for confronting readers in this way, see Stanley Fish, *Surprised by Sin: The Reader in 'Paradise Lost'* (Berkeley and Los Angeles: Univ. of California Press, 1971), *Passim.*
11. For a discussion of Milton's indebtedness to Spenser for the "iconographies of mental shift," see Angus Fletcher, "Positive Negation: Threshold, Sequence, and Personification in Coleridge," in *New Perspectives on Coleridge and Wordsworth,* ed. Geoffrey Hartman (New York: Columbia Univ. Press, 1972), p. 137.
12. Prose 1, *The Consolation of Philosophy,* tr. Richard Green, The Library of Liberal Arts (Indianapolis and New York: Bobbs Merrill Co., 1962), p. 3.
13. Edward Said, *Beginnings: Intention and Method* (New York: Basic Books, 1975), p. 280.
14. For a discussion of Dante's typology, see Erich Auerbach, *Mimesis: The Representation of Reality in Western Literature,* tr. Willard R. Trask (1953; rpt. New York: Doubleday, 1957), pp. 169–173; see also my *Language of Allegory,* pp. 101–109.

George Herbert:
The Word of God
and the
Words of Man

Robert B. Shaw

As a trained rhetorician, for seven years Public Orator of the university in Cambridge, George Herbert was amply equipped to assess the powers and discern the limits of language.[1] Subsequently, as a priest and devotional poet, he put his verbal ability to the most exacting of tests by addressing it to sacred things. Like all writers in divinity, no matter whether they pursue their theme in a scholarly or an imaginative vein, Herbert by writing his poems was wres-tling with paradox. He was applying all his efforts of expression to things which the common consent of believers deems inexpressible. Herbert's awareness of this problem places him in a long and august tradition. St. Paul, the consum-mate preacher who declares that "faith cometh by hearing, and hearing by the word of God," is forced to abandon language in the face of direct experience of the divine: he can say only that he was "caught up into paradise, and heard unspeakable words, which it is not lawful for a man to utter." The early martyr St. Ignatius of Antioch writes soberly of the weakness and corruption of human words, stating a contemplative's preference for silence to speech:

> It is better to be silent and real, than to talk and to be unreal. Teaching is good, if the teacher does what he says. There is one teacher who "spoke and it came to pass," and what he has done even in silence is worthy of the Father. He who has the word of Jesus for a true possession can also hear his silence, that he may be perfect, that he may act through his speech, and be understood through his silence.[2]

St. Augustine, like Herbert a rhetorician, sets standards for Christian eloquence in his *De Doctrina Christiana,* but remarks acutely in passing upon the apparent anomaly of such a task. The heavenly glory that compels man's praise is one which at the same time bafflingly transcends it:

Have I spoken of God, or uttered His praise, in any worthy way? Nay, I feel that I have done nothing more than desire to speak; and if I have said anything, it is not what I desired to say. How do I know this, except from the fact that God is unspeakable? But what I have said, if it had been unspeakable, could not have been spoken. And so God is not even to be called "unspeakable," because to say even this is to speak of Him. Thus there arises a curious contradiction of words, because if the unspeakable is what cannot be spoken of, it is not unspeakable if it can be called unspeakable. And this opposition of words is rather to be avoided by silence than to be explained away by speech.[3]

Several of Herbert's poems in *The Temple* employ the trope which rhetoricians of his time would have called "adynaton." As the etymology of the word suggests, this figure is an admission on the part of the speaker that what he has to say is beyond the power of words to convey. In "Miserie" he complains,

> My God, Man cannot praise thy name:
> Thou art all brightnesse, perfect puritie;
> The sunne holds down his head for shame,
> Dead with eclipses, when we speak of thee:
>   How shall infection
>   Presume on thy perfection?[4]

The closing lines of "Grief" express with more personal feeling the same sense of futility. The final exclamation, unrhymed and extrametrical, virtually embodies the speaker's helplessness:

> Verses, ye are too fine a thing, too wise
> For my rough sorrows: cease, be dumbe and mute,
> Give up your feet and running to mine eyes,
> And keep your measures for some lovers lute,
> Whose grief allows him musick and a ryme:
> For mine excludes both measure, tune, and time.
>   Alas, my God!

The titles of these two poems are entirely apt in relation to the theme of language: upon man, whose ability to speak sets him apart from all other animals, a failure of language to attain its end inflicts perturbation, and at times even agony of spirit. Like Augustine and others before him, Herbert scouts the idea of silence as a medium more eloquent than speech. One of his finer critics has remarked upon an apparent "aspiration to muteness" in his poetry.[5] Herbert's deliberate plainness of style in many poems gives the effect of language coming as close to silence as words can come. Words are imperfect representations of the things they name; they are most effective in pointing to those things when they do not point ostentatiously to themselves. We might say (figuratively) that words applied with disciplined precision are less noisy than others. The unique transparency of Herbert's style will continue to elude analysis; but it can at least be said that a philosophic judgment of the ideal relation of words to their referents, and not a puritanical distrust of sensuous ornamentation, was the shaping force of his esthetic. His persistent care as a stylist is to narrow the unavoidable gap which exists not merely between human words and holy mysteries but also and just as definitely between words and the visible creation.

Herbert starts from a perception that language is fallen even as man is fallen; the divine gift by which Adam named the beasts in Paradise has become a tainted and a fractured idiom, duplicitous as the serpent's forking tongue. "Frailtie," not among Herbert's better-known poems, is striking for the severity with which it calls language to account:

> Lord, in my silence how do I despise
> What upon trust
> Is styled *honour, riches,* or *fair eyes*;
> But is *fair dust*!
> I surname them *guilded clay,*
> *Deare earth, fine grasse* or *hay*;
> In all, I think my foot doth ever tread
> Upon their head.
>
> But when I view abroad both Regiments;
> The worlds, and thine:
> Thine clad with simplenesse, and sad events;
> The other fine,
> Full of glorie and gay weeds,
> Brave language, braver deeds:
> That which was dust before, doth quickly rise,
> And prick mine eyes.
>
> O brook not this, lest if what even now
> My foot did tread,
> Affront those joyes, wherewith thou didst endow
> And long since wed
> My poore soul, ev'n sick of love:
> It may a Babel prove
> Commodious to conquer heav'n and thee
> Planted in me.

The poem begins by opposing meditative silence to the speech which deceives those who trust in it. The poet "sees through" the high-sounding names which mask the world's vanities; knowing them to be in reality but dust, he confidently proceeds to set the record straight by "surnaming" them—calling them what he with his superior insight perceives them in fact to be. "*Guilded clay,/ Deare earth, fine grasse* or *hay*"—he takes pleasure in the wit of his ironical adjectives. The first stanza ends, it appears, with the speaker in a comfortable position. He is able (to adapt the Prayer Book's phrase) to beat down Satan under his feet. But the rest of the poem demonstrates how illusory such confidence is bound to be. The second stanza returns to silence, but it is a silence beset by doubts and temptations. "That which was dust before, doth quickly rise"—and, risen, it proves a formidable opponent. It is not simply that the speaker's victory was too easily won; rather it was not a victory at all. By abandoning the stability of silence, by indulging in the act of "surnaming," the speaker has been seduced by the ambiguous power of language of which he was at first so wisely wary. The very fact that two opposing names can plausibly be applied to the same thing leads the speaker into confusion, into a realm of giddy relativity where things cannot be easily seen through or even easily seen. He is a mortal man, made of dust, and his own premature triumphal march has put dust in his eyes. He has in his ears the conflicting echoes of a confusion of tongues, of the Tower of Babel which his own pride was rashly attempting to erect. The world's vanity is directed towards the earth; his own may have aimed up towards heaven, but it was more rather than less vain for all that. The victory, if there is to be one, must be that of the Word of God in him, not that of his own words triumphing over the world. "Brave words"—his own as much as anyone's—are discredited in this poem; the silence which the speaker's utterance interrupted, which he misguidedly attempted to extol, was a more effective reproof to vanity than any words, simple or brave. In the face of the silence in which the Word of God is heard, the human voice runs the gravest risk of adding to the cacaphony of Babel, even when it is determined to speak truly.

"Frailtie" represents one extreme in Herbert's thinking about language. Since he did not, as a poet or preacher, abandon the use of language in despair over its frailty or his own, his poetry provides numerous examples of his attempts to bring words into harmony with unsayable truth. As he was well aware, the story of Babel was not the only one in the Bible treating the theme of language. The story of Pentecost redresses the balance; for there, instead of divine power confounding the tongues of men, men find themselves enabled, by the coming of the Holy Ghost in tongues of fire, to preach the gospel to people of all nations. The possibility of language which despite its inherent frailty is capable of pointing toward the truth is what Herbert as a Christian is bound to believe in. As a poet his aim is to dramatize the efforts of language to realize its full potential, to exchange the confusions of Babel for the ecstatic clarity of Pentecost.

In early editions of *The Temple* (and in the standard edition made by F. E. Hutchinson) the poems are listed not according to place but alphabetically by title. To look at the contents page in such cases is likely to remind the reader of a dictionary, and that all the more forcefully when Herbert's overwhelming preference for one-word titles is observed. "Complaining," "Confession," "Conscience," "Constancie," "Content"—the lists of substantives appear at once forthright and taciturn, requiring the sort of elucidation which a set of definitions might supply. One might ask how Herbert's task as a poet compares with that of lexicographer. The analogy presents itself unavoidably in the case of "Prayer (I)":

Prayer the Churches banquet, Angels age,
  Gods breath in man returning to his birth,
  The soul in paraphrase, heart in pilgrimage,
The Christian plummet sounding heav'n and earth;
Engine against th' Almightie, sinners towre,
  Reversed thunder, Christ-side-piercing spear,
  The six-daies world transposing in an houre,
A kinde of tune, which all things heare and fear;
Softnesse, and peace, and joy, and love, and blisse,
  Exalted Manna, gladnesse of the best,
  Heaven in ordinarie, man well drest,
The milkie way, the bird of Paradise,
  Church-bels beyond the starres heard, the souls bloud,
  The land of spices; something understood.

The poet attempts definition by metaphor, and in the event the reader may not see the point of one figurative phrase, he is tirelessly obliging in providing others. Or perhaps he is indulging his own recurrent taste which he confesses in another poem, "Jordan (II)," for "quaint words and trim invention." The effect of this profusion of figures is ambiguous. On the one hand, the fact that so many startling but apt metaphors can be found testifies to the apparently limitless potency of language. On the other hand, an uneasiness develops in us as readers as trope is heaped upon trope. We realize that if any one of these metaphors were a truly successful definition, the poem would come to a stop. The further the sequence of figures is extended, the "richer" the language becomes, the more paradoxically poverty-stricken language must come to appear. What began by seeming the speaker's exuberance has come by the final line to seem his desperation, a vain attempt of language to encompass the ineffable. His desperation is the more acute because he has chosen to express himself within the confines of the sonnet form: having come to the fourteenth line, he knows it is his last chance to make himself plain. It is with an almost physical sense of relief, which we can imagine the poet himself to have felt, that we come to the last words, "something understood." Placed as they are, they succeed in bringing to a stop an incomplete sentence whose suspended syntax and accelerating rhythms had become nearly intolerable.

Grammatically, the poem is no more a complete sentence than it was before its last two words were written. We might ask why "something understood" gives to the poem the effect, if not the fact, of completeness. Certainly the climactic shock of contrast counts as a key factor. This is the one phrase in the poem that is not evidently a metaphor; our impression is that it seems "truer" than the characterizations which precede it. It is not that the previous metaphors are *untrue*; for the phrase "something understood" need not be taken as excluding any of them. Rather, it seems to include them and point beyond them and itself, beyond that wished-for full stop on which it brings the restless efforts of language to rest. By placement, style, and sense, it is at home with the silence that follows the poem. As an isolated phrase the words ought by reason to strike us as vague; yet in this context they sound definitive. It must be because they frankly accept their indeterminacy that we are inclined to trust them more than their daring and colorful predecessors. They attain authority by refusing to claim it; their strength is made perfect in weakness. By moving closer to silence they move closer to the essence of what they seek to define. The thinking that brought this poem to its resolution finds a striking analogue in the following passage from St. Augustine:

> ... We have been commanded to pray in closed chambers, by which is meant our inmost mind, for no other reason than that God does not seek to be reminded or taught by our speech in order that he may give us what we desire. He who speaks gives by articulate sounds an external sign of what he wants. But God is to be sought and prayed to in the secret place of the rational soul, which is called "the inner man." This he wants to be his temple. Have you not read in the Apostle: "Know ye not that ye are the temple of God, and the Spirit of God dwelleth in you?" (I Cor. 3:16) and "that Christ may dwell in the inner man" (Eph. 3:17)? Have you not observed in the Prophet: "Commune with your own hearts and be stricken on your beds. Offer the sacrifice of righteousness and hope in the Lord" (Ps. 4:4–5)? Where do you think the sacrifice of righteousness is offered save in the temple of the mind and on the bed of the heart? Where sacrifice is offered, there prayer is to be made. Wherefore when we pray there is no need of speech, that is of articulate words, except perhaps as priests use words to give a sign of what is in their minds, not that God may hear, but that men may hear and, being put in remembrance, may with some consent be brought into dependence on God.[6]

Several explanations, none altogether convincing, have been offered for Herbert's choice of The Temple as the title for his book. I would not claim that he necessarily had this particular passage from Augustine in mind; but certainly as an argument it is congenial with Herbert's strategy throughout his book. If we think of a lexicographer's task as being that of setting limits to meaning, then Herbert's procedure is at the opposite extreme. He sets words at liberty to gesture freely toward meanings that transcend articulation. He employs words to usher the reader into the contemplative silence that lies beyond them, into a realm in which metaphor becomes identity, all signs being at one with what they signify.

Human language can only approximate this consummation; The Temple remains a book of words, not a book of blank pages. In so far as words can be trusted to prepare a reader for the silent colloquies which take place in the temple of the mind, they derive their power not from human invention but divine inspiration. The process of inspiration is one which Herbert, with charm and audacity, delights to dramatize. More than once he employs the conceit that God is his collaborator in the writing of a poem. In "A true Hymne" the speaker is stymied in his attempt at sacred poetry when he reflects upon the dubiousness of his own ability to be true to what he is saying.

> He who craves all the minde,
> And all the soul, and strength, and time,
> If the words onely ryme,
> Justly complains, that somewhat is behinde
> To make his verse, or write a hymne in kinde.

The problem is resolved when he discovers that he need not rely on his own artistry but that of God. As co-author God enables the hymn to speak truly by "rhyming" the motions of the heart with the words which alone would be inadequate as praise:

> Whereas if th' heart be moved,
> Although the verse be somewhat scant,
> God doth supplie the want.
> As when th' heart sayes (sighing to be approved)
> *O, could I love!* and stops: God writeth, *Loved.*

In "Deniall" the form of the poem leaves the notion of divine collaboration implicit, but all to greater effect, perhaps, for being so. The speaker recalls a time of spiritual dryness:

> When my devotions could not pierce
> Thy silent eares;
> Then was my heart broken, as was my verse:
> My breast was full of fears
> And disorder. . . .

The verse in this and the next four stanzas is "broken" in that the final line of each fails to rhyme. Until the last stanza, in which, as in "A true Hymne," "God doth supplie the want":

> O cheer and tune my heartlesse breast,
> Deferre no time;
> That so thy favours granting my request,
> They and my minde may chime,
> And mend my ryme.

The petition, we see, is "something understood" and granted in the course of its utterance. That the final word "ryme" should be performing here the very action it names is a signal token of the ideal harmony God's presence is able to confer on the discord of human speech. Once again, in this instance, the figurative is made actual, if only for the time it takes to utter a single word. The brevity of the feat takes away nothing from its sufficiency.

The peculiarly satisfying rhyming which takes place at the end of "Deniall"—a rhyming of concepts as well as sounds—is an example of how Herbert turns to his advantage the limits of his form. By at once meeting and surpassing those limits, he offers in his own practice an image of transcendence. It is remarkable that he is so frequently able to achieve such images within the confines of lyric. Such an imaginative fusion of terms with the qualities they name is more naturally the action of allegory. The allegorist, whether he is writing in prose or verse, has a vast canvas unrolled before him on which to pursue his effects—as vast, it may be, as *The Faerie Queene*. The burden of allegory may be conveyed by the presentation and interweaving of symbolic actions and characters extending over many pages. The message is fully conveyed to the reader only when the final layer of many layers of meaning has been absorbed, and the work is viewed as a whole. By choosing to address his themes in lyric form, Herbert was adding greatly to the difficulty of his enterprise. Foregoing the allegorist's generous proliferation of meaningful detail, he commits himself to deliver his ultimate meanings in the most compact way possible—often in a single word, or a short phrase. The more we read Herbert, the more we come to realize the extraordinary vividness with which words impressed themselves upon him. In his imaginative appreciation of their import, words took on for him the animation that an allegorist brings to abstractions by creating and setting characters in motion.

Herbert's effort to extend the reach of language through what I have called a rhyming of concepts explains some features of his style which might seem anomalous in the work of one dedicated to plainness. At times he uses devices which can strike the modern reader as strained bits of cleverness. Dryden anticipated such reactions when he wrote of Herbert as one who could "torture one poor word Ten thousand ways."[7] Herbert's ingenuity did not in fact extend quite so far; but he was not one to overlook a somewhat shopworn pun when it revealed something of the truth. Consider the following:

The Sonne.

Let forrain nations of their language boast,
What fine varietie each tongue affords:
I like our language, as our men and coast:
Who cannot dresse it well, want wit, not words.
How neatly doe we give one onely name
To parents issue and the sunnes bright starre!
A sonne is light and fruit; a fruitfull flame
Chasing the fathers dimnesse, carri'd farre
From the first man in th' East, to fresh and new
Western discov'ries of posteritie.
So in one word our Lords humilitie
We turn upon him in a sense most true:
  For what Christ once in humblenesse began,
  We him in glorie call, *The Sonne of Man.*

One notices that in this poem there is nothing of the self-distrust, the leeriness of language, that is so evident elsewhere. With relief, the speaker realizes that his metaphor is made for him already, woven into the texture of his native speech, that his penchant for "surnaming" of which he was dubious in "Frail-tie" is here permissible, when he speaks of his Lord as the Son of Man. He feels that he is discovering rather than inventing. The pun "neatly" encompasses both the glory and the humility of the Incarnation. That the single word should contain two disparate but equally apt meanings will put the alert reader in mind of the greater paradox: the inherence of a divine and a human nature in Jesus Christ. Such a pun, as Herbert exploits it, seems not so much a mark of rhetorical skill as of spiritual insight on the poet's part: a momentary glimpse of the wholeness of meaning which language expressed before the Fall.

When Herbert writes his poems of discovery—discovery of divine collabo-ration, or of sacred meaning inherent in words—he is following the advice recorded at the end of "Jordan (II)." That poem (titled "Invention" in manu-script) recalls the initial exuberance with which the poet sought out the most lustrous words he could find to celebrate heavenly joys, "Curling with meta-phors a plain intention, decking the sense, as if it were to sell." In his pursuit of gorgeous ornament he was hard put to please himself:

> I often blotted what I had begunne;
> This was not quick enough, and that was dead.
> Nothing could seem too rich to clothe the sunne,
> Much less those joyes which trample on his head.

But these esthetic aspirations are exposed in the final stanza as pride rather than zeal; and the divine counsel that concludes the piece gently reproves the poet for imposing higher standards on language than God himself requires:

> As flames do work and winde, when they ascend,
> So did I weave my self into the sense.
> But while I bustled, I might heare a friend
> Whisper, *How wide is all this long pretence!*
> *There is in love a sweetnesse readie penn'd:*
> *Copie out onely that, and save expense.*

By "copying" Herbert means making human words reverberant of the Divine Word. Once his talent has been sacrificed to this purpose it is the presence of the Word itself that allows for trustworthy copying. Such writing performs within the sphere of art the same role which the celebration of sacraments effects in the worship of the Church. By faithful and inspired copying it makes an inward and spiritual grace manifest by an outward and visible sign. A briefer way of saying that in Herbert's poetry signs strain toward union with what they signify is to say that his language is sacramental.

Ignatius of Antioch spoke of the Incarnation of the Word as "a cry which [was] wrought in the stillness of God."[8] Herbert's poems, like the sacraments, are witnesses to the Incarnation. As Herbert believes that the fallen nature of man has been redeemed by the Word becoming flesh, so he also believes that fallen language may be redeemed through the willingness of the Word to assume the burden of human utterance. In the inspired writings of the Bible, language has become a living force so that men do not so much read scrip- ture as they are read by it. Text and reader, life and letters, are surprisingly transposable:

> Such are thy secrets, which my life makes good,
>   And comments on thee: for in ev'ry thing
>   Thy words do finde me out, & parallels bring,
> And in another make me understood.
>   ("The H. Scriptures. II.")

A similar melding of God's "eternall word" with human words is what gives Christian preaching its efficacy, according to "The Windows":

> Lord, how can man preach thy eternall word?
>   He is a brittle crazie glasse:
> Yet in thy temple thou dost him afford
>   This glorious and transcendent place,
>   To be a window, through thy grace.
>
> But when thou dost anneal in glasse thy storie,
>   Making thy life to shine within
> The holy Preachers; then the light and glorie
>   More rev'rend grows, & more doth win:
>   Which else shows watrish, bleak, & thin.
>
> Doctrine and life, colours and light, in one
>   When they combine and mingle, bring
> A strong regard and aw: but speech alone
>   Doth vanish like a flaring thing,
>   And in the eare, not conscience ring.

In his own preaching Herbert knew better than to rely on "speech alone": the prayer he composed for delivery before his sermons includes a fervent invoca- tion of the *Logos*:

> Especially, blesse this portion here assembled together, with thy unworthy Ser- vant speaking unto them: Lord Jesu! teach thou me, that I may teach them: Sanctifie, and inable all my powers, that in their full strength they may deliver thy message reverently, redily, faithfully, & fruitfully. O make thy word a swift word, passing from the ear to the heart, from the heart to the life and conversa- tion: that as the rain returns not empty, so neither may thy word, but accomplish that for which it is given.
>
>   (*Works*, p. 289)

Such passages as those just quoted are important examples of Herbert's think- ing on the role of language in the life of the Church. But he carries his thinking

through to the level of personal devotion; and it is there, since he has to master
his own skepticism of its powers, that language meets its most stringent test.
The author of "Frailtie," as we have seen, was cautious in accepting even claims
advanced by himself for language as a medium of devotion. Herbert discovers
that the Word of God speaks to his unique condition as it does to mankind at
large. He finds that prayer is not merely human utterance, directed to God, but
"God's breath in man returning to his birth." It is easy to be charmed by the
moments of serendipity in Herbert, in which he perceives the hand of God
taking up the pen to add the final touch to a poem. What is more difficult, for
both Herbert and his readers, is to realize that the Word is no less present in
those poems which lament its absence. This conclusion, which follows necessarily from a belief in the Incarnation, is expressed in poems in which the theme
of language figures prominently. "Affliction (III)" begins:

> My heart did heave, and there came forth, O God!
> By that I knew that thou wast in the grief,,
> To guide and govern it to my relief,
>   Making a scepter of the rod:
>   Hadst thou not had thy part,
> Sure the unruly sigh had broke my heart.

As the Christian speaker is a man "in Christ," so Christ is present in his grief.
The afflicted man's cry is involuntary; he does not feel himself to be the author
of it. As it makes sorrow audible it announces the presence of the incarnate
Word in man's sufferings. It echoes the cry of dereliction from the Cross, "My
God, my God, why hast thou forsaken me?" Indeed, the discovery the poem
makes is that the cry *is* virtually the same, that the affliction of Christians is a
kind of sacrament in which the Lord's Passion is shown forth in the suffering
"members" of his Body:

> Thy life on earth was grief, and thou art still
> Constant unto it, making it to be
> A point of honour, now to grieve in me,
>   And in thy members suffer ill.
>   They who lament one crosse,
> Thou dying dayly, praise thee to thy losse.

The same insight appears at the end of "The Crosse." For five stanzas
Herbert laments the inscrutable "crosse actions" of Providence: after years of
hesitation, he has taken Holy Orders only to be struck down by illness so
debilitating as to prevent him from laboring in his ministry. It appears that
his destiny is "in Paradise to be a weed." In the last stanza he accepts the
will of God toward him with the words of another, which he adopts for his
own:

> Ah my deare Father, ease my smart!
> These contrarieties crush me: these crosse actions
> Doe winde a rope about, and cut my heart:
> And yet since these thy contradictions
> Are properly a crosse felt by thy Sonne,
> With but foure words, my words, *Thy will be done.*

Again, Herbert's words reach an impasse where his only recourse can be to "copying." Such copying is to literature what the *imitatio Christi* is to life; it is to take up one's cross. What Herbert learns by hard trial is that by attempting to put his plight in words, the poet adds further strands to the web of contrarieties that ensnares him. Each word is potentially a sign of contradiction; language itself is the Christian poet's cross. It is an awesome affliction; at the same time it is one which he has chosen as the way to salvation. It is only through words, however frail and inconstant, that Herbert can approach the eternal and immutable Word, and enter into that understanding silence in which it makes itself known to men of faith.

NOTES

1. Among the more valuable studies of Herbert's thought and style in his poetry are the following: Rosemond Tuve, *A Reading of George Herbert* (Chicago: Univ. of Chicago Press, 1952); Louis L. Martz, Chapters 7–8, *The Poetry of Meditation: A Study in English Religious Literature of the Seventeenth-Century* (1954; rev. New Haven and London: Yale Univ. Press, 1962); Joseph H. Summers, *George Herbert: His Religion and Art* (1954; rpt. Cambridge, Mass.: Harvard Univ. Press, 1968); Mary Ellen Rickey, *Utmost Art: Complexity in the Verse of George Herbert* (Lexington, Ky.: Univ. of Kentucky Press, 1966); Rosalie Colie, Chapter 6, *"Logos in The Temple,"* in *Paradoxia Epidemica: The Renaissance Tradition of Paradox* (Princeton: Princeton Univ. Press, 1966); Arnold Stein, *George Herbert's Lyrics* (Baltimore: Johns Hopkins Univ. Press, 1968); Stanley E. Fish, Chapter 3, "Letting Go: The Dialectic of the Self in Herbert's Poetry," in *Self-Consuming Artifacts: The Experience of Seventeenth Century Literature* (Berkeley and Los Angles: Univ. of Clifornia Press, 1972); the same author's *The Living Temple: George Herbert and Catechizing* (Berkeley and Los Angeles: Univ. of California Press, 1978); Helen Vendler, *The Poetry of George Herbert* (Cambridge and London: Harvard Univ. Press, 1975); and Barbara Leah Harman, "George Herbert's 'Affliction (I)': The Limits of Representation' (*ELH*, 44, 1977), 267–285.
2. Ignatius of Antioch, *Epist, ad Ephesios,* 15, 1–2, ed. and trans. Kirsopp Lake in *The Apostolic Fathers* (London: W. Heinemann, 1912), 2 vols., Loeb Classical Library, vol. 1. This passage is discussed by J. A. Mazzeo, "St. Augustine's Rhetoric of Silence: Truth vs. Eloquence and Things vs. Signs" in his *Renaissance and Seventeenth-Century Studies* (New York and London: Columbia Univ. Press, 1964), pp. 22–23.
3. Augustine of Hippo, *De Doctrina Christiana,* I, 6, trans. J. F. Shaw in *A Select Library of the Nicene and Post-Nicene Fathers of the Christian Church,* First Series, ed. Philip Schaff

(1887; rpt. Grand Rapids: William B. Eerdmans Pub. Comp., 1974); vol. 2, p. 524. Mazzeo's essay, cited above, is a penetrating analysis of this line of thought in the writings of Augustine.

4. Quotations from Herbert are from *The Works of George Herbert,* ed. F. E. Hutchinson (1941; rpt. Oxford: Clarendon Press, 1953).

5. Rosalie Colie, *Paradoxia Epidemica,* p. 201.

6. Augustine of Hippo, *De Magistro,* i, 2, trans. J. H. S. Burleigh in *The Library of Christian Classics,* 26 vols. (Philadelphia: Westminster Press, 1953–1966), vol. 6, p. 70.

7. "MacFlecknoe," 1. 208.

8. *Epist. ad Ephesios,* 19, 1.

Typology and the Ineffable: Henry Vaughan and the "Word in Characters"

Linda Ching Sledge

In order to create a private grammar of the ineffable out of his own synthesis of occult and Christian mysticism and various strands of seventeenth-century English Protestantism, Henry Vaughan experimented boldly with typology, the ancient hermeneutical system of interpreting Old Testament characters and events as prefigurations of the New.[1] What Vaughan calls "types," "figures," "shadows," "characters," and "hieroglyphics" constitute a sugges-tive, imagistic discourse grounded in the Hebrew Scriptures which enabled him to treat a wide variety of devotional topics. In the highly political figurative poems, "The King Disguis'd" and "Jacob's Pillow, and Pillar," Biblical history is seen to anticipate "anti-typical" events in the poet's own life, the eclipse of Charles I and the English civil wars that ensued. Especially pertinent to a discussion of the ineffable, however, is Vaughan's apprehension of God through the lens of the Bible, particularly the Old Testament. One aspect of Vaughan's decided originality as religious poet is his ability to impart an aura of numinous encounter and mystical negation to typological or figurative diction which, as Erich Auerbach has convincingly shown in his classic essay on "Figura," is denotative and historically derived.[2] Vaughan's controversial poem "The Night," for example, can only in the most superficial sense be considered a depiction of the traditional negative mystic's withdrawal into "the dark night of the soul." The poem's little-noticed typological associations also display the poet's debt to the dramatic, world- and self-affirming figurative style of the Reformers. Vaughan's remarkably eclectic use of the figurative method suggests that the general literary issue of verbally rendering the deity must be approached cautiously, since the language of ineffability is not the same for a seventeenth-century Protestant as for a medieval or Renaissance Catholic poet.

The purpose of this essay will be to examine the long-established exegeti-cal method of delineating God's attributes through types or figures, which produced a syntax of God-wrought Scriptural signs that the Protestant Reform-ers seem to have especially favored in their writings.[3] Because of his virtuosity in seeing and using types, Vaughan's works serve as a pre-eminent illustration

both of the figurative method in poetry and of what I would call the "Nominative" language of ineffability. I will in the course of this essay re-examine the
broad assumption that the forms of language are incapable of articulating the
divine who is, by implication, a mysterious and transcendent Other.[4] I would
agree instead with the contemporary philosopher and theoretician of religious
language Frederick Ferré whose brilliant attempt to construct a logical "model"
of religious discourse reminds us that there are many forms of speaking of the
deity other than that of mystical negation. Ferré gives special attention to
typology or "the open and abundant use of models, analogues, similitudes
[which] seem to be an entrenched part of the religious mentality."[5] The provocative debate among Logical Positivists and their opponents in the decades since
the 1920s over the very question of the verifiable forms of religious discourse
suggests that any study of literary typology, and indeed any discussion of the
language of ineffability, cannot proceed without a general description of the
basic "grammar," that is, the chief categories and forms of language depicting
the deity.

Let me briefly sketch a few categories here.[6] The most obvious, which we
might call the "Adjectival," includes the attempt of religious language to describe God through superlatives—all powerful, infinitely wise and loving, perfectly beautiful. The second category we might call "Conjunctive" or oppositional.
It uses paradoxical language to assert the unity of God's attributes as well as
his utter transcendence: it maintains both "and" and "neither."[7] A third class
of religious language, however, has not been so well defined or thoroughly
investigated by literary critics as the others, although twentieth-century theologians have given it great attention. This category we might call the "Nominative" because it treats the radical transformation of religious discourse in the
restructuring of language by God's acts, that is, the signs, names and events by
which God's active presence in Scriptural history—his "Word"—was made real
and vivid. As A. C. Charity asserts in his discussion of literary typology in Dante,
this form of speech is ruminative, sign-forming and existential.[8] The logical
problem inherent in the "Nominative" language is that of verification.[9] And the
poetic form of this speech is figurative and analogical in the way exemplified
by Vaughan's typological verse.

In fact, this third, or Nominative, form of discourse of the ineffable was
not new to the seventeenth century, but available from the time of St. Paul to
Christian writers attempting to give the deity a historic, verifiable character. It
is well known that St. Augustine discussed at length the profound distinction
between God's Word in Christ and the imperfect human words men use in their
vain attempts to know God. Yet he also gave great attention to types, "similitudes" or Scriptural "allegories," placing these in a separate and higher rhetorical category than mortal words and identifying them with the Word itself. For
Augustine, as for all exegetes until the Deists' attack on the traditions of Biblical
interpretation, the literal context of Scripture in which types were imbedded

was historically true as well as eternally real. It is important to realize that types were not human metaphors for God. They *were* God's verbal and historical acts. In *De Vera Religione,* Augustine describes types as actual, not literary events, which verify an ineffable God's miraculous intrusion into human affairs. This was God's *own* language, the holy Wisdom by which he taught men repeatedly the lesson of the Incarnation—his entrance into and transformation of human history in Christ:

> Let us use the steps which divine providence has deigned to make for us. When we delighted over much in silly figments, and grew vain in our thoughts, and turned our whole life into vain dreams, the ineffable mercy of God did not disdain to use rational angelic creatures to teach us by means of sounds and letters, by fire and smoke and cloudy pillar, as by visible words. So with parables and similitudes in a fashion he played with us when we were children, and sought to heal our inward eyes by smearing them with clay.[10]

But although typology was never neglected by the medieval exegetes who followed St. Augustine, it was overshadowed by the more abstract medieval allegorical exegesis until the post-Reformation zeal for seeing the "Word in Character," to use Vaughan's own terms, re-cast figurative language in a more literal, dramatic, and persuasive form.

This method of expressing the deity, the *via eminentiae,* is radically different from the *via negativa,* the mystical way of apprehending God by denying him finite or creaturely characteristics.[11] For the negative way, which, in seeking God through paradox and silence is one of the primary examples of the conjunctive method, offers only one narrow way of approaching God and speaking about him. For the devotional poet, such an approach assumes that God is unknowable and wholly Other and that language because of its finiteness is inadequate to describe him. The *via eminentiae,* by contrast, assumes that God is indeed ineffable in his essence, yet knowable in the world through his acts, words, and angelic or natural agents, and that a "code" of signs can be established for men to understand. The system of emanations rests on two pillars of doctrine: God's entering history in the Incarnation of Christ and the revelation of his will in Scripture.

The way of emanations became the Thomist doctrine of analogies, the ascendant means of talking about God in medieval theology and poetry. It is this doctrine which supported the well-known fourfold system of allegorical exegesis into which typology fits. Even after the Reformers attacked the excessive abstraction of the medieval Biblical allegorists, the exegetical system of "spiritualizing" or drawing abstract meaning from the literal level of the Biblical texts still survived in more restricted form in seventeenth-century typology. Luther and Calvin distrusted medieval allegory but reserved special affection for types because of their fidelity to the Biblical letter. Both Reformers shared the medieval Christian view of Old Testament types and their Gospel

"antitypes" as "God's handwriting"—the deity's visible imprint in the Hebrew
and Christian past, in the present, and in the millennium to come. Yet departing
from medieval exegetes, Luther and Calvin saw typology as more distinctive
and useful than all the other allegorical "senses" which had eclipsed it in the
Middle Ages, for it wove Biblical history into the very fabric of peoples lives.[12]
So real was the impact of Biblical *littera* on the lives of seventeenth-century
Protestants of all camps that typology became for them a way of bringing a
divine analogical order to bear on the maelstrom of common experience. This
was particularly true for seventeenth-century Puritans, who, according to the
historian Willian Haller, saw the Old Testament as "the perfect typological
mirror in which to make their hearers see themselves and the crises and
predicaments through which they themselves were passing."[13] Over a century
before Vaughan's *Silex Scintillans* was published, the Reformer William Tyndale
had praised figures for containing "the secrets of God hid in Christ," and
further asserted that they were the "root and ground of us all," an anchor to
the Bible from whence faith and salvation sprang.[14] By Vaughan's time, this
attitude was firmly entrenched in the popular imagination, especially among
the Puritans, for whom typology became, as Thomas Davis observes, "as
important a method of Biblical exegesis as medieval allegory had been to the
Scholastics."[15] The seventeenth-century Christian had become so familiar with
figurative discourse through sermons, diaries, devotional manuals and even
political polemics that he, too, understood and practiced the "code" by which
typology spoke of the salvific process underlying history, which emanated from
the deity himself and entered even commonplace human experience. If Vaughan,
as a staunch Anglican Royalist, abhorred the anti-Stuart jeremiads hurled from
Puritan pulpits, he nevertheless as a poet seemed to assent to the Puritans'
fervent espousal of "a world slick't up in types."[16]

    By the time Vaughan began to write in the 1640s and 1650s, the issue of
the inadequacy of language to describe the deity survived primarily as a poetic
cliché, a standard literary disclaimer prefacing the religious poet's wholeheart-
ed deployment of the sensuous language of the physical world. Nor is the issue
a valid rhetorical concern for a figurative poet like Vaughan, who sees God and
Christ indirectly through the spectacles of the Bible. Even the iconoclastic
Puritans, who in politics and in doctrine had the most reason to oppose the
inherent sensuousness of verse and idolatry of symbolmaking, in poetic practice gave that issue little real attention.[17] A case in point is the Puritan thinker
Richard Baxter, who simply dismisses the problem. In his meditation *The Saints
Everlasting Rest,* Baxter admits that words (and types in particular) are imperfect
representations of divine truth, as if making an expected bow to religious
convention and perhaps to the prevailing Puritan authorities. Then he continues with his elaborate, extended defense of types, reasoning that although the
senses could be a potential trap, sensuous language had a proper use sanctioned
by God: since God himself had resorted to types when speaking to mankind

in the Bible, sensuous language was "necessary" and could appropriately be used to articulate the invisible qualities of the deity:

> And it is very considerable how the holy Ghost doth condescend in the phrase of Scripture, in bringing things down to the reach of sense; how he sets forth the excellencies of Spiritual things in words that are borrowed from the objects of sense; how he describeth the glory of the New Jerusalem in expressions that might take even with flesh itself: As that the Streets and Buildings are pure Gold, that the gates are Pearl. . . . That we shall eat and drink with Christ at his Table in his Kingdom: that he will drink with us the fruit of the Vine new; that we shall shine as the Sun in the firmament of our Father; These with most other descriptions of our Glory are expressed, as if it were the very flesh and Sense; which though they are all improper and figurative, yet doubtless if such expressions had not been best, and to us necessary, the Holy Ghost would not have so frequently used them.[18]

The issue of the inadequacy of language arises, then, when one is addressing the special question of direct communion with God and attempting to define the essence of that sublime being. Although this is a crucial problem in Catholic mysticism, especially among practitioners of the negative way, it is not an important issue in much Protestant poetry, which is Christocentric, and world-affirming, and thereby focused on God's revelation in history. The general epistemological question, as I see it, is not simply how we may speak of the deity who is beyond knowing, but how Christian poets have attempted to translate what an immanent God is revealing continually in the world. The second but salient aspect of knowing God through a conventional or "Nominative" syntax of signs is how this knowledge becomes instrumental for salvation.[19] Vaughan, as seventeenth-century Protestant poet, takes on both tasks, and typology is one of his major and most brilliant techniques.

In "The Holy Scriptures," Vaughan argues that the art of divine poetry is typological by definition, for it rests on the poet's ability to utter the "Word in Characters." He uses typology to dramatize this point: Old Testament altar stone, manna, and wine prefigure the Word in the Bible, in the body and blood of Christ, and in the bread and wine of communion. Echoing Calvin, Vaughan calls the Scriptures a "key" as embodied in the figure of Christ as Logos, the manifestation of the deity at creation, and in the disembodied "voices" that spoke to the patriarchs out of whirlwind and fire. Just as Calvin believed that the etched heart was a type of Old Testament law,[20] Vaughan himself fulfills in the sacrificial notion of his art the promise of the Word in the holy texts: the poet's heart is etched painfully with "God's penning" and his volume of verse, stained with the poet's own sin, figures the Saviour's agony at Golgotha:

> In thee the hidden stone, the Manna lies,
>   Thou art the great Elixir, rare and Choice;
>   The Key that opens to all Mysteries,
> The Word in Characters, God in the Voice.

O that I had deep Cut in my hard heart
    Each line in thee! Then would I plead in groans
Of my Lords penning, and by sweetest Art
Return upon himself the Law, and Stones.
    Read here, my faults are thine. This Book, and I
    Will tell thee so; Sweet Savior thou didst dye![21]

Despite the fact that figures provided Vaughan with a nexus of intricately linked spiritual and historical meanings which helped him discover an "easie access" to God, they limited him to a set of prescribed interpretations, especially when used in their more restricted Protestant sense. They revealed, too, the pivotal role that the Protestant notion of regeneration played in unlocking the meaning of types and in bridging the enormous gulf that yawned between *dévot* and deity.[22] In "Vanity of Spirit," Vaughan's most complete statement on devotional poetics, the limitations which types imposed on the Christian poet are clearly defined. The task of the poet was not to re-create by his own efforts God's truth but to discover and to utter a "truth readie penn'd," the Biblical types themselves. Nevertheless, utterance or poetry did not depend on man's will but on God's alone. Without the God-wrought power to bring meaningless human words into proper aesthetic alignment with God's Word, Christ himself, the types contained in the Biblical texts, the "peece of much antiquity," appear to the unregenerate poet as a heap of indecipherable "Hieroglyphicks quite dismembered/ And broken letters scarce remembered":

Weake beames, and fires flashed to my sight,
Like a young East, or Moone-shine night,
Which shew'd me in a nook cast by
A peece of much antiquity,
With Hieroglyphicks quite dismembered,
And broken letters scarce remembered.
I tooke them up, and (much Joy'd), went about
T'unite these pieces, hoping to find out
The mystery; but this neer done,
That little light I had was gone:
It griev'd me much. At last, said I,
Since in these veyls my Ecclips'd Eye
May not approach thee, (for at night
Who can have commerce with the light?)
I'le disapparell and to buy
But one half glaunce, most gladly dye.
                    ("Vanity of Spirit," ll. 19–34)

An examination of one of the most complex of Vaughan's types, the Biblical Jacob, shows how the poet solved in one instance the technical restrictions and devotional imperatives imposed by typological language. Vaughan

sympathized keenly with the human struggles of the patriarch, while recognizing his roles as percursor of Christ and gifted Biblical dreamer able to pierce
nature's veils in visionary commerce with the deity. More important to our
study of Vaughan's numinous poetics and to his use of the "Nominative"
language of ineffability, however, is his view of Jacob as a type of the regenerate
Christian poet fulfilled in the present by the "antitypes" of Vaughan himself
and of his poetic creations. In "The World (II)," Vaughan's own struggles to
create what he describes in his Preface to *Silex Scintillans* (1655 version) as a "true
hymn" is identified with Jacob's distress on the eve of his battle with the angel
at Peniel before meeting Esau, the brother whom he had betrayed years before.
Jacob's difficult passage over Jordan before his nocturnal duel with the angel
(Genesis 32:10) is the poet's longed-for rebirth in Christ as "hagiographer" or
Christian poet. The staff with which Jacob calms the Jordan's turbulent waters
is the poet's pen summoning the Logos into concrete form. Vaughan carefully
constructs a parallel between God's creation of a Christian poet out of a
depraved soul and God's creation of Israel, founder of a great nation, out of
the badly frightened Jacob. The comparison implies that poetry is far more
than incarnation; it is "regeneration," the poet's rebirth through conversion
after an agonizing interior battle to abandon the vanity of "Witt" and "de-
prav'd tastes" for the proper subjects of poetry—"thy dear Word as thou has
dress'd it," the Word-made-Flesh as seen in Biblical types.

It is important to note that types enter the poem only at its conclusion,
after the poet has attempted unsuccessfully to apprehend God through various
kinds of religious language. Vaughan adopts the "conjunctive" language of
mystical negation, but this only leads him toward rather than away from trivial
worldly concerns. The poet cannot free himself through negation from earthly
trappings, and his comparisons seem heavy, dull, and lifeless:

> Thou art not Riches; for that Trash
> Which one age hoords, the next doth wash
> And so severely sweep away;
> That few remember, where it lay.
> So rapid streams the wealthy land
> About them, have at their command:
> And shifting channels here restore,
> There break down, what they bank'd before.
> Thou art not Honour; for those gay
> Feathers will wear, and drop away;
> And princes to some upstart line
> Give new ones, that are full as fine.
> Thou art not pleasure; for thy Rose
> Upon a thorn doth still repose;
> Which if not cropt, will quickly shed;
> But soon as cropt, grows dull and dead.
> ("The World [II]," ll. 33–48)

Vaughan turns next to "adjectival" language—poetic similitudes and metaphors of God drawn from nature—but his efforts here also seem vain, ending
in an unwieldy colloquial paraphrase of a common proverb: "swallows, like
false friends, fly away upon the approach of winter."

> Thou art the sand, which fills one glass,
> And then doth to another pass;
> And could I put thee to a stay,
> Thou art but dust! then go thy way,
> And leave me clean and bright, though poor;
> Who stops thee, doth but dawb his floor,
> And Swallow-like, when he hath done,
> To unknown dwellings must be gone!
>
> (ll. 49–56)

Vaughan turns finally to types—the figure of the soon-to-be regenerate
Jacob waving his staff magus-like over Jordan (and thereby anticipating Moses
and the parting of the Red Sea), bringing order to the unwieldy matter of a
fallen world. When used here, the figure of Jacob renders the poem far more
than an evocation of God's visible attributes in nature. The poem becomes a
manual for salvation, an antitype of Jacob at Peniel, offering the reader a means
of approaching God by rejecting the world for the "narrow way" laid open to
heaven by Jacob's staff and by the poet's own regeneration through types, the
proper "words" of his holy art.

> Give me my staff, then, as it stood
> When green and growing in the Wood.
> (Those stones which for the Altar serv'd,
> Might not be smooth'd, nor finely carv'd:)
> With this poor stick I'le pass the Foord
> As Jacob did; and thy dear word
> As thou hast dress'd it: not as Witt
> And deprav'd tastes have poyson'd it:
> Shall in the passage be my meat,
> And none else will thy Servant eat.
> Thus, thus and in no other sort
> Will I set forth, though laugh'd at for't:
> And leaving the wise World their way,
> Go through; though Judg'd to go astray.
>
> (ll. 80–91)

For our purpose of illustrating how types as a "Nominative" language can
reveal an ineffable deity, Vaughan's original and brilliant use of figures in "The
Night" is especially illuminating. The poem in theme denies the efficacy of
positive approaches to God, yet it couches its anti-rhetorical argument in the
concrete form of typology. Figures are used as generalized symbols relating to
the theme of nocturnal theophany and are absorbed into the language of occult

and Christian mysticism. Vaughan's eclectic poetic method is especially evident in this poem. The deity is seen through the "veils" of night and day, clouds and stars. These images derive from sources as diverse as medieval and hermetic mystical texts and the Book of Revelation, although their exact doctrinal or philosophical sources are not easy to pinpoint;[23] nevertheless they are knit into an integral, allusive poetic design with a remarkably evocative emotional effect. To my mind, the poem is neither a vehicle for mystical doctrine nor a tissue of poetic images, as various scholars have argued;[24] nor is it what it suggests on the surface—a paean to the night. Rather, I find that it is a lyric praising the Incarnation which draws its images of the deity's presence in nature from a wide range of sources, including the Old Testament. Typology is an impor-tant, though inobtrusive technique to anchor incarnational nature-images in a Scriptural context. The Biblical event directly treated in the poem, Christ's appearance to Nicodemus in the Book of John, must be seen as an antitype of other nocturnal theophanies in the Old Testament to which Vaughan constant-ly alludes in his *oeuvre*; the most significant of these, of course, is Jacob's dream of the angelic ladder at Bethel. The Old Testament dream-vision provides the "shade" or "true Night" which the New Testament theophany (Christ to Nicodemus) fulfills. Without figural correspondences, the poem would seem structurally weak and the literal New Testament event which provides the poem's basic narrative would appear merely an unimportant, quickly aban-doned plot-device and preamble for the extended mystical apostrophe to night.

Yet Vaughan himself suggests that the poem ought to be considered in a typological light. The nocturnal vision of Nicodemus suggests far more than the actual event described in the Gospel of John. Vaughan enlarges the Scriptural framework of the poem to encompass the Old Testament by declaring that only "Angels wing or voice" disturbs the peace of night: this reference suggests that Nicodemus's real-life meeting with Christ (unheralded by angels) has been foreshadowed by Jacob's dreams of angelic ladder and angelic assailant, the archetypal angelic and nocturnal theophanies in church tradition. "Sacred vail," "Angels wing," "dark Tent," "dazling darkness" seem more than allusive poetic images borrowed from various mystical traditions. They are figures clearly alluding to the Biblical patriarch Jacob and his nocturnal visions, affirming that Christ's and Nicodemus's meeting is a fulfillment of prophetic events in Old Testament history in which the deity through divine agents deigned to reveal himself to a particularly gifted mortal:

> Were all my loud, evil days
> Calm and unhaunted as is thy dark Tent,
> Whose peace but by some Angels wing or voice
>   Is seldom rent;
>   Then I in Heaven all the long year
> Would keep, and never wander here.

> But living where the Sun
> Doth all things wake, and where all mix and tyre
> Themselves and others, I consent and run
> 　　To ev'ry myre,
> And by this worlds ill-guiding light,
> Erre more than I can do by night.
> 　　　　　　　　　("The Night," ll. 37–68)

For Vaughan, night is a hallowed "Virgin-shrine," an emblem of the Incarnation. As such, Vaughan's phrase "dazling darkness" relates indirectly to Jacob's vision of the angelic ladder at Bethel, for the Old Testament vision, too, was commonly understood in Vaughan's time to be a figure of the Incarnation, the mystery described by the seventeenth-century Puritan James Ussher as "the only ladder whereby Heaven may be scaled by us."[25] I would further argue that the entire poem is an anti-type of the incarnate Word. The poem's tri-partite structure is obvious: two long expository passages separated by a central two-stanza passage using Welsh *dyfalu* form and setting forth a catalogue of the numinous aspects of night. To my mind, this three-part form serves a different purpose than logical coherence or prosodic diversity. The central mystical section is a "still point" at the very heart of the poem embodying the "heart" of Christian doctrine, night's Christological essence. Night is, in other words, Christ himself. Typological echoes of the Song of Songs occur in the extended reference to Christ as Bridegroom summoning the spouse with "his still, soft call." Here, at the poem's very center, is the figure of the Word uttering itself into being at the Incarnation, as seen throught the "glass" of the most sensual of Scriptural texts

Yet there is a deeper music at the heart of night's fruitful silence. A caesura bisects virtually every line of the center section into two hemstichs. Because of the incremental repetition of the "still points" in each line, one hears the interior pauses as audible sounds of the ineffable deity himself.

> Dear night! this worlds defeat;
> The stop to busie fools; cares check and curb;
> The day of Spirits; my souls calm retreat
> 　　Which none disturb!
> Christs progress, and his prayer time;
> The hours to which high Heaven doth chime.
>
> Gods silent, searching flight:
> When my Lords head is fill'd with dew, and all
> His locks are wet with the clear drops of night;
> 　　His still, soft call;
> His knocking time; the souls dumb watch,
> When spirits their fair kindred catch.
> 　　　　　　　　　(ll. 25–36)

It seems to me that "The Night" is a poetic *tour-de-force,* for in attempting to make concrete the invisible essence of God, the entire work becomes a figure of the Word-made-Flesh. The two narrative side-sections in which the poet treats realistic historical concerns are the fleshly vessel enclosing the numinous and silent "heart" of the poem, the catalogue evoking the spiritual essence of Christ penetrated by brief moments of divine quiet. "The Night" is Vaughan's paean to the incarnate Christ, the *Verbum infans,* the inarticulate Word of God, in its figural language and poetic devices and in the figural form of the work itself:

> There is in God (some say)
> A deep, but dazling darkness; as men here
> Say it is late and dusky, because they
>   See not all clear;
> O for that night! where I in him
> Might live invisible and dim.
>   (ll. 49–54)

In the final analysis, what I believe Vaughan's figurative verse intends is something far more than the mere cataloging of God's omni-attributes or the re-creation by means of paradoxical language of the mystical union of self and divine Other. Rather, it attempts the construction of what the philosopher Frederick Ferré describes as a "metaphysical model," a concrete rhetorical structure articulating the deity which can be discovered through typology or what I would call the "Nominative" language of the ineffable.

> When the Judeo-Christian scriptures set about representing the nature of ultimate reality, this enterprise is not approached through abstract theory but through epistemologically vivid stories and anthropomorphically immediate images. Ideas drawn from one area of experience are put to work in another area—an area in which, we are explicitly warned, these ideas have no proper place. The keystone of the biblical ontological scheme, the concept of God, is beyond human conception: "His ways are not our ways, nor His thoughts our thoughts." But in spite of such reminders, the theoretical term "God" is constantly interpreted in terms of epistemologically vivid personal models. The very warnings against supposing our concepts of God to be literally representative are themselves couched in the language of the model: the personal *His,* the anthropomorphic attribution of *thoughts* to God.[26]

This "model" can be seen in the typological poem "The Night," for the work satisfies both Biblical truth and revelation, has historical deific verification, and issues in an existential choice—the adoption of a regenerate life. Frederick Ferré, in his analysis of the logical consistency of "metaphysical models," could have been speaking of Vaughan's valiant personal and poetic attempt to elucidate the ineffable in types and to utter the "Word in Characters."

NOTES

1. The best treatment of Vaughan's typology is by Barbara Lewalski in "Typology and Poetry: A Consideration of Herbert, Vaughan and Marvell" in *Illustrious Evidence: Approaches to English Literature of the Early 17th Century,* ed. Earl Miner (Berkeley: Univ. of California Press, 1975), pp. 41–69. Lewalski's discussion is cogent but very brief.

2. The definitive discussion of literary typology is Auerbach's "Figura " tr. Ralph Manheim, *Scenes from the Drama of European Literature* (New York: Meridian Press, 1959); see especially pp. 11–76. I am using the terms "type" and "figure" synonymously.

3. An excellent summary of how Reformation typology evolved from medieval allegory is contained in Thomas M. Davis's essay, "The Traditions of Puritan Typology," *Typology and Early American Literature,* ed. Sacvan Bercovitch (Amherst: Univ. of Massachusetts Press, 1972), pp. 42–45. For an extended treatment of this issue, see James Preus, *From Shadow to Promise* (Cambridge: Harvard Univ. Press, 1969.)

4. This assumption may have its source in St. Augustine's notion of a "sacred rhetoric" aimed at a numinous encounter beyond language. See Stanley Fish, *Self-Consuming Artifacts: The Experience of 17th Century Literature* (Berkeley: Univ. of California Press, 1972), pp.1–4; 21–42; 72–77. See also J. A. Mazzeo, "St. Augustine's Rhetoric of Silence," *Renaissance and Seventeenth-Century Studies* (New York: Columbia Univ. Press, 1964), pp. 1–28.

5. Frederick Ferré, "Mapping the Logic of Models in Science and Theology," in *New Essays on Religious Language,* ed. Dallas High (New York: Oxford Univ. Press, 1969), p. 75. See also Ferré, *Language, Logic and God* (New York: Harper, 1961), ch. 12; and Ferré and K. Berdall, *Exploring the Logic of Faith* (New York: Association Press, 1962), chs. 2, 4.

6. The following three-part "grammar" is my own summary and systematizing of various categories of religious language described by other contemporary theologians; I am particularly indebted to Ferré's adaptation of Ernest Nagel's description of scientific language "models" to the language of religion. The terms and descriptions are my own. (See Ernest Nagel, *The Structure of Science: Problems in the Logic of Scientific Explanation* [New York: Harcourt, Brace, 1961], ch. 5; Ferré, note 6.) The preliminary construction of a "grammar" of language about the ineffable derives its historic antecedents from Aristotle's hylomorphic metaphysical system which uses a formal-conceptual model of reality rooted in the grammatical relationship between subject and predicate, and the Thomist embellishment of this tradition in Aquinas' formulation of the analogical or "proportional" language about God.

7. For a good discussion from a theological standpoint of this kind of language, see I. A. Ramsey, "Paradox in Religion," *New Essays in Religious Language,* p. 147ff.

8. A. C. Charity, *Events and Their Afterlife: The Dialectics of Christian Typology in the Bible and Dante* (Cambridge: Cambridge Univ. Press, 1960), pp. 1–9; 13–20.

9. See C. B. Daly's discussion of the problem of verification as it arises out of Aquinas' notion of the "adequacy" versus the "correspondences" of truth—"Metaphysics and the Limits of Language," *New Essays in Religious Language,* p. 122.

10. Augustine, *De Vera Religione,* L, 98, in *Augustine: Earlier Writings,* ed. J. H. S. Burleigh (Philadelphia: Westminster Press, 1953, [The Library of Christian Classics]), p. 275.

11. The process on a psychological level can best be described as "cognitive overload"—verbal repetition or a sequence of reductive assertions leading to negation

which makes the mind "blank out," i.e., cease to derive logical meaning from known terms. The union that one achieves with the deity by this method, however, is temporary—rationality ultimately reasserts itself. In a poet like Vaughan, temporary union with the deity was difficult and unsatisfying, and he sought a volitional response, or an ethical and historical imperative in the "antitype" of the self, as we shall see. It is my further contention that the figure of Jacob becomes for him the basis of a personal mythology of exile, isolation and dreaming (see especially "Jacob's Pillow, and Pillar").

12. Martin Luther, *Works*, ed. Jaroslav Pelikan (Philadelphia: Fortress Press, 1960), XXXVII, p. 109. (Luther's earlier works on the sacraments 1524-1527.) John Calvin, *Institutes of the Christian Religion*, tr. Ford Lewis Baltes, ed. John T. Mc Neill (Philadelphia: Westminster Press, 1960), II, x, 20; II, xi, 3-6.

13. William Haller, *Liberty and Reformation in the Puritan Revolution* (New York: Columbia Univ. Press, 1963), p. 26.

14. William Tyndale, "Prologue to the Book of Leviticus," *The Work of William Tyndale*, ed. G. E. Duffield (Appleford: Sutton Courtenay Press, 1964), I, p. 60.

15. Davis, "The Traditions of Puritan Typology," p. 28.

16. The quotation is taken from the American Puritan poet Edward Taylor, "Preparatory Meditations."

17. This important and often misunderstood point is convincingly argued in Robert Daly's recent book on Puritan poetics, *God's Altar: The World and the Flesh in Puritan Poetry* (Berkeley: Univ. of California Press, 1978), pp. 44-71.

18. Richard Baxter, *The Saints Everlasting Rest*, Part IV (London, 1650).

19. In the Nominative form of religious discourse, the logical problem of verification has at least the possibility of psychological success, as the negative way, with its temporary duration, does not. The verification of the subjective perception of God lies in the poet's or *dévot*'s volitional response to discovered signs. Vaughan weaves the historical types into a personal mythology which has the force of an ethical imperative for "regeneration"; an entire study can be done, for example, on how Vaughan uses the figure of Jacob in this manner.

20. Calvin, *Institutes*, II, xi, 7.

21. Henry Vaughan, "The Holy Scriptures," *The Complete Poetry of Henry Vaughan*, ed. French Fogle (New York: New York Univ. Press, 1965). All subsequent references to Vaughan's works are from this edition.

22. For a contrasting view of Vaughan's "oppositional structure" deriving from the Reformation's transformation of Augustinianism and the subsequent emphasis on a theology of grace, conversion, and regeneration, see William Halewood, *The Poetry of Grace* (New Haven: Yale Univ. Press, 1970), pp. 33-70; pp. 125-137 (on Vaughan and Marvell).

23. For a discussion of Vaughan's use of hermetic images in this poem, see A. W. Rudrum, "Vaughan's 'The Night': Some Hermetic Notes," *MLR*, 64 (1969), 11-19. The best recent article on "The Night" is by Jonathan Post, who treats the poem as an elaboration of Vaughan's understanding of the Book of Revelation: "Vaughan's 'The Night' and his 'late and dusky age'," *SEL*, 19 (1979), 127-141.

24. For the notion that Vaughan is a mystic, see R. A. Durr, *On the Mystical Poetry of Henry Vaughan* (Cambridge: Harvard Univ. Press, 1962), pp. 112-122; for a suggestion of a debt to St. John of the Cross, see R. Sencourt, *Carmelite and Poet* (New York: Macmillan, 1944). Such views are countered by Frank Kermode's argument that Vaughan's images are less the product of doctrine or devotion than "a highly personal (and poetic) synthesis of his own making, in "The Private Imagery of Henry Vaughan," *RES*, 7 (1950), 206-225.

25. James Ussher, "On the Incarnation," *Introduction to Puritan Theology,* ed. Edward Hindson (Grand Rapids: Baker Book House, 1976), pp. 126–127.

26. Frederick Ferré, "Mapping the Logic of Models," *New Essays on Religious Language,* p. 77. See pp. 75–86 for his discussion of "metaphysical models" in religious discourse.

"Something" in Wordsworth

William Shullenberger

To pose the question of "ineffability" in Wordsworth's writing is to place that writing under a certain hermeneutic pressure, for "the Ineffable" seems the sort of term which Wordsworth would have gone out of his way to avoid. The lofty abstract precision of "the Ineffable" compacts the entire classical-Christian ontological structure in its syllables: a Being whose presence can only be suggested by the negation of human speech, who is nevertheless the foundation for everything which can be spoken and spoken about. The Wordsworth who matters most to us was engaged in the Romantic project of translating the triadic structure of Christian metaphysics, which bound God, Man and Nature together, into the dyadic secular framework announced in the Prospectus to *The Excursion*:

> my voice proclaims
> How exquisitely the individual Mind
> And the progressive powers perhaps no less
> (Of the whole species) to the external World
> Is fitted:—and how exquisitely, too—
> Theme but little heard of among men—
> The external World is fitted to the Mind;
> And the creation (by no lower name
> Can it be called) which they with blended might
> Accomplish.[1]

Musing on "ineffability" in Wordsworth, then, involves a correspondent and continuous project of translation. Wordsworth's idea of "ineffability" pertains not to the Christian soul's self-quieting communion with God but to the phenomenology of the Wordsworthian creation, imagination's commerce with "the external World."

"A sense sublime/ Of something far more deeply interfused,/ Whose dwelling is the light of setting suns" ("Tintern Abbey," ll. 96–7) might stand for Wordsworth's experiential equivalent of "the Ineffable"; that is, both Wordsworth's phrase and the classical term intimate the same problem faced by language. If we briefly compare the two as responses to that problem, we can make a rough measure of Wordsworth's resistance to the classic ontology and of his commitment to "words/ Which speak of nothing more than what we are"

(Prospectus to *The Excursion,* ll. 58–9). "Ineffable" is a strictly Latinate term which is derived by placing the negative prefix *in-* before the adjective *effabilis,* itself a compound of *ex* (out) and *fari* (to speak).[2] The antithetical structure of the word neatly embeds the classical dialectic between this world, which can be spoken, and transcendent Being, which cannot. Wordsworth's phrasing translates this structure of definite opposition into a vernacular grammar of the indefinite, which tends to dissolve oppositions into continuities, and to broach the problem of what cannot be uttered yet must be attested to by generating a language of potentially infinite metonymic extension. This is not to say that Wordsworth renounces the etymological density and tension of Latinate terms, but that he places those terms, like "sublime" and "interfused," in a word string which approaches its subject by accretion, by stretching beyond itself, rather than by concentration and internalized antithesis.[3]

Wordsworth's whole phrase, then, articulates that which is marked by the classical term "the Ineffable," and in Wordsworth's phrase no single term carries thematic force equivalent to the classical term. "Something," however, may be provisionally isolated because of its syntactic importance as the term upon which the subsequent clauses and appositions depend:

> A sense sublime
> Of something far more deeply interfused,
> Whose dwelling is the light of setting suns,
> And the round ocean, and the living air,
> And the blue sky, and in the mind of man:
> A motion and a spirit, that impels
> All thinking things, all objects of all thought,
> And rolls through all things.
> (ll. 95–102)

The etymological origination of "something" is as indefinite as its referential function:[4] a word apparently without origin, it serves as a syntactic place-holder upon which Wordsworth's language turns in its desire to account for the origins of "all thinking things, all objects of all thought. . . ." The strategically indefinite "something"—"O joy! that in our embers/ Is something that doth live"— ("Intimations Ode," ll. 130–131)—generates Wordsworth's particular rhetorical sublimity, as it is the occasion for the extended predication, the syntactic pauses and appositive returns which characterize the "turnings intricate" (*The Prelude* Bk. V, l. 63) of Wordsworth's verse in its most elevated mood.[5]

Although Wordsworth refers this "something" to an experience of "A presence that disturbs me with the joy/ Of elevated thoughts" ("Tintern Abbey," ll. 94–95), the metonymic circuit of his meditation calls attention less to an epiphanic moment than to what language attempts to make of it. The referential vacancy of "something" indicates the impossibility of retrieving "presence" in language, and provokes Wordsworth's own deeply breathed phrases of predication and apposition as the inaugural gestures of an interpretative desire sustained by each of his readers. Evading any definitive account, "something" is a linguistic cipher which makes meaning come into being even as it remains conceptually indeterminate; it stands for an impenetrable space or irrecoverable moment which interpretation desires to claim, to infiltrate, to flood with meaning. To analyze or attempt to describe the structure of what is covered by "something" in Wordsworth's discourse is not to approach the truth of it more closely, but to extend Wordsworth's initial meditation, to supplement his desire to explain. Even to designate in spatial or temporal terms that which cannot be located in space or time is to recur to metaphor in order to be able to speak of it at all, and every metaphor carries the temptation to valorize the signifier, the known term, in the place of that which it cannot quite signify. "Juncture," "site," "spacing," "interval," "trace," are all terms provided by contemporary critical discourse which might be substituted for that "something" mentioned by Wordsworth, and all are latent metaphors, all must account for the problem which Kenneth Burke notes in the traditional rhetoric of religion: the necessity of speaking in borrowed language.[6] Thus even Derrida's rigorous effort to collapse the transcendental structure of "presence" into the secular play of "différance" risks being read as a version of negative theology.[7] I risk the use of such language in approaching Wordsworth, however, because it tends to speak not of essences or identities, but of differential states, and of the function of a "betweenness" which, nothing in itself, constitutes language as a system of differences[8] and consciousness as a quest of language for its own origination.

Wordsworth's designation for his epiphanic moments is "Spots of time," "those passages of life that give/ Profoundest knowledge to what point, and how,/ The mind is lord and master—outward sense/ The obedient servant of her will" (The Prelude Bk. XII, ll. 220-223). By implicating space and time in one another, Wordsworth acknowledges the limits of these provisional metaphors, and opposes, even as he exposes, the primary difference by which our life on earth is composed. A "spot of time" is neither a moment nor a space, yet both at once, yet more than this, an occasion of rupture, a disclosure of difference: mind knows at once its difference from outward sense, imagination discovers its unearthly power over earthly phenomena. Further than this, the mind learns its own difference from itself, for the recognition of a "spot of time" is retrospective, and the mind constitutes itself as a memory of its own glorious emergence. "Such moments," Wordsworth says, "Are scattered everywhere, taking their date/ From our first childhood" (The Prelude Bk. XII, ll. 223-225). It might be said that any moment, closely considered, is the occasion of the "ineffable" for Wordsworth, for the "passage" out of which language emerges latently structures all phenomenal experience, from beholding daffodils to traversing the Vale of Gondo, and composes Wordsworthian consciousness as consciousness engaged in a retrospective quest for its own origination in loss.

"It was Wordsworth," Thomas Weiskel put it, "who first attempted to assimilate the perception of everyday reality to the affective structure of the sublime in his great program of defamiliarization."[9] The kind of imaginative rupture which accounts for the sublime experience is a potential element of the homeliest of Wordsworth's moments of recognition, generating the "defects" of writing for which Coleridge was the first to take Wordsworth to task: "occasional prolixity, repetition, and an eddying, instead of progression, of thought . . . ; thoughts and images too great for the subject . . . what might be called mental bombast, as distinguished from verbal; for, as in the latter there is a disproportion of the expressions to the thoughts, so in this there is a disproportion of thought to the circumstance and occasion."[10] Prolixity and bombast are exaggerated versions of a language dislodged from its own moment of origin, yet compelled to encircle, to eddy about that moment, as if its very linguistic inviolability challenged the poet to his greatest efforts in hortatory and deliberative rhetoric.

Against Coleridge's critique we might pose David Perkins's recognition that "Wordsworth's outpourings of direct, extremely powerful emotion come in passages of argument and summary—not, in other words, when he presents experience, but when he interprets it."[11] The problem with the sublime experience, for Wordsworth, is that it depends for its renovating virtue upon a language which, as the agent of designation and of memory, Wordsworth deems sadly incompetent. The experience of sublimity is immediately, necessarily displaced by interpretative reaction, which claims the imaginative energy released in the sublime moment for the language which, desiring to recover the sublime, can only defer it, can only speak of "something that is gone" ("Intimations Ode," 1. 53), or of "something evermore about to be" (*The Prelude* Bk. VI, 1. 608). Wordsworth's writing refers to the sublime as a necessary fiction, a theoretical or potential moment experienced retrospectively or in prospect, insofar as the language which determines perception can represent it. For language itself can never make the sublime "present" but only represent it as a displaced presence, an absence felt only at the moment of its own disappearance. The sublime for Wordsworth is a rupture in signification which language rushes in to seal, yet language internalizes the rupture, so that Wordsworth's poetry everywhere stresses the limits of its own expressibility.

As a kind of defense against the phenomenological insecurity occasioned by such rupture, Wordsworth interprets the site of rupture as the scene of imaginative transgression of ordinary perception, which momentarily opens the prospect of transcendence:

> Imagination—here the Power so called
> Through sad incompetence of human speech,
> That awful Power rose from the mind's abyss
> Like an unfathered vapour that enwraps,

At once, some lonely traveller. I was lost;
Halted without an effort to break through;
But to my conscious soul I now can say—
"I recognize thy glory:" in such strength
Of usurpation, when the light of sense
Goes out, but with a flash that has revealed
The invisible world, does greatness make abode,
There harbours; whether we be young or old,
Our destiny, our being's heart and home,
Is with infinitude, and only there;
With hope it is, hope that can never die,
Effort, and expectation, and desire,
And something evermore about to be
                    (*The Prelude* Bk. VI, ll. 592–608).

Such is Wordsworth's retrospective assessment of his disappointment at having crossed the Alps without being aware of the passage. Correlative to the intimation of transcendence is the mind's apocalyptic presence unto itself, which blacks out "the light of sense." Yet the myths of transcendence and of the mind's self-presence occur to Wordsworth not on the spot of the "original" experience but as the experience is recollected in composition.[12] Thus Wordsworth's assertion of poetic theme—intimations of transcendence and of the mind's self-presence[13]—seems to be subverted by the tendency of his writing, which gives evidence of the mind as a recollected structure.

The tension between the theme and the tendency of his writing is implicit in Wordsworth's critical theory as well. Stephen K. Land has noted the "semantic dualism" underwriting Wordsworth's critical premises and his lyrical strategies;[14] Wordsworth, as Land explicates him, affirms the priority of mental and emotional experience over the linguistic expression of it, which must always be a diminished version of its riches. Such dualism is implicit in even the apparent organicism of this passage from the third essay "Upon Epitaphs":

> Words are too awful an instrument for good and evil to be trifled with; they hold above all other external powers a dominion over thoughts. If words be not (recurring to a metaphor before used) an incarnation of the thought, but only a clothing for it, then surely will they prove an ill gift; such a one as those possessed vestments, read of in the stories of superstitious times, which had power to consume and to alienate from his right mind the victim who put them on.[15]

Incarnation, Land notes, is a more subtle formation of a dualistic structure than the eighteenth century model of language as a dress for thought. Yet the passage displays Wordsworth's uneasiness over the power of language to erode that dualism, to infiltrate and to "consume" the inner life of thought which Wordsworth wishes to keep sacrosanct, a region of pure conscious intensity. If writing comes to be, for Wordsworth, the making conscious of consciousness itself, consciousness depends upon the "external power" of language for the evidence of its own survival and continuity. Yet as an "external power," language always carries the mark of its alienation from the idea of the mind's self-presence. Thus the consciousness which chooses to disclose itself in writing must always represent itself as divided, alienated from the "right mind" which is ineffable, because it is necessary fiction, a way of composing—by proposing an origin for—the linguistic drift which a poetry bereft of a central self threatens to become.

Perhaps to compensate for the knowledge of exile in which he constitutes himself as a writer, Wordsworth lodges the idea of the "right mind" in a species of figures whose pure consciousness is not infected by language. Land calls our attention to the presence in the *Lyrical Ballads* of "a sequence of rustics, children, and idiots whose cryptic or rambling utterances, often either nonsensical or banal on the surface, are not supposed to *be* poetry but to indicate its inner presence rather as the living body indicates the presence of a soul."[16] Just before he approaches the visionary passage of Snowdon, Wordsworth praises "men for contemplation framed,/ Shy, and unpractised in the strife of phrase":

> Theirs is the language of the heavens, the power,
> The thought, the image, and the silent joy:
> Words are but under-agents in their souls;
> When they are grasping with their greatest strength,
> They do not breathe among them . . .
>   (*The Prelude* Bk. XIII, ll. 271–275).

The paradigm of humanity in its right mind, their integrated contemplation standing for the possibility of the mind's pure self-presence, such figures may be Wordsworth's equivalent to the "impossible possible philosopher's man" imagined by Wallace Stevens:

> The man who has had time to think enough,
> The central man, the human globe, responsive
> As a mirror with a voice, the man of glass,
> Who in a million diamonds sums us up.[17]

Stevens's man is "the transparence of the place in which/ He is and in his poems we find peace." Wordsworth's unlettered bards are similar transparencies, and if their poems could be read, they would make beatitude possible, for "the language of the heavens" would compose a text of pure presence, the impossible possibility toward which Wordsworth's writing yearns.

Escaping the alienation by which the poet's consciousness discovers itself in language, such ideal figures can have no history. The growth of a poet's mind is a growth in exile, a sequence of accessions to consciousness experienced as "anxious visitation" wherein the mind discovers not its transparence to the place in which it is, but its difference: "moon and stars/ Were shining o'er my head. I was alone,/ And seemed to be a trouble to the peace/ That dwelt among them" (*The Prelude* Bk. I, ll. 314–317). In recollecting itself through language, consciousness inscribes as its enduring condition—and as the precondition for the possibility of its growth—the sense of having been cast out from a transcendental quietude. That quietude is proposed not so much as a memory, but as an intimation, for it stands for a condition which precedes the emergence of consciousness itself. The ideal figures of silent rustics personify this condition; never having come into being through the incarnation of thought which is language, it is as if they were never born and can never really die; they represent what the poet would be if he were not bound to language. Words-worth counters these fictive figures who resist the tendency of writing with figures of the dead, upon whom the momentum of his narrative of conscious-ness depends. The moment in which these figures cease to be corresponds to the moment in which the poet discovers himself to be conscious. In this regard, Wordsworth's poetry is a series of epitaphs for imagined others, vestiges of silent selves, in burying whom the poet acknowledges the occasion of his own emergence into language. In dwelling on two of these selves, the Boy of Winander and Lucy, both of whom Wordsworth imagined during his residence in Goslar,[18] I wish to close this excursion toward what Wordsworth called "the hiding-places of man's power" (*The Prelude* Bk. XII, 1. 279).

That the Winander Boy represents an earlier self of Wordsworth, a partic-ular event in the history of his consciousness, is evident from his rewriting the passage from the first to the third person, as if by so doing he could mark the irrecoverable otherness of his own earlier experience.[19] Yet even in the at-tempted recollection of the boy's perception, there is the sense of absence, distance, delay, the suggestion that consciousness emerges as after-effect and can only speak of "immediate" experience as a lost possibility:

> And, when there came a pause
> Of silence such as baffled his best skill:
> Then sometimes, in that silence, while he hung
> Listening, a gentle shock of mild surprise
> Has carried far into his heart the voice
> Of mountain-torrents; or the visible scene
> Would enter unawares into his mind
> With all its solemn imagery, its rocks,
> Its woods, and that uncertain heaven received
> Into the bosom of the steady lake
> (*The Prelude* Bk. V, ll. 379–388).

The sudden silence of the owls, themselves provoked by the boy's "mimic hootings," creates an auditory vacuum so powerful that it assumes the boy's immediate and passive attention altogether. In that moment of his occupation with a perceptual emptiness, the world registers impressions which emerge only retrospectively, with "a gentle shock of mild surprise." Wordsworth wrote of the poem, which begins the Poems of The Imagination, that it represents one of the earliest processes of Nature in the development of this faculty. Guided by one of my own primary consciousnesses, I have represented a commutation and transfer of internal feelings, co-operating with external accidents, to plant, for immortality, images of sound and sight, in the celestial soil of the Imagination.[20]

We might say as well that the process represented here is a paradigm of writing, for the world inscribes its imagery in the boy, so that his most intense perceptions are already written as memories. The process of "commutation and transfer of internal feelings, co-operating with external accidents," is a fluctuating movement of disappointment, differentiation, displacement, and substitution performed upon the boy's original desire, which is for a mimetic capability so perfect as to be Orphic: to wake the owls into a sustained responsive harmony would be to achieve confirmation of his full presence among natural presences, a being so at one with the world that he would not need the mediation of language. Between what the boy wishes for and what he receives we can mark the passage of writing, the compensatory imagery of the world profferred at the moment of the boy's discovery of his difference from the world.

Derrida's description of the model of psychic writing developed by Freud applies as well to Wordsworth:

> Writing supplements perception before perception even appears to itself [is conscious of itself]. "Memory" or writing is the opening of that process of appearance itself. The "perceived" may be read only in the past, beneath perception and after it.[21]

In the Winander Boy passage, presence and appearance become interfused in the "solemn imagery" of which the written verse is itself an image; uncertain heaven received into the bosom of the steady lake, perceived by the boy, recollected by the poet, and presented to the reader's attention suggests a potentially endless sequence of representations, out of which it is impossible to explicate an origin, for the apparent origin is itself a reflection of an "uncertain heaven," the traditional origin of origins. As images become irrecoverably implicated in one another, so the feelings bound to images become likewise, through the process of "commutation and transfer," confused with other feelings. What Wordsworth offers as hypothetical in "Nutting"—"unless I now/ Confound my present feelings with the past" (ll. 48–9)—is the inevitable condition out of which he writes: writing originates and gathers its momentum from the pressure of memories welling up simultaneously in the gap where consciousness admits its difference from "immediate perception." Frances Ferguson writes of Wordsworth that

Perception is binding, in that one cannot simultaneously hold two different perceptions of what one takes to be the "same thing" and any new perception thus becomes not merely another perception but a "new existence" for both the mind and the objects of perception.[22]

All of Wordsworth's poetry opposes this statement: one cannot but hold several perceptions of the "same thing" simultaneously, for what is perceived is already lost, and the perception of it already bound to other retrospective "perceptions" planted in what Wordsworth calls "the celestial soil of the Imagination," or inscribed upon the depthless wax of the unconscious in Freud's image of the mind as a "mystic writing-pad."[23] Consciousness composes itself in retrospect, emerging from the multiple losses which constitute perception, fashioning itself in a language which can only speak of what is gone. The reported death of the Winander Boy is a death into nature, a making of the Boy a transparence of the place of his recognition, at the moment of his recognition of his difference. The knowledge which the poet gains, in burying the Boy, and in returning to his grave, is not purchased by the loss of power (*The Prelude* Bk. V, 1. 425), but by the loss of the possibility of immediate perception, of pure presence.

Like the Winander Boy passage, the poems clustered about the name "Lucy" dramatize the moment in which the child becomes a transparency of place, dying into the life of nature, as the moment in which the poet's conscious-ness emerges as a retrospective gazing into the face of loss. Hartman has written, "In the Lucy cycle, death and the humanizing consciousness of death are almost simultaneous: Wordsworth does not dramatize the interval."[24] And yet it is the interval toward which all the poems turn, enacting the repetition-compulsion of a language seeking out the traumatic moment of its own origina-tion. If Lucy lived as "A Maid whom there were none to praise/ And very few to love" ("She Dwelt Among the Untrodden Ways"), her death spurs the poet from imaginative slumber into a lyric capability to praise, but that lyric capabili-ty's cost is Lucy's identity, her status as a determinate poetic object.[25] The poet laments that "she is in her grave, and, oh,/ The difference to me!" The difference, what Hartman calls the "interval," is the sublime rupture from which poetry springs, and the name "Lucy" refers to that difference in the same provocative way that the indeterminate "something" does in "Tintern Abbey."

The poems elaborate the impossibility of locating Lucy in terms of any temporal or spatial reference, until the very failure of reference comes to mark her imaginative status as lost origin, the very principle of lostness which gener-ates the poetry of Wordsworth. Lucy is as identitiless as rock or stone or tree, and the blank she represents as a proper name without identity is a kind of linguistic vacuum which cannot be read without provoking the interpretative desire to fill it, to make of the name a recognizable, if deceased, presence, to recuperate it from its disquieting ghostliness.[26] Wordsworth's own quest in the cluster moves away from the search for an identity, an assurance of Lucy's presence, toward an accommodation with what remains behind. The poems indicate a partial quieting of the restless circuit of desire in a constellation of substitute images, tangible figures which still carry traces of Lucy, by which the world responds to the poet's desire for what is irrecoverable.

The shift from quest to accommodation, curiously enough, begins when the poet still knows Lucy to be alive. The journey of the poet toward Lucy in "Strange Fits of Passion" is gradually slowed, and the poet's attention deferred from his apparent goal to the various landmarks of his journey: the moon, the lea, "those paths so dear to me," the orchardplot, the hill, the cottage. The diffusion of the poet's love for Lucy into the various elements of landscape with which he associates her represents a tacit desire for a steady-state of passion. Unlike the love bound to a lyric object whose rose-like freshness must fade, such a state would be sustained by the metonymic chain, by which all elements in the constellation of desire are bound each to each. The disappearance of a single element—even if it were the primary one, Lucy—would guarantee the survival of affection by crystalizing and intensifying the bonds of those elements which remain. The premonition of Lucy's death to which the poet gives utter-ance in the closing lines has been performing its secret ministry throughout the poem, not only in the metonymic "commutation and transfer of internal feelings" from Lucy to the untrodden ways among which she dwells, but in the poet's desire to prolong his own narrative progress into an endless approach which is never to be culminated in presence. The effect intended by this slowing to virtual stasis is to project Lucy herself outside time in the same way that Keats preserves the beloved on the Grecian Urn: "She cannot fade, though thou hast not thy bliss,/ Forever wilt thou love, and she be fair!"[27] The irony of Words-worth's lyric, and indeed of the whole cluster of Lucy poems, is that the landscape is endeared by the emptying of Lucy's human identity, so that the very idea of Lucy's death which the poet wishes to resist is being accomplished by his own meditative process, the process of linguistic displacement we have been attending to. Thus the commanding voice of Nature in "Three Years She Grew in Sun and Shower" seems an aggrandized projection of the metonymic absorption of Lucy into landscape which the poet has been implicitly working.

Wordsworth sustains the hope that the consciousness which emerges from loss will discover the compensatory blessing of a nature humanized by that loss.[28] Yet the equation in the Lucy cluster remains unbalanced. Lucy's being made a transparence of the place in which she was does not hollow out an internal dimension to landscape, nor render a landscape whose reciprocating presence can be felt by the poet.[29] To be left with heath, calm, and quiet scene, or in the more unyielding imagery of "A Slumber Did My Spirit Seal," among "rocks, and stones, and trees," is to discover one's dwelling-place among exter-nal powers, forever to be excluded from the inner life of things. The language which Wordsworth claims to hold "above all other external powers a dominion over thoughts" sustains this alienation, for the consciousness which writes itself into being does so by positing its own inner life as an inexplicable hypothesis. "Strange Fits of Passion," apparently the most private of the Lucy cluster, represents the prospect of an "inner state" as unaccountable as the identity of Lucy; it suggests language's inability to name its own source. Depending upon interpretative sympathy to account for the startling final ejaculation, the poem leaves its reader at the threshold of an interiority which offers no easier access to consciousness than the silent landscape of "A Slumber Did My Spirit Seal." Whether the consciousness turns inward to account for its origination, or outward to research its destiny, it contemplates an unanswering silence. That human language issues from the "blank abyss" (*The Prelude* Bk. VI, 1. 470) to speak of something, to return to the abyss with its proposals and its questions, is the difference which Lucy makes, whether she stands for a remembered possibility or the possibility of memory. The ghost of Wordsworth's "egotistical sublime,"[30] Lucy reminds the poet and his readers of the creative insufficiency of the language in which they imagine their existence.

NOTES

1. The Romantic project of translating Christian metaphysics and imagery into the dialectic between mind and nature is the central theme of M. H. Abrams's *Natural Supernaturalism: Tradition and Revolution in Romantic Literature* (New York: W. W. Norton and Co., Inc., 1971). Abrams treats the Prospectus to *The Excursion* as a definitive statement of that project. The text to which I shall refer for quotations from Wordsworth's poetry is *Wordsworth: Poetical Works*, ed. Thomas Hutchinson; rev. ed., Ernest de Selincourt (London: Oxford University Press, 1969; repr. 1975). References will be indicated parenthetically in the text of the essay by poem title and line numbers.
2. This etymological construction is provided in the *Compact Edition of the Oxford English Dictionary* (1971).
3. Josephine Miles describes Wordsworth's poetry in terms of its continuities, grada-tions and associations, counter to the eighteenth-century articulation of balance and antithesis. *Wordsworth and the Vocabulary of Emotion* (Berkeley: Univ. of California Press, 1942).
4. The *OED* indicates a vague Teutonic origin for the words "some" and "thing."
5. David Perkins identifies the features of "suspension, subordination, and apposi-tion" in an acute stylistic examination of an earlier passage in "Tintern Abbey" (ll. 22–49). *Wordsworth and the Poetry of Sincerity* (Cambridge, Mass.: Harvard Univ. Press, 1964), pp. 204–210.
6. Kenneth Burke, *The Rhetoric of Religion: Studies in Logology* (Berkeley and Los Angeles: Univ. of California Press, 1970), p. 15.
7. The extent to which Derrida resists being read theologically is an indication of the temptation to do so. He addresses the problem directly in the essay *"Différance,"* in *Speech and Phenomena*, trans. David B. Allison (Evanston: Northwest-ern Univ. Press, 1973), p. 134.

8. That language is a system of differences is one of the central premises of Saussurean linguistics. Ferdinand de Saussure, *Course in General Linguistics,* ed. Charles Bally and Albert Sechahaye in collaboration with Albert Reidlinger, trans. Wade Baskin (New York: Philosophical Library, 1959).

9. Thomas Weiskel, *The Romantic Sublime: Studies in the Structure and Psychology of Transcendence* (Baltimore: The Johns Hopkins Univ. Press, 1976), pp. 18–19. I am indebted to Weiskel for his description of the sublime as a moment of semiotic rupture which sets the mind on its interpretative labors. It would be impossible to condense Weiskel's subtle and provocative appreciation of Wordsworth, yet this essay is in one respect an effort to approach that appreciation.

10. Samuel Taylor Coleridge, *Selected Poetry and Prose,* ed. Elisabeth Schneider (New York: Holt, Rinehart and Winston, Inc., 1951), p. 351.

11. Perkins, p. 217.

12. Wordsworth's often cited remark in the Preface of the Second Edition of the *Lyrical Ballads* is relevant here:

> I have said that poetry is the spontaneous overflow of powerful feelings: it takes its origin from emotion recollected in tranquillity: the emotion is contemplated till, by a species of reaction, the tranquillity gradually disappears, and an emotion, kindred to that which was before the subject of contemplation, is gradually produced, and does itself actually exist in the mind (*Poetical Works,* p. 740).

The supplementary emotion intended to reproduce the "original" emotion gradually displaces it, until the mind comes to dwell not in the "original" moment but in the supplementary moment of composition, that is, in the interpretative longing for the origin.

13. The identity of transcendence with the mind's presence to itself is explored by Albert Wlecke, *Wordsworth and the Sublime* (Berkeley and Los Angeles: Univ. of California Press, 1973). Wlecke's description of the structure of "sublime self-consciousness" follows Wordsworth's desire to valorize the self in resistance to the tendency of the writing, which calls the self into question.

14. Stephen K. Land, "The Silent Poet: An Aspect of Wordsworth's Semantic Theory," *University of Toronto Quarterly,* 52 (Winter 1973), 157–169.

15. *The Prose Works of William Wordsworth,* ed. W. J. B. Owen and Jane Worthington Smyser (Oxford: The Clarendon Press, 1974), v. 2, pp. 84–85.

16. Land, 166.

17. "Asides on the Oboe," in *The Collected Poems of Wallace Stevens* (New York: Alfred A. Knopf, Inc., 1969), pp. 250–251.

18. Richard E. Matlak, "Wordsworth's Lucy Poems in Psychobiographical Context," *PMLA,* 93 (January 1978), 46.

19. "In the first extant version of ll. 389–413 ["There was a Boy . . . the steady Lake"] the first personal pronoun is used throughout in place of the third, indicating that W. W. was himself the boy who 'blew mimic hootings to the silent owls'." *Wordsworth: The Prelude or Growth of a Poet's Mind* (Text of 1805), ed. Ernest de Selincourt; new ed., corrected by Stephen Gill (London: Oxford Univ. Press, 1970), p. 267.

20. *Prose Works,* v. 3, p. 35.

21. Jacques Derrida, "Freud and the Scene of Writing," *Writing and Difference,* trans. Alan Bass (Chicago: Univ. of Chicago Press, 1978), p. 224.

22. Frances Ferguson, *Wordsworth: Language as Counter-Spirit* (New Haven and London: Yale Univ. Press, 1977), p. 247.

23. Quoted and elaborated by Derrida, pp. 223–231.

24. Geoffrey H. Hartman, *Wordsworth's Poetry 1787–1814* (New Haven and London: Yale Univ. Press, 1971), p. 161.

25. See "The Lucy Poems: Wordsworth's Quest for a Poetic Object" in Ferguson, pp. 173–194, for a subtle examination of the way in which the poems seem to write Lucy out of existence.

26. Although Geoffrey Durrant suggested in 1969 that the question "Who was Lucy?" is irrelevant (*William Wordsworth* [London: Cambridge Univ. Press, 1969], p. 60), the desire to supply her an identity is unlikely to be quenched. For a fresh approach to Lucy's association with Dorothy Wordsworth, see the article by Richard E. Matlak referred to above (n. 18).

27. John Keats, *Selected Poems and Letters,* ed. Douglas Bush (Boston: Houghton Mifflin Co., The Riverside Press), p. 208.

28. In writing of Emerson, Harold Bloom mentions "what is most vital in Romantic tradition, the double program of the naturalization of the human heart and the humanization of the natural world." *The Ringers in the Tower: Studies in Romantic Tradition* (Chicago: Univ. of Chicago Press, 1971; repr. 1973), p. 225. Bloom could have described Wordsworth's project in particular this way, for it is the major theme of his reading of Wordsworth in *The Visionary Company: A Reading of English Romantic Poetry* (Garden City, N.Y.: Doubleday & Company, Inc.; Anchor Books Edition, 1963), pp. 132–210.

29. "It is through Lucy's death that Wordsworth learns that Nature does betray the heart which loves her." Hartman, p. 161.

30. The phrase, of course, is Keats's, from the letter to Richard Woodhouse dated 27 October 1818, *Selected Poems and Letters,* p. 279.

The Two Languages and the Ineffable in Shelley's Major Poetry

Stuart Peterfreund

Ineffability—the failure of language in its referential capacity to express the numinous or transcendent—is an important concept in Shelley's major poetry. Both Shelley and his commentators have in fact noted the presence and significance of this impasse of language in a number of works. In *Alastor*, for example, the narrator describes the young poet-protagonist's dream of the Indian maiden, remarking in the process that her "wild numbers"—her poetry—told an "ineffable tale."[1] Earl R. Wasserman also describes Shelley's "choral dance of the Hours and Spirits of the Human Mind" in *Prometheus Unbound*, Act IV, as a dance that "corresponds to the 'order,' 'arrangement,' or 'combination' of particulars that, according to Shelley, the poet effects under the compulsion of his extraordinary and ineffable apprehension of absolute unity."[2]

Wasserman's comments contain two insights particularly germane to this subject. First, his emphasis on the " 'order,' 'arrangement,' or 'combination' of particulars" reflected in Shelley's language indicates that even though the referential capacity of his poetry to express its object may break down in the apprehension of the ineffable, the formal component of that language somehow remains intact and assumes the burden of linguistic meaning. Second, the joyfulness of both the ineffable moment and its rendering suggest that the onset of the inexpressible draws the speaker closer to his object rather than distancing him from it; there is none of the plangency and self-deprecation found in other poetry. These two insights have a cause and effect relationship to one another. Because Shelley believes in two modes of language, one of which "means" referentially, the other formally[3]—and because the formal mode of language precedes and gives rise to the referential mode[4]—the ability of language to body forth meaningful utterance is not extinguished in the face of the ineffable. Accordingly, joy rises up in response to the inexpressible because it is in precisely such a moment that the priority of the formal mode over the referential is established, with the result that the speaker and the hearer alike are granted an apprehension (although not a vision) of the informing principle of the universe. Shelley at first calls this principle "Necessity," but later comes to recognize it as "Eternal Love"[5]; like the "determinate ideas" of Plato's

Parmenides, it places the Logos within the created universe, rather than prior to, or outside, it.[6]

Shelley's unique sense of joy in the ineffable can best be understood by contrasting him with Dante, perhaps the greatest poet of the ineffable. Out of this contrast will emerge a sense of Shelley's concept of the proper mode of poetic speech, as well as a sense of how the aspirant to such language seeks its full attainment. With a grasp of Shelley's complex notion of language it will then be possible to identify moments of ineffability in some of the major poetry and then to comment on their peculiar characteristics.

In the *Paradiso* the poet speaks haltingly, in language which is full of self-negation and deprecation, of the inability of his language to assume its expressive burden. Granted a vision of the "Living Light" of the Trinity, he laments, 'O how inadequate is speech, and how feeble toward my conception! and this toward what I saw is such that it suffices not to call it little.'[7] At the moment of greatest ineffability identified by Wasserman in *Prometheus Unbound*, Act IV, on the other hand, the Chorus of Spirits and Hours sings out in the imperative, apparently confident that its speech will prove adequate to its object:

> Then weave the web of the mystic measure;
> From the depths of the sky and the ends of the earth,
>   Come, swift Spirits of might and of pleasure,
> Fill the dance and the music of mirth,
>   As the waves of a thousand streams rush by
> To an ocean of splendour and harmony!
>
> (129-134)

The different attitudes of these two approaches to the ineffable may be accounted for in part by the diametrically opposed positions of the two poets regarding the inter-relationship of vision, thought, and language. In the *Paradiso* speech is regarded as inadequate to express the speaker's vision primarily because it exists only after the fact of vision, with thought-process interposed as metaphor between the two. Dante's narrator first sees, then perceives (thinks), then speaks. Vision precedes thought, and thought precedes speech, each of the former overwhelming in its turn the latter. In *Prometheus Unbound*, however, speech is adequate to express the chorus's vision because words precede and inform it—there is no prior "seen." Incantatory language, characterized by rhythm, rhyme, alliteration, and other modes of recurrence and equivalence,[8] is spoken by the chorus to create equivalence of another sort, in the form of an object—not of vision, but of thought. Elsewhere in *Prometheus Unbound* Asia underscores the priority of language in her description of the Promethean gift: "He gave man speech, and speech created thought,/ Which is the measure of the universe" (II.iv.72-73). Shelley's speaker first uses language, then thinks, by subjecting speech to the bodily eye, then (and only then) sees by bodying forth what he has thought.

The problem of this kind of notion of the relationship of language, thought, and vision is that it is valid only for the formal mode of language, and not for the referential. The formal mode works to conjure up the "seen"; the referential, on the other hand, takes the "seen" as a given, a point of departure, and takes as its task the analysis and classification of it. The distinction between these two languages is essentially that drawn by Shelley in *A Defence of Poetry* between the formal activity of the imagination and the referential activity of reason: "Reason is the enumeration of quantities already known; imagination is the perception of the value of those quantities, both separately and as a whole. Reason respects the differences, imagination the similitudes of things" (C, p. 277). On the matter of which of these two languages is properly of poetry, as well as of which is prior, Shelley is perfectly clear: "Poetry, in a general sense, may be defined to be 'the expression of the imagination,' and poetry is connate with the origin of man" (C, p. 277).

Human nature being what it is, all but the first human speakers have had the tendency to confuse these two modes of speech, thereby falling prey to the delusion of material priority, the delusion that there is a "real" visible world that preceded the first speaker, when in fact it is the right and responsibility of each speaker to create the world anew, for himself, by means of the three-step process of language, thought, and vision. The delusion of such priority—of an "originary moment," prior to human consciousness, of " 'real presence,' or 'original plenitude' "—is what Derrida characterizes as the "always already,"[9] and what Blake attacks as coercive and reductive in *The Book of Urizen* and *Milton.*

But if material priority is ultimately nothing more than a delusion, as Shelley says repeatedly in *Prometheus Unbound,* and if the formal language of poetry is mimetic from the first, then there arises the question of what it is that poetry either imitates or ought to imitate. The question is by no means trivial, for in Shelley, no less than in Dante, ineffability arises as the result of actual or failed poetic mimesis, at the moment when all delusion or interference are removed from between the poet and the object of imitation. But of course it is exactly that object which differs so radically in Dante and Shelley, as does the experience of inexpressibility arising from the confrontation of the pristine and unmediated.

At the conclusion of the *Divine Comedy,* the speaker has a vision of the source and mystery of the universe, the Trinity, in unmediated radiance. This is, for Dante, the cause, the deep truth of the universe, existing outside and prior to him. The speaker of the *Paradiso* has this vision, conceives its significance, and then attempts to imitate both vision and conception in language which proves unequal to its task. As a result, the speaker's vision of the Trinity gives rise to the experience of ineffability. According to Shelley, however, human speech comes first, not last, because agency, mystery, and deep truth, if they exist at all, are prior to human awareness, in a voiceless, imageless, and inconceivable condition. Furthermore, neither the status nor the "message" of this first cause is accessible to the one who would attempt to "decode" the invisible in terms of the visible. As Shelley's avatar, Demogorgon, says in response to one of Asia's questions about the causality and teleology of the world,

> —If the Abysm
> Could vomit forth its secrets:—but a voice
> Is wanting, the deep truth is imageless;
> For what would it avail to bid thee gaze
> On the revolving world? what to bid speak
> Fate, Time, Occasion, Chance, and Change? To these
> All things are subject but eternal Love.
>
> (II.114–120)

In commenting on this passage, Wasserman observes that "mind, therefore, cannot gain knowledge from external intuitions pretending to ultimate truths, but must derive its knowledge from itself, even though that self-examination reveals, skeptically, the mind's ignorance of what lies outside existence."[10] And yet, to argue against Wasserman in this instance: if the individual is able to intuit the force of Eternal Love—or, rather, to rid himself of delusions so that Love acts upon him in a direct and unmediated manner—would he not have gained access to the "ultimate truth" that Wasserman has deemed unapproachable? In gaining whatever access that he can to such a truth, the individual might be said to have transcended the limits of his own existence, to have "reached" the ineffable by speaking himself into unison with Eternal Love.

Just what Shelley meant by this Love is difficult to say. Demogorgon is perfectly clear about what it is not, in distinguishing it from "Fate, Time, Occasion, Chance, and Change." Fate would seem to imply *telos,* ultimacy, finality. Time might imply the same, but it would seem more obviously to connote an imposed system of measurement, a quantification and reduction of the rhythms of existence to the fixed or arbitrary. Occasion implies singularity, the assignment of value to the discrete, individual, and momentary rather than to the massed, collective, and eternal. Chance suggests momentary inconsistency and unaccountable variation; Change, a variation which also possesses a telic component—a variation, that is, which is positive or negative only in the sense that it moves toward a certain end. Eternal Love, then, is endless, with its own principle of self-begetting, a rhythm which marks, but does not measure, its continued existence.

Whatever the differences between Dante's understanding of the ineffable and that of Shelley, both spring from the recognition of an intense feeling of love for the object of perception. This love arises in response to the object's beauty and a desire on the part of the speaker-subject for self-transcendence and union with the object. The differences between the two poets with regard to this moment have to do with their estimates of the power of love to help them to achieve self-transcendence, as well as with their diverse conceptions of the nature of the beauty which gives rise to desire. In the case of Dante, the object of love has priority over the subject, and is seen by him only in a moment of miraculous and exalted vision. While the moment confirms the reality of the object, it also confirms the subject's inability to do justice to his experience either in conception or in language. Dante's love is of the unattainable; he will never possess Beatrice, much less the Trinity. It is clearly not within the speaker-subject's own power to achieve self-transcendence or to attain unity with the object of his desire.

With Shelley, however, the speaker has priority over the object of beauty; predisposed to love, he begins to achieve self-transcendence through the very act of speaking, and continues to do so until he achieves union with his object—a union which is nothing less than the manifestation of eternal Love. Because thought and sense impressions are elaborated in the process of speech, they too have the power of transcendence. Thus in *A Defence* Shelley states that the moral efficacy of poetry depends on the ability of the imagination, via language, to achieve transcendence in the pursuit of love:

> The great secret of morals is love, or a going out of our own nature and an identification of ourselves with the beautiful which exists in thought, action, or person, not our own. A man, to be greatly good, must imagine intensely and comprehensively; he must put himself in the place of another and of many others; the pains and pleasures of his species must become his own.
>
> (C, pp. 282–283)

The love that Dante experiences rises up in response to an object of beauty that is indescribable because it is unique. There is only one Trinity, as there is, on the level of the creature, only one Beatrice. The love that Shelley experiences, on the other hand, arises in response to a beauty both multiple and recurrent. The speaker of *Epipsychidion* says that

> True Love in this differs from gold and clay,
> That to divide is not to take away.
> Love is like understanding, that grows bright,
> Gazing on many truths; 'tis like the light,
> Imagination! which from earth and sky
> And from the depths of human phantasy,
> As from a thousand prisms and mirrors, fills
> The Universe with glorious beams, and kills
> Error, the worm, with many a sun-like arrow
> Of its reverberated lightning. Narrow
> The heart that loves, the brain that contemplates,
> The life that wears, the spirit that creates
> One object, and one form, and builds thereby
> A sepulchre for its eternity.
>
> (ll. 160–173)

A language of reference, whose task is to denote clearly the discrete object, simply cannot be the "reverberated lightning" of "a thousand prisms and mirrors." It remains, rather, for the language of poetry to express the multiplic- ity and recurrence of reality. In fact, in *A Defence* Shelley says that "the language of poets has ever affected a certain uniform and harmonious recurrence of sound, without which it were not poetry, and which is scarcely less indispensi- ble to the communication of its influence than the words themselves, without reference to that peculiar order" (C, p. 280). Words themselves are "peculiar" in that by naming an object or action they emphasize its singularity. The effect of poetry does not reside in such naming, however, but rather in a "uniform and harmonious recurrence of sound"—that is, in the formal properties of language. Those formal properties precede the establishment of denotation, which is arbitrary and derivative. Language, in the uniform and harmoniously recurrent dispensation found in poetry, "is connate with the origin of man." It is "arbitrarily produced by the imagination and has relation to thoughts alone" (C, pp. 277, 279).

In conclusion, it is possible from even this brief discussion to identify and characterize the ineffable moment in Shelley's poetry. Affectively, it is marked by the presence of love, whether mentioned specifically or simply enacted in context. The presence of such love leads the speaker to strive for self-transcen- dence by means of speech in order to attain the beautiful object. Formally, it is characterized by a heightened verbal patterning which reveals a lowered emphasis on the referential properties of language. What Shelley gives us in these many colored refractions of speech, therefore, is a sense of the white radiance of ineffability—a sense not of loss or failure, but of joy.

NOTES

1. *The Complete Poetical Works of Percy Bysshe Shelley,* ed. Thomas Hutchinson, introd. Benjamin P. Kurtz (New York: Oxford Univ. Press, 1933), l. 168. Subsequent references to Shelley's poetry by line, and by act and scene where appropriate, will appear in the text.

2. *Shelley: A Critical Reading* (Baltimore and London: Johns Hopkins Univ. Press, 1971), p. 369. Less charitable is Carlos Baker, *Shelley's Major Poetry* (Princeton: Princeton Univ. Press, 1948), p. 14, who sees the poetry as being "full of 'ragged breaches'— syntactic disorders, obscurities, images carelessly thrown down or so changeable and various that they are scarcely caught before they are bewilderingly superseded by others."

3. Numerous commentators have recently discussed the concept of "two-languages" in relation to Shelley's poetry. See Norman Thurston, "The Second Language of *Prometheus Unbound,*" *PQ,* 55 (1976), 126–133; Richard Cronin, "Shelley's Language of Dissent," *EiC,* 27 (1977), 203–215; Susan Hawk Brisman, ' 'Unsaying His High

Language': The Problem of Voice in *Prometheus Unbound,*" *SiR,* 16 (1977), 51–86; and V. A. DeLuca, "The Style of Millennial Announcement in *Prometheus Unbound,* " *K-SJ,* 28 (1979), 78–101. A brilliant and useful book, which provides Brisman with a basis for her description of the two languages is Gerald L. Bruns, *Modern Poetry and the Idea of Language: A Critical and Historical Study* (New Haven and London: Yale Univ. Press, 1974). See especially pp. 44–45ff., p. 206.

4. The argument is made in *A Defence of Poetry,* in *Shelley's Prose, or, the Trumpet of a Prophecy,* ed. David Lee Clark (Albuquerque: Univ. of New Mexico Press, 1954), p. 277. Subsequent references to *A Defence* will be to (C, p. xxx), and will appear in the text.

5. These terms and Shelley's recognition that they describe the same phenomenon seen from two different points of view, are discussed by Wasserman in *Shelley: A Critical Reading.* See especially chapter 10, "*Prometheus Unbound:* Power, Necessity, and Love," pp. 306–325.

6. Tr. Benjamin Jowett, in *Plato,* Great Books of the Western World, vol. 7, ed. Robert Maynard Hutchins (Chicago: Encyclopedia Britannica, 1952), pp. 488–489. A good discussion of the "inside-outside" controversy, as it is generated by contradictory positions elaborated in Platonic dialogues, is Harry A. Wolfson, "Extradeical and Intradeical Interpretations of Platonic Ideas," in *Religious History: A Group of Essays* (Cambridge, Mass.: Harvard Univ. Press, 1961), pp. 27–68.

7. Tr. Charles Eliot Norton, in *The Divine Comedy of Dante Alighieri,* Great Books of the Western World, vol. 21, ed. Robert Maynard Hutchins (Chicago: Encyclopedia Britannica, 1952), canto 33, sts. 121–123.

8. Shelley cites recurrence as a cardinal characteristic of poetry in *A Defence* (C, p. 280). Roman Jakobson makes a similar point about poetic language in "Linguistics and Poetics," in *Style in Language,* ed. Thomas A. Sebeok (Cambridge, Mass.: M.I.T. Press, 1960), pp. 358ff.

9. Jacques Derrida, *L'Ecriture et la différence* (Paris: Seuil, 1967), pp. 303, 314. See also Leslie Brisman, *Romantic Origins* (Ithaca and London: Cornell Univ. Press, 1978), pp. 238, 294.

10. Wasserman, *Shelley,* p. 323.

Interpreting the Uncitable Text:
The Literary Criticism
of Thomas De Quincey

Timothy Corrigan

> Criticism . . . if it is to be conscientious and
> profound, and if it is applied to an object as
> unlimited as poetry, must be almost as
> unattainable by any hasty effort as fine
> poetry itself.
> > De Quincey, "On Wordsworth's Poetry"

> It is not because I have said that the effect
> of interpretation is to isolate in the subject
> a heart, a *kern* . . . of *non*-sense, that
> interpretation is itself a non-sense.
> > Lacan, "De l'interpretation"

One of the chief projects of the Romantic poets was to make the visible difficult to see and the word difficult to say, to capture a vision beyond sight and a speech beyond language. Harold Bloom, among others, has described part of this effort in a study of poetic vision in Blake, Shelley, and other Romantics,[1] and a good deal of attention has recently been devoted to investigating the contingent problem, the Romantic's search for a new cosmic syntax.[2] Overlooked among these valuable investigations, however, has been the effect that this revised conception of poetry had on the literary criticism of the time, an effect whose seriousness and profundity is best evidenced by the paucity of major critical documents to appear during this period and the strange nature of those, such as Coleridge's *Biographia Literaria,* that do appear. That this crisis in Romantic criticism has not been given much attention, moreover, accounts in many ways for the general devaluation and misunderstanding of the work of Thomas De Quincey, a critic whose sensitivity to those unspeakable, visionary powers of poetry was matched by an indefatigable but ultimately hopeless struggle to describe them with the fallen language of critical prose.

For De Quincey the dilemma originates in his celebrated distinction between a literature of knowledge and a literature of power. This distinction, like much of De Quincey's thinking about language and poetics, resembles most closely Coleridge's differentiation between the faculty of reason and the faculty of understanding. Yet clearly this kind of aesthetic dichotomy is not confined to these two German-influenced Romantics and can be found in different forms in many of the other Romantic writers. "All that is literature seeks to communicate power," De Quincey says; "all that is not literature, to communicate knowledge." And echoing the Romantic suspicion of logical thought, he notes that "literature is the direct and adequate antithesis of Books of Knowledge" since the latter "speaks to the *mere* discursive understanding."[3] While a literature of power speaks to the emotions and imagination, its chief characteristic being the energy and imaginative movement it initiates. Shakespeare and Milton are two primary examples:

> When, in King Lear, the height, and depth, and breadth, of human passion is revealed to us, and, for the purposes of a sublime antagonism, is revealed in the weaknesses of an old man's nature, and in one night two worlds of storm are brought face to face—the human world, and the world of physical nature— mirrors of each other, semichoral antiphonies, strophe and antistrophe heaving with rival convulsions, and with the double darkness of night and madness,— when I am thus suddenly startled into a feeling of the infinity of the world within me, is this power, or what may I call it? Space, again, what is it in most men's minds? The lifeless form of the world without us, a postulate of the geometrician, with no more vitality or real existence to their feelings than the square root two. But, if Milton has been able to *inform* this empty theatre, peopling it with Titanic shadows, forms that sat at the eldest counsels of the infant world, chaos and original night . . . so that, from being a thing to inscribe with diagrams, it has become under his hands a vital agent on the human mind,—I presume that I may justly express the tendency of Paradise Lost by saying that it communicates power; a pretension far above all communication of knowledge.
>
> (X, 49)

The dynamics and vital movement that De Quincey describes here as central to great literature are again typical Romantic concerns. But for De Quincey they become by far the salient feature of his affective aesthetics and consequently the key to his critical response to art. Intricately related to this movement is his "law of antagonism," that "great cardinal law on which philosophical criticism . . . must hereafter mainly depend" (X, 436); and these contraries or antagonisms serve primarily to generate a movement forward and usually upward, as in the poetry of Milton:

> What you owe to Milton is not any knowledge, of which a million separate items are still but a million of advancing steps on the same earthly level; what you owe is *power,*—that is exercise and expansion to your own latent capacity of sympathy with the infinite, where every pulse and each separate influx is a step upwards, a step ascending as upon a Jacob's ladder from earth to the mysterious altitudes

above the earth. *All* the steps of knowledge, from first to last, carry you further on the same plane, but could never raise you one foot above your ancient level of earth: whereas the very *first* step in power is a flight—is an ascending movement into another element where earth is forgotten.

(XI, 56)

This movement generated by literature and directed towards the infinite has a second dimension which is equally important to De Quincey's poetics, namely, its visual nature. This too is a dominant concern in Romantic poetry; but it is continually forefronted by De Quincey, both in his theories and practical criticism, and consistently united with the dynamics of movement. In one of his more striking passages about the literature of power, he remarks: "it may travel towards an object seated in what Lord Bacon calls *dry* light; but, proximately, it does and must operate . . . on and through the *humid* light which clothes itself in mists and glittering *iris* of human passions, desires, and genial emotions" (XI, 54–55). This unrolling of light and images is what Bloom perceptively calls the "visionary cinema" of the Romantics, and for De Quincey, the poetic text that results is as uncitable as it is spectacular, creating an imaginative flight and joy that "linger and reproduce . . . in reverberations and endless mirrors" (XI, 301). Perhaps the finest illustration of this visionary movement is a passage from *Confessions of an Opium-Eater* in which images of power are quite significantly coupled with the drive of desire towards an object which again and again shifts out of reach. That these elements are presented through a pictorial medium which is explicitly associated with dreams makes this description, moreover, a direct allegory for the form and function of De Quincey's psycho-aesthetic. Here Piranesi leads the imagination:

> Many years ago, when I was looking over Piranesi's *Antiquities of Rome,* Coleridge, then standing by, described to me a set of plates from the artist, called his "Dreams," and which record the scenery of his own visions during the delirium of a fever. Some of these . . . represented vast Gothic halls; on the floor of which stood mighty engines and machinery, wheels, cables, catapults, & c., expressive of enormous power put forth, or resistance overcome. Creeping along the sides of the walls, you perceived a staircase; and upon this, groping his way upwards, was Piranesi himself. Follow the stairs a little farther, and you perceive them reaching an abrupt termination, without balustrade, and allowing no step onwards to him who should reach the extremity, except into the depths below. Whatever is to become of poor Piranesi, at least you suppose his labours must now in some way terminate. But raise your eyes, and behold a second flight of stairs still higher. . . . Once again elevate your eye, and a still more aerial flight of stairs is descried; and there again is the delirious Piranesi, busy on his aspiring labours: and so on until the unfinished stairs and the hopeless Piranesi both are lost in the upper gloom of the hall. With the same power of endless growth and reproduction did my architecture proceed in dreams.

(III, 438–39)

The aesthetic and linguistic problem that arises from this perception of poetry is unmistakable: the vision and movement attributed to a poem are simply incompatible with the static, denotative function of conventional language. De Quincey's theoretical solution to this problem, however, is not difficult on one level: he argues that poetic language is not conventional language but language which can capture and communicate powers and feelings beyond the reach of a discursive tongue. Poetic experience and its language, in other words, are associated with the intuitive faculty, which is qualitatively distinguished from discursive modes of thought and language: "An *intuition* is any knowledge whatsoever, sensuous or intellectual, which is apprehended *immediately*: a notion, on the other hand, or product of the discursive faculty, is any knowledge whatsoever which is apprehended *mediately*. All reasoning is carried on discursively" (X, 103). Poetic language is "hieroglyphic suggestion" (XI,88), intelligible and communicable intuitively and, unlike many discursive uses of language, is bound to poetic style in a subtle and ineffable manner. De Quincey explains:

> Whatsoever is entirely independent of the mind, and external to it, is generally equal to its own enunciation. Ponderable facts and external realities are intelligible in almost any language: they are self-explained and self-sustained. But, the more closely any exercise of mind is connected with what is internal and individual in the sensibilities . . . precisely in that degree, and more subtly, does the style or the embodying of the thoughts cease to be a mere separable ornament, and in fact the more does the manner . . . become confluent with the matter. . . . The union is too subtle, the intertexture too ineffable,—each co-existing not merely *with* the other, but each *in* and *through* the other.
>
> (X, 229, 230)

In a similar passage, De Quincey then relates this stylistic transformation of language to the all important need to present the flux of power:

> In very many subjective exercises of the mind . . . the problem before the writer is to project his own inner mind; to bring out consciously what yet lurks by involution in many unanalysed feelings; in short, to pass through a prism and radiate into distinct elements what previously had been even to himself but dim and confused ideas intermixed with each other. Now, in such cases, the skill with which detention or conscious arrest is given to the evanescent, external projection to what is internal, outline to what is fluxionary, and body to what is vague,—all this depends entirely on the command over language as the one sole means of embodying ideas . . . those who rest upon external facts, tangible realities, and circumstantial details,—in short, generally upon the objective, . . . must be forever less dependent upon style than those who have to draw upon their own understandings and their own peculiar feelings for the furniture and matter of their composition.
>
> (X, 226–227)

A very specific example of this poetic use of language is the word "amphithe-
atre" combined with "hills" and "forests" in *Paradise Lost*. Employing his law
of antagonism, De Quincey writes about the visionary flux that a single word
initiates:

> In the word *theatre* is contained an evanescent image of a great audience, of a
> populous multitude. Now, this image—half-withdrawn, half-flashed upon the eye,
> and combined with the words *hills* and *forests*—is thrown into powerful collision
> with the silence of the hills, with the solitude of forests; each image, forms
> reciprocal contradiction, brightens and vivifies the other. The two images act, and
> react, by strong repulsion and antagonism. . . . Paradise could not in any other
> way, or by any artifice less profound, have been made to give up its essential and
> differential characteristics in a form palpable to the imagination.
>
> (X, 403–404)

Yet, while the poetic idiom skillfully used can thus transcend the bounds
of ordinary language and create experiences which strictly speaking belong to
another semiotic system (one defined by visual motion), the critical idiom
cannot do so. Critical languages are discursive and pedestrian; consequently
their attempt to explain, apprehend, or describe the poetic experience will
inevitably be frustrated by the qualitative difference between the poetic experience and the critical language. De Quincey lucidly describes this limitation of
non-poetic words in his essay on the poetry of Pope:

> What are words to thoughts? Every word has a thought corresponding to it, so
> that not by so much as one solitary counter can the words outrun the thoughts.
> But every thought has *not* a word corresponding to it: so that the thoughts may
> outrun the words by many a thousand counters. In a developed nature, they *do*
> so. But what are the thoughts when set against the modifications of thoughts by
> feelings, hidden even from him that feels them, or against the inter-combinations
> of such modifications with others—complex with complex, decomplex with decom-
> plex? These can be unravelled by no human eye.
>
> (XI, 80–81)

In terms of quotidian speech, the thoughts and feelings of poetry are unspeakable, without words. Poetry uses "an alphabet of new and infinite symbols" (I,
129) which the reader-critic must try to translate into a prosaic language. Yet,
as De Quincy noted so frequently, the very point of a literature of power is that
it is not "adequately communicable by translation."[4] Whereas a literature of
knowledge "is translateable, and translateable without one atom of loss" (X,
50), great literature defies translation and leaves the critic mute before its power
of vision.

Therefore while the astute reader-critic may grasp the power of literature
through the intuitive faculty, a conflict and crisis occur when he or she must

present that intuited knowledge discursively. This fundamentally linguistic crisis is apparent even when De Quincey attempts to define a literature of power,
as most of the definition becomes a rhetorical detour or evasion in which he
attempts to suggest obliquely what he cannot adequately denote with words:

> Now if it is asked what is meant by communicating power, I, in my turn, would
> ask by what name a man would designate the case in which I should be made
> to feel vividly, and with a vital consciousness, emotions which ordinary life rarely
> or never supplies occasions for exciting, and which had previously lain unawa-
> kened, and hardly within the dawn of consciousness—as myriads of modes of
> feeling are at this moment in every human mind for want of a poet to organize
> them?
>
> (X, 48)

Or even more to the point is De Quincey's description of his relation with the
mysterious "Ladies of Sorrow." Like poetry, they inhabit the realm of intuition
and dreams, remaining silently apart from their reader in vague, moving signs.
To intepret them, consequently, De Quincey must struggle without much hope
to bridge that gap between their meaning and mere words:

> Do they talk, then? O no! Mighty phantoms like these disdain the infirmities of
> language. They may utter voices through the organs of man when they dwell in
> human hearts, but amongst themselves is no voice nor sound; eternal silence
> reigns in *their* kingdoms. . . . I upon earth had heard their mysteries oftentimes
> deciphered by harp and timbrel, by dulcimer and organ. Like God, whose ser-
> vants they are, they utter their pleasure not by sounds that perish, or by words
> that go astray, but by signs in heaven, by changes on earth, by pulses in secret
> rivers, heraldries painted on darkness, and hieroglyphics written on the tablets
> of the brain. *They* wheeled in mazes; *I* spelled the steps. *They* telegraphed from
> afar; *I* read the signals. *They* conspired together; and on the mirrors of darkness
> *my* eye traced the plots. *Theirs* were the symbols; mine are the words.
>
> (XIII, 364–65)

This struggle to understand his "Ladies of Sorrow" and, by analogy, to
translate any poetic experience into a discursive language, is at the heart of
most of De Quincey's writing. In its most general sense, the tension is usually
described in terms of De Quincey's dual personality as a dreamer and a
logician. But more important is what propels his writing through this dichotomy: a persistent desire to unite the two tendencies in a single act, the desire,
that is, to display the shadowy dream vision in the concrete analytical material
of words. In this regard, I would like to suggest here that one key to De
Quincey's thought and criticism is to be found in the models of Freud and
Lacan. A purely psychoanalytic study of De Quincey's entire work based on
these models would doubtless be a fruitful pursuit, particularly in light of the
strong emphasis De Quincey places on the psychological components of the
mind and of the extraordinarily rich record he has left of his own mind and

dreams.[5] I will confine myself here, however, to De Quincey's literary criticism, and will focus simply on the psychoanalytic concept of desire and the play of language around that desire in its attempt to produce meaning. A good prece-dent for this approach has been set by Gayatri Spivak in a recent essay on Coleridge.[6] I am not, however, as convinced as she of the universal truth of Lacan's models, and instead of using De Quincey as evidence for Lacan's theories, I shall use Lacan's metapsychological approach to language only as a source of insight into the linguistic intricacies of De Quincey's literary criticisms.

The specific subject of Spivak's essay is Coleridge's *Biographia Literaria,* particularly the annoying and brilliant chapters twelve and thirteen. Using Lacanian linguistics as a framework, she concentrates on the narrative strategy of Coleridge's work, which she correctly sees as characteristic of many of his contemporarties: "The entire *Biographia* inhabits the narrative structure of pro-motion and *post*ponement (today we might say difference, certainly avoidance and longing) that so many Romantics share."[7] The whole *Biographia,* especially the two central chapters, moves toward a climactic revelation of truth and unity, both psychological and metaphysical. Yet all along the way the disclosure of this promised oneness (which for Lacan is the property of the imaginary) is delayed and detoured through a series of rhetorical and structural maneuvers. Writing becomes a hiding-in-disclosure and an endless anticipation of what is beyond writing. "The narrative declaration of the status of the *Biographia Liter-aria* is thus deliberately evasive, the writing reminder of a gap."[8] And the spurious letter that interrupts Coleridge's argument both serves as the crucial act in that argument and provides the possibility of ending it: "A reader of Lacan can interpret this textual gesture" as "the eruption of the Other onto the text of the subject. Read this way, what is otherwise seen as an interruption of the development of the argument about the imagination may not only be seen as a keeping alive, by unfulfillment, of the desire that moves the argument, but also as the ruse that makes possible the establishment of the Raw of the imagination."[9]

Writing about poetry, De Quincey faces a problem similar to that which Spivak delineates in *Biographia Literaria.* Motivated by a desire not only for the fluidity, power, and unity that poetry represents, but for the means to recount it, De Quincey must confront the impossibility of locating that experience in a discursive language. This desire for sense propels every reader and particular-ly a reader as sensitive and demanding as De Quincey. For reading is a desire for sense from signs, just as interpretation is a desire for meaning from a text. To communicate with another reader through criticism means therefore to communicate not only the spiritual force that the reader-critic originally experi-ences but the yearning that motivates that experience. And the desire for sense is thus compounded by a desire to communicate a meaning whose primary text is defined as linguistically uncitable. De Quincey, like Coleridge, must consequently resort to techniques that would permit him to say the unsayable in language, so that, in the desire to speak the ineffable, verbal postponement will substitute for verbal fulfillment. Like Coleridge, De Quincey makes his criticism ultimately a "hiding-in-disclosure, [with] the signifier creating 'the effect of the signified' by rusing anticipation."[10] But De Quincey's solution is significantly different from Coleridge's in that his posturing is a product far less of a narrative persona than of narrative structuring and style, both of which relate to that dynamic movement of literature that persistently eludes De Quincey.

Desire is metonymy, Lacan states in his essay on "The Insistence of the Letter."[11] And the two halves of this assertion are the two pillars of De Quincey's literary criticism. "Desire," Lacan continues, "is to be conceived as *significative mediation* of a *fundamental antinomy*. Thus it participates in need insofar as it is relatively satisfied by an object, but only sustains itself insofar as it participates in demand by its perennially unsatisfied quest of the being of the Other, *locus of the signifier*."[12] The desire of a reader-critic, as the Piranesi passage suggests, is accordingly a movement which becomes a series of partial fulfillments that seeks to "achieve" a literary object that continually moves and directs the reader towards an unassailable goal—the Other, the primary signifier. Hence De Quincey rightly feels the strain in his self as writer about literature and his self as experiencer of its power since his acquisition of language is exactly what exiles him from that mute experience and places him in the metonymic grip of desire. The "moment in which desire becomes human is also that in which the child is born into language," says Lacan.[13] And consequently for De Quincey the only maneuver available is a metonymic courtship in which his longing to speak his vision is never consummated and in which the linguistic displacement of the romance is necessarily a veering off from any final meaning.

The practical consequences of this predicament are evident throughout De Quincey's writings. De Quincey himself often seems perfectly aware of the predicament and the endless postponements that it forces him to adopt. In one essay, for instance, he abruptly addresses the reader as he recognizes in him or her the mirror image of his own detoured yearnings:

> Reader, you are beginning to suspect us. 'How long do we purpose to detain people?' For anything that appears we may be designing to write on to the twentieth century,—for twice thirty years. 'And *whither* are we going? toward what object?'—which is as urgent a quaere as *how far*. . . . You feel symptoms of doubt and restiveness; and, like Hamlet with his father's ghost, you will follow us no further, unless we explain what it is that we are in quest of.
>
> (X, 189–190)[14]

Since the poetic truth that De Quincey wishes to share is outside the denotative scope of his language, he must be content to lead the reader along the path of his language. De Quincey can thus draw him into the momentum of his desire, and then hope the reader can make the non-verbal leap into the central vision: "We shall endeavor to bring up our reader to the fence, and persuade him, if possible, to take the leap which still remains to be taken. . . . But as we have reason to believe that he will 'refuse' it, we shall wheel him round and bring him up to it from another quarter. A gentle touch of the spur may perhaps carry him over" (X, 191). Viewed as aesthetic stimulant rather than as aesthetic meaning or explanation, critical language subsequently becomes a kind of teasing process in which the digression can become the point of the writing. "But this (you say) is a digression," De Quincey anticipates in one essay, "why, true; and a digression is often the cream of an article."[15] Indeed no essay better demonstrates this strategy and its success as a tool for critical exegesis than De Quincey's "On the Knocking on the Gate in *Macbeth*."

Most analysts of this classic essay have described it as an example of the author's usual method, which is, according to John E. Jordan, "to feel an effect, analyse its cause, attempt to make it concrete or to recreate it, and then to trace it back to some precept or reconstruct the age or individual which produced it."[16] Correct as this description may be on one level, it nevertheless ignores that linguistic anxiety and incompleteness that informs most of De Quincey's writings about great literature. This anxiety is announced in the first paragraph of the essay on *Macbeth* where he explicitly says that the attraction of this particular scene lies in the fact that it virtually frustrated him into silence for many years, remaining outside the abilities of a discursive understanding or language: "From my boyish days I had always felt a great perplexity on one point in *Macbeth*. It was this:—The knocking at the gate which succeeds to the murder of Duncan produced to my feelings an effect for which I never could account. The effect was that it reflected back upon the murder of a peculiar awfulness and a depth of solemnity; yet however obstinately I endeavoured with my understanding to comprehend this, for many years I never could see *why* it should produce such an effect" (X, 389). Immediately, though, De Quincey warns against this discursive faculty, which should never distract one from an imaginative apprehension of poetic truth. A reader should "never pay any attention to his understanding when it stands in opposition to any other faculty of his mind. The mere understanding, however useful and indispensible, is the meanest faculty in the human mind, and the most to be distrusted" (X, 389). As an example, he chooses a simple visual perception, which is especially fitting since, for both De Quincey and Lacan, vision is the plane on which the verbal/non-verbal confrontation begins and on which, unfortunately, "the understanding is positively allowed to obliterate the eyes" (X, 390).

De Quincey then returns to his argument; he returns, that is, from one digression only to move the reader into another: "My understanding could furnish no reason why the knocking at the gate in Macbeth should produce any effect, direct or reflected. In fact, my understanding said positively that it could not produce any effect. But I knew better, I felt that it did; and I waited and clung to the problem until further knowledge should enable me to solve it" (X, 390). This knowledge is furnished obliquely at best, appearing in the form of a metaphoric episode which also functions metonymically, condensing and displacing the original experience of the drama. This new digression is a story of an actual murder, and as such draws the poetic experience onto the level of society and language where the unspeakable is accommodated or natural-ized. De Quincey explains:

> At length, in 1812, Mr. Williams made his *debut* on the stage of Ratcliffe Highway, and executed those unparalleled murders which have procured him such a bril-liant and undying reputation. . . . All other murders look pale by the deep crim-son of his; and, as an amateur once said to me in a querulous tone, 'There has been absolutely nothing *doing* since his time, or nothing that's worth speaking of.' But this is wrong; for it is unreasonable to expect all men to be great artists, and born with the genius of Mr. Williams. Now it will be remembered that in the first of these murders (that of Marrs) the same incident (of a knocking at a door soon after the work of extermination was complete) did actually occur which the genius of Shakspere has invented; and all good judges, and the most eminent dilettanti, acknowledged this felicity of Shakspere's suggestion as soon as it was actually realized."
>
> (X, 390–391)

The very language of this passage—Williams as a stage actor and "murder considered as one of the fine arts"—suggests the metaphoric transformation that is taking place here. The narrative quality of the passage and the entire essay, peppered with explanatory events from daily life, becomes a metonymic displacement of the *Macbeth* incident onto an objectively novelistic level. De Quincey interjects two further analogies, for instance:

> If the reader has ever witnessed a wife, daughter, or sister in a fainting fit, he may chance to have observed that the most affecting moment in such a spectacle is *that* in which a sigh and stirring announce the recommencement of suspended life. Or, if the reader has ever been present in a vast metropolis on the day when some great national idol was carried in funeral pomp to his grave, and, chancing to walk near the course through which it passed, has felt powerfully, in the silence and desertion of the streets, and in the stagnation of ordinary business, the deep interest which at the moment was possessing the heart of man,—if all at once he should hear the death—like stillness broken up by the sound of wheels rattling away from the scene, and making known that the transitory vision was dissolved, he will be aware that at no moment was his sense of the complete suspension and pause in ordinary human concerns so full and affecting as at that moment when the suspension ceases, and the goings-on of human life are suddenly resumed.
>
> (X, 392–93)

Having translated his aesthetic experience into a societal language, De Quincey is now able to analyze his experience and almost scientifically discuss how murder elicits sympathy and how Shakespeare manipulates that sympathy towards Macbeth (X, 392). The once unspeakable dramatic effect can thus be transformed into a literary maxim, a critical law that neatly contains the experience in a verbal definition. The flood of verbal substitutions and clausal extensions that follows indicates, however, the inadequacy of even this definition:

> All action in any direction is best expounded, measured, and made apprehensi-
> ble, by reaction. Now, apply this to the case in *Macbeth*. Here, as I have said, the
> retiring of the human heart and the entrance of the fiendish heart was to be
> expressed and made sensible. Another world has stept in; and the murders are
> taken out of the region of human things, human purposes, human desires. . . . But
> how shall this be conveyed and made palpable? In order that a new world may
> step in, this world for a time must disappear. The murderers and the murder must
> be insulated—cut off by an immeasurable gulf from the ordinary tide and succes-
> sion of human affairs—locked up and sequestered in some deep recess; we must
> be made sensible that the world of ordinary life is suddenly arrested, laid asleep,
> tranced, racked into a dread armistice; time must be annihilated, relation to things
> without abolished; and all must pass self-withdrawn into a deep syncope and
> suspension of earthly passion. Hence it is that, when the deed is done, when the
> work of darkness is perfect, then the world of darkness passes away like a
> pageantry in the clouds: the knocking at the gate is heard, and it makes known
> audibly that the reaction has commenced; the human has made its reflux upon
> the fiendish; the pulses of life are beginning to beat again; and the re-establish-
> ment of the goings-on of the world in which we live first makes us profoundly
> sensible of the awful parenthesis that had suspended them.
>
> (X, 393)

Yet, as this series of redundancies suggests, language can be only a temporary seating place for the drive of the desire and the movement of literature, and this lyrical summary is accordingly usurped and displaced in the next para-graph by a rhythmic paean to Shakespeare, the god-like man whose mysterious power resembles that of a silent and vibrant nature: "O mighty poet! Thy works are not those of other men, simply and merely great works of art, but are also like the phenomena of nature, like the sun and the sea, the stars and the flowers, like frost and snow, rain and dew, hail-storm and thunder, which are to be studied with entire submission of our own faculties"(X, 393–94).

While the naturalization and displacement of the scene from *Macbeth* is the most striking feature of this remarkable essay, its stylistic maneuvering is equally important. In this regard, V. A. De Luca notes that the essay "resembles a dream experienced, recognized, and then forgotten, and the process as a whole, preserved in prose, provides the essay with its formal shape."[17] The structure and the style of the writing, in short, seeks to mirror the dynamics of the poetic experience at which De Quincey aims. This attempt to accomplish with stylistics what is normally beyond the scope of a lifeless prose is common to much of De Quincey's critical writing, and contributes a large part of its fluid poetic flavor. Despite what many critics believe, however, the attempt does not accomplish its task, and this failure to capture its object is precisely what causes the prose to generate and regenerate itself as poetic pursuit. Virginia Woolf, who praised De Quincey's use of language with characteristic discrimination, describes this style and indicates perhaps unwittingly the desire for the unreachable vision that underlies it: "[in his writing] the idea of hurry and trepidation, of reaching towards something that for ever flies, intensifies the impression of stillness and eternity." For, she says, De Quincey "could not tell the simplest story without qualifying and illustrating and introducing additional information which until the point that was to be cleared up has long since become extinct in the dim mists of the distance. . . . Then suddenly the smooth narrative parts asunder, arch opens beyond arch" towards "the vision of something forever flying, forever escaping."[18]

The development of this "pursuing" prose style has its roots, as I have indicated, in the crisis precipitated by that inexpressible quality in a literature of power. De Quincey's ubiquitous concern with style in his theoretical and practical essays, moreover, suggests in itself a sort of subtle displacement from the matter to the manner of poetry, from the signified to the signifier. And, although this way of describing his use of style somewhat oversimplifies De Quincey's highly intelligent theory of style, it does indicate his very tentative and indirect play around the concrete and massive centers of art which Johnson and Coleridge focus on more directly, and further, his effort to remain on a second linguistic layer apart from those centers.

In a more conscious and practical fashion, De Quincey's style becomes a method and tool to vitalize a discursive language so that it can track the vision of literature. Stylists are thus "the *discoverers* of truth. . . . Light to *see* the road, power to *advance along* it—such being amongst the promises and proper functions of style, it is a capital error . . . to undervalue this great organ of the advancing intellect—an organ which is equally important considered as a tool for the culture and *popularization* of truth" (X, 261). To support this theory De Quincey makes a Coleridgean distinction between an organic style and a mechanic style, the first aptly being the only use of words suited for dealing with power, motion, and thoughts, the three dimensions of great literature:

> Style may be viewed as an *organic* thing and as a *mechanic* thing. By organic, we mean that which, being acted upon, reacts, and which propagates the communicated power without loss. By mechanic, that which, being impressed with motion, cannot throw it back without loss, and therefore soon comes to an end. . . . Now, the use of words is an organic thing, in so far as language is connected with thoughts, and modified by thoughts. It is a mechanic thing, in so far as words in combination determine or modify each other. The science of style as an organ of thought, of style in relation to the ideas and feelings, might be called the *organology* of style. The science of style considered as a machine, in which words act upon words, and through a particular grammar, might be called the mechanology of style.   (X, 163–64)

An organic style thus allows the critic to approximate the ever-moving, ever-vanishing power of art, and while never actually containing that transcending force which is "essentially ineffable and unutterable in vulgar ears" (X, 263), it can actuate the desire of the reader-critic as it engages literary power. This actuated desire may then be able to illuminate—though not copy—its object, "to brighten the intelligibility of a subject which is obscure to the understanding" and "to regenerate the normal *power* and impressiveness of a subject which has become dormant to the sensibilities" (X, 260). De Quincey himself recognizes that frequently this stylistic effort means simply creating an energetic redundancy such as he does in the essay on *Macbeth,* where the accumulation of words is able to signify, only through their superfluity, what is beyond language. De Quincey's windy and circular sentences, loaded with clauses qualifying and extending other clauses, hence become indicators of an inadequacy, reminders of a gap in the writing. For a good stylist, then, "tautology becomes a merit: variation of words, with a substantial identity of sense and dilution of truth, is oftentimes a necessity. A man who should content himself with a single condensed enunciation of a perplexed doctrine would be a madman" (X, 139). And, continuing this excellent description of how style becomes a displacer of truth, De Quincey appropriately shifts to a visual metaphor, since the elusive power is generally visual:

> Like boys who are throwing the sun's rays into the eyes of a mob by means of a mirror, you must shift your lights and vibrate your reflections at every possible angle.... Time must be given for the intellect to eddy about a truth, and to appropriate its bearings. There is a sort of previous lubrication ... which is requisite to familiarize the mind with a startling or complex novelty. And this is obtained for the intellect by varying the modes of presenting it,—now putting it directly before the eye, now obliquely, now in abstract shape, now in the concrete.... The true art for such popular display is to contrive the best forms for appearing to say something new when in reality you are but echoing yourself; to break up massy chords into running variation; and to mask, by slight differences in manner, a virtual identity in the substance.
>
> (X, 139–40)

Not surprisingly, this active use of words becomes the touchstone for many of De Quincey's judgments on the value of other writers. In discussing Jeremy Taylor's writing, he mentions one remarkable characteristic of his style: "... the everlasting strife and fluctuation between his rhetoric and his eloquence, which maintain their alternations with force and inevitable recurrence, like the systole and diastole, the contraction and expansion, of some living organ" (X, 108). Similarly, his criticism of Burton and Milton relies fundamentally on the relation of their language to the imaginative movement it should present: "Agile movement, and a certain degree of fancifulness, are indispensable to rhetoric. But Burton is not so much fanciful as capricious; his motion is not the motion of freedom, but of lawlessness; he does not dance, but caper. Milton, on the other hand, *polonaises* with a grand Castilian air, in paces too sequacious and processional: . . . his thoughts and his imagery . . . move to the music of the organ" (X, 102). De Quincey is fairly consistent with this kind of criticism, whereby the power suggested is the product of the movement of the critical language. At his best, he not only describes this power but keeps pace with it, as he does in the following passage on JeremyTaylor and Sir Thomas Browne: "in them alone, are the two opposite forces of a eloquent passion and rhetorical fancy brought into an exquisite equilibrium,—approaching, receding,—attracting repelling,—blending separating,—chasing and chased, as in a fugue,—and again lost in delightful interfusion" (X, 104-105).

Once again, the movement of the visionary text he pursues necessitates that De Quincey's language always fall short. Yet the intense desire for that fleeing vision enlivens the critical idiom for De Quincey as for no other critic. As I have tried to demonstrate, his practical and theoretical criticism is full of examples of this "passionate prose." But perhaps the finest instance of it is his analysis of Pope's "Eloisa to Abelard." To Pope's work in general, he extends unenthusiastic approval, generally because the visual power that the poet presents lacks the steady, consistent development of the power of art. "I admire Pope in the very highest degree," he explains, "but I admire him as a pyrotechnic artist for producing brilliant and evanescent effects out of elements that have hardly a moment's life within them. There is a flash and a startling explosion; then there is a dazzling coruscation, all purple and gold; the eye aches under the suddeness of a display that, springing like a burning arrow—out of darkness, rushes back into darkness with arrowy speed, and in a moment all is over" (XI, 119). But "Eloisa to Abelard" is another case: De Quincey misreads the poem as being more Romantic than ironic, but in that misreading he finds the maintained power and vision that he seeks in great poetry. His attempt to put that visionary power in words will of course be frustrated, as all linguistic arts of desire must be. Yet in this instance he comes as close as any critic has to what Jordan calls "an artistic recreation, a reevocation of the aesthetic effect."[19] Here his prose virtually moves with the emotions and struggles he discusses, and the exacting narrative quality focuses on minute details, thus nearly creating a verbal cinema out of the "lyrical tumult of the changes":

> The self-conflict—the flux and reflux of the poor agitated heart—the spectacle of Eloisa now bending penitentially before the shadowy austerities of a monastic future, now raving upon the remembrances of a guilty past—one moment reconciled by the very anguish of her soul to the grandeurs of religion and of prostrate adoration, the next moment revolting to perilous retrospects of her treacherous happiness—the recognition, by shining gleams through the very storm and darkness evoked by her earthly sensibilities, of a sensibility deeper far in its ground, and that trembled towards holier objects—the lyrical tumult of changes, the hope,

the tears, the rapture, the penitence, the despair—place the reader in tumultuous sympathy with the poor distracted nun.

(XI, 66)

In light of this and other examples of De Quincey's best literary criticism we can recognize what has usually been regarded as his critical failing—his verbosity, his long narrative digressions, and his lack of attention to the specific textual intricacies of poetry—as instead an idiosyncratic but triumphant solu-tion to the general crisis in the language of criticism during the Romantic period. It seems certain that most of the great Romantics felt in their own particular ways that ineffable energy of art which De Quincey termed and visualized as "power." Yet to translate it or accommodate it in criticism re-quired individual solutions: Blake could abandon words altogether and express his best criticism in a dialectic between the text and his visual commentary, as he does in his presentation of Dante's *Divine Comedy* or Young's *Night Thoughts*; Coleridge could resign himself to a kind of translation process through which the silent visions of art are transferred, with loss, to more profane tongues like the scientific idiom of *Biographia Literaria*.[20] Neither as methodical as Coleridge nor as radical as Blake, De Quincey is driven nonetheless by as great a desire for poetic truth as any Romantic, and his solution to the crisis is, if less striking, equally effective.

Located primarily in style and narrative naturalizations, this critical solu-tion is clearly not the aesthetic experience itself. And to appreciate the full significance of De Quincey's work, his reader must see and hear past the language and towards the vision that the critical language seeks to retrieve. To follow De Quincey, in short, the reader's own desire must penetrate the palimp-sest that De Quincey's critical discourse ultimately becomes. And while this palimpsest may not be the aesthetic experience itself, it is, nevertheless, very much a primary experience. De Quincey's critical discourse should never be misprized for its inherent frustration, since it is only through an appreciation of his skill in manipulating the precise sense of words that the power of his vision and the visionary non-sense of his meanings are communicated. Criti-cism is, above all else, language, and that language must be the first site of meaning, especially in the critical work of writers such as De Quincey. In this regard, what Lacan has noted about the unconscious might also be said of the force which so powerfully informs De Quincey's writings about art: "No doubt that we have to lend an ear to the 'not-said' which lies in the holes of discourse, but this does not mean that we are to do our listening as if it were someone knocking from the other side of the wall. For if from this point on we are no longer to concern ourselves except with these noises . . . it must be admitted that we will not have put ourselves in the most propitious set of conditions to decipher their sense. Without first racking our brains to comprehend . . . how is one supposed to *translate* what is not of itself language?"[21]

NOTES

1. "The Visionary Cinema of Romantic Poetry," in *William Blake: Essays for S. Foster Damon,* ed. Alvin Rosenfeld (Providence: Brown Univ. Press, 1969).
2. See for example, Earl R. Wasserman, "Metaphors for Poetry," in *The Subtler Language* (Baltimore: Johns Hopkins Univ. Press, 1959), pp. 169–195, and Heinrich Bosse, "The Marvellous and Romantic Semantics," *SiR,* 14 (1975), 211–234.
3. *The Collected Writings of Thomas De Quincey,* ed. David Masson (1889–90; rpt. New York: AMS Press, 1968), X, 47–48; XI, 54. All further references to this edition will be abbreviated in the text.
4. Quoted in John E. Jordan, *Thomas De Quincey, Literary Critic* (Berkeley: Univ. of California Press, 1952), p. 253.
5. One could add to this De Quincey's use of the Lacanian notion of a "primary language," and both Lacan and De Quincey's idea that any language speaks to the subject's Other.
6. "The Letter as Cutting Edge," *YFS,* 55–56 (1977), 208–226.
7. Spivak, pp. 209–210.
8. Spivak, p. 210.
9. Spivak, p. 218.
10. Spivak, p. 212.
11. Jacques Lacan, *Ecrits* (Paris: Editions de Seuil, 1966), p. 518.
12. Lacan, p. 386–390.
13. Lacan, p. 319.
14. I recognize the journalistic pressures and exigencies that inform these delays and digressions, but they are obviously not incompatible with my argument.
15. *Posthumous Works of Thomas De Quincey,* ed. Alexander Japp (London: U. S. Book Company, 1891), II, 22.
16. Jordan, p. 4.
17. "De Quincey's 'Knocking on the Gate in *Macbeth*': Dream and Prose Art," *ELN,* 13 (1976), 277–278.
18. *The Second Common Reader* (New York: Harcourt, Brace & World, 1932), pp. 120–123.
19. Jordan, p. 269.
20. See Timothy Corrigan, "Coleridge as Reader: Language in a Combustible Mind," *PQ,* 59 (1979), and "The *Biographia Literaria* and the Language of Science," *JHI,* 41 (1980), 399–419. These are chapters in *Coleridge, Language, and Criticism* (Athens: Univ. of Georgia Press, 1982).
21. Lacan, p. 307.

The Poetics of "Black on White": Stéphane Mallarmé's *Un Coup de dés*

Kathleen Henderson Staudt

DEDICATED TO THE MEMORY OF PAUL DE MAN

Critics who write about "ineffability" in poetry are usually concerned, implicitly or explicitly, with the relationship between language and something beyond it, an ideal or a dimension of experience that is by definition inexpressible in language. They consider poetic language as a medium through which higher things are partially apprehended. Stéphane Mallarmé's work occupies a peculiar place within the discussion of ineffability and literature because of its radical denial that poetry can express *any* ineffable or transcendental truth. Far from developing a poetic technique that could mediate an ineffable ideal, Mallarmé's poetics seeks a new language that would free itself altogether from mediation and become an end in itself.

The place of Mallarmé's poetics in such a context is explored quite thoroughly in Gerald Bruns's *Modern Poetry and the Idea of Language*: Bruns places Mallarmé's poetic theory at one pole of a dialectic between "Orphic" and "Hermetic" modes. The "Orphic" mode, which governs most theories of language as mediation, conceives of "creating a world" by means of the poetic word. Although many writers in the Romantic tradition recognize the impossibility of literally "speaking things into being," the Orphic myth of language is clearly akin to the belief that words make accessible to the mind certain dimensions of thought that would otherwise elude it. The Orphic mode assumes, in short, that there is something beyond language that needs to be expressed, brought to consciousness, or "created."[1]

In contrast, the "Hermetic" mode includes those theories which view the poetic structure as an end in itself, rather than as a medium expressing some "idea" or "reality" beyond language.[2] For Bruns, Mallarmé is the *daimon* or spiritual ancestor of a group of modern poets and critics who have sought a radically self-referential, autonomous language, transcendent in itself. He connects Mallarmé, through Valéry, Saussure, and Jakobson, to the radical questioning of "transcendental signifieds" found in Jacques Derrida.[3] My own essay will follow Bruns's lead in reading Mallarmé as a forerunner of certain contemporary structuralist and post-structuralist theorists, and will try to show how Mallarmé's resistance to the concept of language as a means of communication gives rise to his search for a poetic language "transcendent in its own right."[4] I shall, however, depart from Bruns somewhat by giving more attention to the "Hermetic" than to the "Orphic" aspects of Mallarmé's poetic practice.

Mallarmé's fascination with the possibility of an autonomous poetic work is evident in "Solennité," his review of Théodore de Banville's *Le Forgeron*. Here he praises de Banville's work for its obedience "to the dialectic that belongs to poetry alone (*au seul dialectique du vers*)."[5] He is especially impressed by the calculated impersonality of the text, which allows the language to move in its own world. Mallarmé's review praises, in particular, the liberation in the poem of "the principle which is only Poetry" (*le principe qui n'est—que le Vers*), and calls this principle "Signe," the sign. The emergence of this autonomous sign (*lancé de soi*) reveals a mystery that is somehow inherent in words themselves.[6] This desire to construct a "pure" work, independent of the world and made up of signs that evoke each other through a power inherent in language itself, is implicit in much of Mallarmé's writing about poetry. To comprehend fully his reasons for seeking this hidden purity, it is necessary to identify the other aspects of language that Mallarmé's poetry of "pure signs" is constructed to resist.[7]

In an early essay entitled "Hérésies artistiques: l'Art pour tous," Mallarmé inveighs against the popular notion that poetic language ought to be "intelligible" to all people simply because it uses the grammar and vocabulary of their native tongue. On the contrary, he argues, the art of poetry should be viewed as a sacred mystery, accessible only to a devoted few. In their effort to discover "une langue immaculée," Mallarmé insists, poets should eschew the "intelligibility" that the masses demand of literature, and should instead imitate the obscurity of ancient hieroglyphic manuscripts. Moreover, poets must avoid all the formal ugliness of mass-produced literature, especially the columns of the newspapers and the monotonous uniformity of the cheap booksellers' editions of great poets.[8]

By resisting the conventional character of written language, Mallarmé hopes to uncover a unique mystery that belongs to language alone. He writes in "Le mystère dans les lettres" that the language of the masses, in its insistence on communicating messages, overlooks a more essential mystery inherent in language. "What they fail to spread," he writes "is the priceless mist that floats about the secret abyss of every human thought."[9] The poet's mission, then, is not to communicate thought, but to enable this mysterious dimension of language itself to emerge, by discovering new relationships among pure signs.

Thus the poet's awareness of the "principle which is only Poetry" depends on his sensitivity to attributes of language that are overlooked in popular forms of literature and verbal communication. The most important of these, for Mallarmé, is the status of language as a visible form, as black ink on white paper. He is especially fascinated by the capacity of these black forms to establish relationships among themselves, to "signify" according to the rules of a self-contained linguistic system. This "signifying" power of words is quite different, for Mallarmé, from their mere "intelligibility" to the masses. Thus he rebukes poets who write only in order to be "understood" and readers who wish only to "understand." Rather, he insists, the poem should be viewed as a sacred end in itself. As he puts it in one particularly vivid passage, those who write to be understood seek "intelligibility" in "an inkwell without darkness."[10] This image is a rich one for Mallarmé's purposes. Words written in ink whose blackness is not noticed are words whose only purpose is to serve as mediators. They are effaced by the message they communicate. Mallarmé thus insists on the status of the poetic word as a thing in itself, as a form on paper, a blackness against white.

The substantiality of poetry in Mallarmé's thinking is underscored in "L'Action restreinte,"[11] an essay which describes to a would-be writer the poet's confrontation with ink and paper, the materials of his craft. Instead of an "inkwell without darkness," the poet here faces a crystalline inkwell, "clear as consciousness (*clair comme une conscience*)," containing a drop of shadow ("*une goutte de ténèbres*").[12] This dark drop of ink will become the poetic word, some-thing even more substantial than the meditation of which it is a trace. In pursuing "black on white," the poet works in a world of pure darkness and light, the exact negative of the stars against a black sky. Black ink and white paper are his materials, and these represent, for Mallarmé, something as myste-rious and elemental as the stars.[13] The language of the poem must somehow present the mystery that accompanies its own emergence, "le rien de mystère, indispensable, qui demeure, exprimé, quelque peu."[14] This sense of mystery is due in large measure to the semiotic character of words themselves, as black marks which are at the same time, inexplicably, "signs" evoking other signs. The poet who pursues "black on white" must learn how to manipulate these signs so that the mystery of poetry itself will emerge from their interrela-tionships, overriding whatever other meanings arbitrary convention has as-signed to the poet's words.

The theoretical implications of the poetic problem facing Mallarmé are explored with remarkable lucidity in the work of Jan Mukařovsky, a member of the Prague Linguistic School who was influenced by both Saussure and Jakobson. Mukařovsky's essay "On Poetic Language" studies closely the rela-tionship between the role of poetic language as the "material" of a work of art and its tendency, at the same time, to point beyond itself to other signs. Mukařovsky insists, first, that poetic language defines itself as different from "standard literary language" by deliberately deviating from the patterns of language to which readers are accustomed.[15] This deviation from the norm tends to bring to the foreground language's status as a complex of sounds and forms out of which a poet builds a work, its status as the "material" of a work of art. Yet the capacity of poetic language to "signify" and to "mean" within the conventions of standard language distinguishes poetry inescapably from the other arts:

> What is language in literature? It is a *material* like metal and stone in sculpture, like pigment and the material of the pictorial plane in painting . . . Nevertheless, there is a considerable difference between other artistic materials and language. Stone, metal and pigment enter art as mere natural phenomena which gain a semiotic character only in art; they begin to "mean" something. Language in its very essence is already a sign. (p.9)

Like artists working in other media, Mallarmé regards language as a material that needs to be molded into a work of art. The fundamentally semiotic character of language which Mukařovsky describes is clearly a source of poetry's unique richness, but it also presents a difficult problem to the poet.[16] It obliges him to adapt for his own purposes that aspect of the common, or "standard," language which he seeks most to transcend: its tendency toward "mere intelligibility." Paradoxically, Mallarmé attempts to make use of language's function as a medium of communication in his effort to construct a "pure work."

The challenge presented by the material and semiotic properties of language is most developed in Mallarmé's discussions of "Le Livre," the "Great Work" that he dreams of completing. This Great Book will be an expansion of the autonomous sign described in "Solennité."[17] Its power will lie not in what it says about the world, but in the new and uniquely poetic significance that it will discover in the language of the world. He envisions the Great Work as an ultimate form that could subsume everything that conventional language reveals as "the world," replacing ordinary reference with a language of pure signs. In a letter written to Verlaine in 1885, Mallarmé explains his dream of the "Great Work," emphasizing not what it will say, but what it will be. He describes the Book as "architectural and premeditated," based on "equations" that will capture the mysterious rhythms inherent in the form of a book— especially the rhythm created by the turning of the leaves and by the movement of words across the "black on white" page. The Book embodies for Mallarmé a purity of form that all poets seek, whether or not they do so consciously, whenever they try to construct works of art out of language. In describing his poetic project, Mallarmé pictures himself as a mathematician and an alchemist rather than as a poet in the Romantic sense; far from attempting to express inspired thoughts, he seeks to reveal the mysterious, living patterns that he finds inherent in the relationships among signs within a work.[18]

It is curious that Mallarmé's Great Work is described both as the "Orphic explication of the earth" and as "the literary game *par excellence.*" The former designation attributes to language a prophetic and creative power analogous to what Bruns calls the "Orphic" mode in poetry, and implies that the Book would have a radically referential function, "naming" the existing world in order to re-create it in the image of poetry. This conception of the poet's task is also implicit in Mallarmé's statement elsewhere that "the world is made to end in a beautiful Book" (*le monde est fait pour aboutir à un beau Livre*).[19]

The view of the Book's "Orphic" function seems quite distinct from its role as "literary game *par excellence*," which corresponds to what Bruns calls the "Hermetic" conception of poetry as a game of words transcendent in itself. Mallarmé insists elsewhere that the poetic work neither imitates nor adds to the world of objects and experience. Its role is to abstract from the world systems of pure relationships out of which a work of art can be constructed.[20] This would seem to be humbler project than the "Orphic explication of the earth," which gives the work power to transcend and replace the world. Yet both claims—the prophetic drive to explain and transcend the world through poetry and the insistence that the poet must confine his attention to purely formal relationships among words—coexist in Mallarmé's writings on poetry. This tension between two poetic goals is one source of the enigmatic combination of formal beauty and thematic opacity that characterizes Mallarmé's best and most difficult works.

If Mallarmé is so committed to the elimination of mere intelligibility, why does he continue to use the French language, the native language of the masses whose irreverence he so vehemently criticizes? Why does he not seek a purely architectonic form like that developed in the early twentieth century's "concrete poetry"—poetry whose sound and shape took precedence over meaning? Mallarmé's continued fidelity to French grammar and syntax is an essential part of his technique. Paradoxically, he exploits language's tendency to "mean" as one of a number of linguistic properties that must be revealed in the poet's effort to overcome referentiality. For Mallarmé, the referential meanings of words are due entirely to arbitrary convention or "chance" (*le hasard*), an entity that is beyond the poet's control. The pure form would present "le hasard vaincu mot par mot," chance defeated one word at a time, through the gradual construction of a work governed by its own internal laws.[21]

In its effort to "abolish chance" in this sense, Mallarmé's poetry employs a complex mixture of visual, auditory, spatial, and thematic effects that explication can only partly elucidate. His occasional writings on poetic technique do, however, suggest some of the methods by which a poet can hope to achieve a work that is at once "the Orphic explication of the Earth" and "the literary game *par excellence*."

The essay published under the title "Crise de vers" offers one of Mallarmé's most concise descriptions of the form a "pure work" would take. "The ideal," he writes, "would be a reasonable number of words stretched beneath our mastering glance, arranged in enduring figures, and followed by silence."[22] In this one sentence, Mallarmé touches on most of the techniques that determine his concept of poetry: he emphasizes the importance of typographic form, the appeal of the poem to the eye, and the interplay of words with silence.

The essay goes on to assert that the pure poem should have no personal voice that would distract from its architectonic form. Its words should be set in motion by their own internal imbalances (*par le heurt de leur in-égalité mobilisés*), not by the will of the poet. In practice, the poet must be guided by the demands of syntax and by the graphic and sonorous relations and differences among words. By thus exploiting the dynamic relationships inher-ent in language, Mallarmé hopes to bring about an art form motivated from within itself. The "collision" of words with one another and the rhythmic and sonorous effects that this produces will take the place of the driving personal emotion or the voice of Nature that motivated Romantic poetry. The beauty of the new poetry will be crystalline, pure: it will be like the glitter of firelight on the facets of precious stones, a beauty that comes about solely through the impersonal structural relationships of form to form, light to darkness.[23]

This interest in pure relationships among words is the basis for Mallarmé's preoccupation with analogies between poetry and the non-repre-sentational arts of music and architecture.[24] For him, music is a language based on relationships (*des rapports*), and uncontaminated by what he calls "l'universel reportage" of ordinary language. Poetry must strive, like music, to stress rela-tionships rather than meanings. It must bring to the reader's attention the sounds, shapes, and forms of the words, the rhythmic effect produced by the intervention of silence in poetic lines and by the movement of words across the page. By thus transposing musical techniques to language, the poet can hope to reveal a mysterious, primitive harmony that lies hidden within his words. Although he believes that the new poetry can learn a great deal from the structure of symphonic forms, Mallarmé insists that it will be a form superior to music. Poetry uses printed words on paper which, unlike performed music, do not fade over time. The written word, arranged and developed in relation-ships that imitate the symphony's variety of timbres and rhythms, is capable of creating a more enduring music, one that can be re-mobilized, in silence, with each fresh reading.[25]

Like music, then, the pure poem can only be related to the world of objects and experiences through its infinite "suggestiveness." Thus, to say the ordinary name of a known object in the context of pure poetry is to make of it something utterly new, to place it in a world of its own. In a well-known passage from "Crise de vers," Mallarmé claims that by pronouncing the name of a flower, "une fleur," he can remove that word from its function in everyday language and hence abolish its connection to any object to which it might have referred. The word becomes a pure sign independent of referentiality, "l'absente de tous bouquets."[26] By thus linking the name of a flower to an entity that is absent from the world of experience, the poet hopes to give that word a new function in a completely autonomous verbal universe.

It is clear, however, that such an absolute transposition of the everyday word into a universe of pure fictions is not possible so long as words retain their function as "names" of things in the common language. Even to understand the concept implied by "l'absente de tous bouquets," one needs to know what the usual referent of "fleur" is, and to understand the rules of ordinary French that make "fleur" the grammatical referent of "l'absente." In contrast to the musical note, the word always retains, as a kind of residue, the referential function that convention has assigned to it. Similarly, the relationships among words in a poem are necessarily governed in part by the same conventions of grammar and syntax that rule the language of "reportage." This conflict between the controlled, autonomous universe of words that the poet envisions and the conventions within which the same words usually function is evident in the closing paragraph of "Crise de vers":

> Out of a number of words, poetry fashions a single new word which is total in itself and foreign to the language—a kind of incantation. Thus the desired isolation of language is effected; and chance (which might still have governed these elements, despite their artful and alternating renewal through meaning and sound) is thereby instantly and thoroughly abolished. Then we realize, to our amazement, that we had never truly heard this or that ordinary poetic fragment; and, at the same time, our recollection of the object thus conjured up bathes in a totally new atmosphere.[27]

The new "total word," completely isolated from the existing language, is here presented as a triumph of poetry over "chance" (*le hasard demeuré aux termes*),[28] the conventional associations that contaminate the poet's materials and limit his control over his work. The final sentence of this paragraph, however, seems to contradict Mallarmé's claim that poetry can completely "abolish chance" in this sense. Here his allusion to the recollection of the object conjured up (*l'objet nommé*, the object *named*) reveals that the word cannot be utterly dissociated from the object it used to name. By focusing for a moment on the thing referred to rather than on the word itself, Mallarmé tacitly acknowledges that poetry cannot free itself entirely from the assumptions governing the language of denomination or reference. Because he continues to use the "contaminated" French language in the construction of his "pure" poetic works, Mallarmé is obliged to come to terms with this inevitable tendency of his words to retain "traces" of their function as names of objects and events.

The tension between the poet's drive to create a "pure work" on the one hand and the inevitable "intelligibility" of his materials on the other is a source of the rich mystery and formal beauty of Mallarmé's last complete work, *Un Coup de dés jamais n'abolira le hasard*. Although there seems to be little basis for assuming that he intended it to be his "Great Work,"[29] the poem does present some fascinating illustrations of Mallarmé's poetics of the "pure work" in action. The poet's struggle against "le hasard demeuré aux termes" here enters both the philosophical theme and the physical form of his work. The conflicts between typographic and syntactical forms, as between thematic and visual effects, reveal the paradoxical futility of the poet's continuous struggle to "defeat chance" by constructing an autonomous language.

The poem's physical appearance immediately reveals a fascination with the typographical form of words as "black marks on white." Groups of words are related to one another by distinct typefaces and by visual configurations that frequently disrupt syntax and distract our attention from the meanings of the words to the shapes that they form on the page. The title sentence, UN COUP DE DÉS JAMAIS N'ABOLIRA LE HASARD, unifies the poem both visually and thematically. Its large upper-case type provides a graphic focus around which all the other typographical "themes" in the poem organize themselves.[30] At the same time, the enigmatic meaning of this sentence provides a key to the poem's total significance. It proclaims in tautological fashion that chance will never be abolished by a single game of a chance, that a roll of the dice (*un coup de dés*) cannot defeat the chance which made it possible. The deeper poetic significance of this statement becomes clear if we recall Mallarmé's reference to the "chance" that poetry resists in its confrontation with ordinary language (*le hasard demeuré aux termes*). Though the form of the poem proclaims its attempt to construct something new out of words, the title sentence proclaims the ultimate futility of the work's linguistic act. Thus the work, a form constructed out of words, vainly attempts to resist the conventionality and arbitrariness by which those words exist in the language.

Between the words of this key sentence emerge the fragments of a narrative, recounted in language whose syntax is remarkably clear, despite the disruptive effect of typographical configurations and white spaces. Both thematically and visually, page 3 presents the first scene and the first stage of the poem's fragmentary narrative action. Here the white abyss of the sea opens to receive the sinking ship announced on page 2.[31] The shape of the lines on the page clearly repeats the steep drop into the abyss, and invites us to picture the sinking ship (*un naufrage*) poised on the edge of destruction:

    l'Abîme

blanchi
    étale
      furieux

        sous une inclinaison
          plane déséspérement

            d'aile

         la sienne
          par

              avance retombée d'un mal à dresser le vol
                  et couvrant les jaillissements
                  coupant au ras les bonds.
                 (*O.c.,* pp. 460–461)

The visual image of a drop into blackness, and other versions of this same shape—thin at the left, denser at the lower right—will recur in the poem for varying purposes. This image is repeated, for example, on page 7, where a plumed hat is described in the text, and on pages 10 and 11 where the "constellation" of the Great Bear will be described.

As page 3 set the scene, page 4 narrates the primary action of the poem's second "movement" in the sentence "LE MAITRE . . . hésite" (The Master . . . hesitates). The sentence structure and typographical form of this page deliberately disperse this central sentence, interrupting and covering the action that it narrates, so that the materiality of the text itself will seem more immediate than the events of the narrative. The most striking source of the fragmented effect is the separation of the subject, "LE MAITRE," from its predicate, "hésite." Because of this separation, the intervening phrases that modify "LE MAITRE," offering sketchy descriptions of his origins and purpose here, initially seem to be random parentheses. Meanwhile, the white spaces and typographical configurations create a symmetrical, winglike shape that repeats itself in the lower half of the page. This graphic symmetry contrasts markedly with the disorder in the production of sense on this page. The white spaces of the visual design and the median line of the page break up sentences and phrases when grammar and syntax demand most strenuously to keep words together. This contrast between fragmented syntax and balanced visual form forces the reader to notice the text for its own sake, and deliberately frustrates conventional efforts to "understand." At the same time, the syntax, while complex, is correct and decipherable, so that the reader is kept aware of a meaning that is struggling to escape, a "sens enseveli" or buried sense.[32]

This buried sense reveals the traces of a highly charged dramatic situation which is central to the narrative. "Le Maître," who has already been located at an ultimate moment (*dans les circonstances éternelles, du fond d'un naufrage* [p. 2]), hesitates before rolling the dice. As he does so, the dice clenched in his fist, we learn that he once controlled the ship, but has now lost control (*jadis il empoignait la barre*), and that his fate is inevitable. His fist, which once guided the tiller, now clutches the dice which can have no effect on his fate, but which he must nonetheless roll. As in *Igitur,* the protagonist here finds himself at a critical moment in which he becomes aware, during a prolonged hesitation, of his own existence and of the utter futility of his final act, a roll of the dice in vain resistance to "le hasard."[33]

But here, chance is more vividly symbolized by the white neutrality of the sea, which will swallow up Master and ship and leave no evidence that they ever existed. The words that trail off at the end of page 4,

naufrage cela
       direct de l'homme
           sans nef
            n'importe
             où vaine
          (*O.c.,* pp. 462–463),

stress the utter vanity of the action contemplated, and the inevitability of the shipwreck regardless of the Master's actions. The shape of these lines allows us to see the whiteness of the page "swallowing up" the text's effort to explain the master's gesture, just as the sea will swallow up the ship after the dice are rolled.

The Master's situation is presented in a new set of images on pages 7 and 8 of the poem, where the feather and the human figure associated with it take the place of the shipwreck and become the body that is suspended over the abyss. Several readers have noted that the feather, "la plume," which appears alone on the left half of page 7, is also a word for "pen," the instrument of writing.[34] On pages 7 and 8, Mallarmé conflates the "plume" with a new, younger hero-figure. The shape formed by the lines on this page repeat the shape of the plumed hat they describe; at the same time, one can discern an inkwell and quill pen:[35]

plume solitaire éperdue

> *sauf*
> > *que la rencontre ou l'effleure une toque de minuit*
> > *et immobilise*
> > *au velours chiffonné par un esclaffement sombre*

> > *cette blancheur rigide*
> *dérisoire*
> > *en opposition au ciel*
> *trop*
> > *pour ne pas marquer*
> > > *exigüment*
> > > > *quiconque*
> > *prince amer de l'écueil*
> > *s'en coiffe comme de l'héröique*
> > *irrésistible mais contenu*
> > *par sa petite raison virile*
> > > > *en foudre*

(O.c., pp. 468–469)

Both inkwell and black plumed hat are images of blackness against a white background. The subsequent emphasis on the hero's silhouette against the white sea, with its interest in blackness on white, suggests that this hero could be read as self-reflexive image for the text itself—blackness against white, set down by "une plume." The description of the plumed hat against sea and sky (beginning *cette blancheur rigide*) is particularly striking as a double image for the narrative situation and the graphic form of *Un Coup de dés*. The "blancheur rigide" of the feather opposing the white sky is also the white feather of a quill pen about to blot the whiteness of the page, and an image of an overblown masculinity, "une petite raison virile," trying to master something beyond its powers. Like the pen, the "blancheur rigide" "marks" the figure of the hero as a black spot which tries vainly to differentiate the whiteness surrounding it, to "impose a boundary on the infinite." The silhouettes of both hero and text are presented as futile efforts to organize an uncontrollable whiteness.[36]

With the appearance of "LE HASARD" on page 9, the narrative action of the poem is completed. The dice are rolled, and the feather/pen falls, to be overwhelmed by the uniform whiteness of the sea (*par la neutralité identique du gouffre*). The coincidence between the dropping of the feather and the sinking of the ship suggests a correspondence between the Master's futile act—the roll of the dice—and the poet's act of writing, which produced the poem called *Un Coup de dés*. This coincidence reveals the poem as an emblem for writing itself, which stops and is replaced by whiteness when the poem ends.

Once the ship/poem has been thus "dissolved," what can remain?[37] The final portion of the work, pages 10 and 11, suggest an image for the text itself—the CONSTELLATION. Both the meaning and the shape of the words on the last page focus on a constellation as an abstract configuration of black points against a white background, the exact negative of the "alphabet des astres" described in *L'Action restreinte*. The text's shape on page 11 repeats the shape that we saw on page 3, but now we recognize both as roughly approximating the shape of the "Septentrion" or "Great Bear" constellation:

EXCEPTÉ
   à l'altitude
      PEUT ÊTRE
        aussi loin qu'un
          endroit
            fusionne avec au-delà

            hors l'intérêt
            quant à lui signalé
                en général
        selon telle obliquité par telle déclivité
                  de feux

      vers
        ce doit être
          le Septentrion aussi Nord

                UNE CONSTELLATION

        froide d'oubli et de désuétude
            pas tant
            quelle n'énumère
     sur quelque surface vacante et supérieure
           le heurt successif
               sidéralement
       d'un compte total en formation
                   (*O.c.*, pp. 476–477)

Here the text, describing the "Septentrion" or Great Bear, refers to its own shape, and explains what is implied by a text that is also a constellation. The constellation is a pure form, the product of chance—produced by certain chance relationships between lights (*selon telle obliquité telle déclivité/de feux*). Like the text that shares its form, the constellation is impersonal. Cold, detached from the lives of mankind, it gives off the light of interstellar events that have taken place beyond memory, millennia before we see its light. It thus represents the preservation in space of a moment in time that is long over. It counts out a series of arbitrary relationships that once existed between adjacent stars and suspends them against a vacant background, much as the text suspends its black marks against white vacancy.[38] Most importantly, the constellation is still "in formation." Its form will never be fixed and determinate, for chance has already dissipated the configuration that we see in the sky now. It is the transitory index of chance events that continue and can never be completely controlled by a pure form.

For this reason, as Bruns, Cohn, and others have shown, the constellation is the epitome of the structure that Mallarmé's text strives to achieve. The text, black form against white, preserves on paper a series of relations in time and space which were once established in an act of writing.[39] This poetic act, now completed, is inscribed in the text, impersonally, on the level of the narrative as well as in the visual connection between the text and the constellation. Thematically, the constellation "survives" the sinking of the ship. It is aloof from this event, yet it was present during the narrative action and persists after it.[40] The correspondence between text and constellation developed in the form of the last page suggests that we should see the text, too, as a "survivor." It was there to record the last moment of Master and ship, which was also the last moment of an act of writing. But it persists after the act of writing is completed, as an entity having its own shape and its own rules, free of the writer's intention or thought. In the text as constellation, there is no trace of the originating inspiration or thought which motivated the act of writing; all we have is the poem, *Un Coup de dés,* which presents itself as a product of chance (*le hasard*), constructed in resistance to chance.

The last line's announcement that "Every thought gives off a roll of the dice" (*Toute Pensée émet un Coup de Dés*), however, admits that the poem originated in an experience outside of language and is thus rooted in the ordinary world of "chance." The fact that C and D in this last line are in the upper case suggests that we are to take "Un Coup de Dés" as a reference to the poem's own title, and an acknowledgement of its origins in thought. The last line thus undercuts the autonomy of the text as constellation by announcing that the poem has told, in spite of itself, the story of its own creation. It has recorded the experience that engendered it by narrating the story of the Master and his dice and by equating the roll of the dice with the poem's appearance. Thus it has not completely overcome "chance" because it still refers beyond itself to a "real" experience: the act of writing *Un Coup de dés,* an act that began before the poem took shape.

Nevertheless, to the extent that the poem comes to resemble the surviving constellation in its form and structure, it succeeds in "transcending" momentarily the human experience of writer and audience, and creates a unique formal language of its own. The poem thus approaches Mallarmé's ideal of an opaque language of pure forms, "black on white," a language that has freed itself from the world of experience and convention to become "transcendent in itself."

The poem's status as an "approach to" or "approximation of" Mallarmé's poetic ideal is the quality that allies it most interestingly to the problem of ineffability in literature. By its effort to "resist chance" in Mallarmé's terms, the poem resists the conventional role of language as a mediator of ideas. Instead, the work's primary goal is to express *itself* as an ineffable ideal. This ideal is ultimately unattainable because the poetic purity suggested by the poem's form and by the self-reflexive image of the constellation remains beyond the reach of "contaminated" linguistic materials. The narrative embedded in this intricate formal structure tells of the vain struggle by which the poet created the work. It thus shows that even the "purest" poetic form must recount, in spite of itself, the story of its own creation; it must "refer to" and "mediate" the story of its own origins in a human experience. Thus, *Un Coup de dés* is a poem of ineffability because it gestures toward a purity of form that remains beyond the reach of its linguistic materials. In spite of itself, the poem acknowledges its bondage to the earthbound, chance-governed "language of the crowd," from which all poetic language is borrowed, and to which even the "purest" poetry must ultimately return.

NOTES

1. *Modern Poetry and the Idea of Language: a Critical and Historical Study* (New Haven and London: Yale Univ. Press, 1974), pp. 1–3.
2. Bruns, p.1.
3. Bruns, esp. pp. 73–74, 96–98 and 101–117. For another perspective on the relation of Mallarmé's thought to contemporary criticism, see Gérard Genette, "Valéry and the Poetics of Language," in Josué V. Harrari, ed., *Textual Strategies: Perspectives in Post-Structuralist Criticism* (Ithaca: Cornell Univ. Press, 1979), originally published as "Valéry et la poétique du langage," *MLN,* 87 (1972).
4. Bruns, p. 98. My reading of Mallarmé is indebted in important ways to Bruns's chapter on Mallarmé, pp. 101-117. In particular, I follow him in stressing the poet's interest in developing an autonomous language, and in studying the importance of typograpy in *Un Coup de dés.*
5. Henri Mondor and G. Jean-Aubry, eds., *Mallarmé: Oeuvres complètes* (Paris: Gallimard, 1945), p. 333. Cf. Bradford Cook, trans., *Mallarmé: Prose Poems, Essays and*

Letters (Baltimore and London: Johns Hopkins Univ. Press, 1956), p. 69. Further references to these works will be abbreviated "*O.c*" and "Cook", respectively.

6. Idem.

7. Although Mallarmé does not himself use the term "pure sign," I feel that this phrase best describes the autonomous, impersonalized word described in "Solennité," one of the units making up what Mallarmé elsewhere calls the "pure work" (*O.c., 366*—"l'ouevre pur"). The term "pure sign" looks forward to Valéry's "pure poetry," which is closely related to Mallarmé's poetic project. See Valéry, *The Art of Poetry,* trans. Denise Folliot (New York: Pantheon Books, 1958), pp. 184-192.

8. *O.c.,* 257; Cook, 9.

9. Cook, 31. Cf. *O.c.,* 384: "... plutôt que tendre le nuage, précieux, flottant sur l'intime gouffre de chaque pensée".

10. Cook, 30, translates "un encrier sans nuit"—an inkwell without darkness—as "nightless well." Cf. the original passage in *O.c.,* 383: "Les individus, à son avis, ont tort ... parce qu'ils puisent à quelque encrier sans Nuit la vaine couche suffisante d'intelligibilité que lui s'oblige, aussi, à observer, mais pas seule. ..."

11. *O.c.,* pp. 369-373.

12. "L'encrier, cristal comme une conscience, avec sa goutte, au fond, de ténèbres relative à ce que quelque chose soit" (*O.c.,* 370).

13. Cf. Idem: "Tu remarquas, on n'écrit pas, lumineusement, sur champ obscur, l'alphabet des astres, seul, ainsi s'indique, ébauché ou interrompu; l'homme poursuit noir sur blanc."

14. *O.c.,* 370. "with the faint trace of mystery which remains, expressed, just a bit."

15. *The Word and Verbal Art,* ed. and trans. John Burbank and Peter Steiner (New Haven and London, Yale Univ. Press, 1977), p. 8.

16. Cf. Bruns, p. 106.

17. Cf. *O.c.,* 380; Cook, 26-27.

18. *O.c.,* 662; Cook, 15.

19. *O.c.,* 872, Cook 24.

20. *O.c.,* 871; Cook 23-24.

21. *O.c.,* 387.

22. Cook, p. 38. Cf. *O.c.,* 364: "Qu'une moyenne étendue de mots, sous la compréhension du regard, se range en traits définitifs, avec quoi le silence."

23. *O.c.,* 366.

24. On the relationship of music to language in Symbolist thought, cf. Joseph Chiari, *Symbolisme from Poe to Mallarmé* (London: Rockliff, 1956), p. 44; Anna Balakian, *The Symbolist Movement: A Critical Appraisal* (New York: Random House, 1967). pp. 86-88, Susanne Bernard, *Mallarmé et la musique* (Paris: Nizet, 1959), p. 153, and Bruns, pp. 101-17.

25. *O.c.,* 367-8; Cook, 42-43.

26. *O.c.,* 368; Cook, 42.

27. Cook, 43. Cf. *O.c.,* 368: "Le vers qui de plusieurs vocables refait un mot total, neuf, étranger à la langue et comme incantatoire, achève cet isolement de la parole: niant, d'un trait souverain, le hasard demeuré aux termes malgré l'artifice de leur retrempe alterné en le sens et la sonorité, et vous cause cette surprise de n'avoir oui jamais tel fragment ordinaire d'élocution, en même temps que la réminiscence de l'objet nommé baigne dans une neuve atmosphère."

28. See previous note. Literally, "the chance that adheres to the words."

29. Jacques Schérer's *Le "Livre" de Mallarmé: recherches sur des documents inédits* (Paris: Gallimard, 1957) suggests that Mallarmé was planning another work, quite different

in form and scope from *Un Coup de dés,* which was in fact the projected "Great Work." A good summary of the ongoing critical debate over this issue appears in Robert Greer Cohn, *Mallarmé's Masterwork: New Findings* (The Hague: Mouton, 1957), pp. 13–20.

30. Bernard develops convincingly the analogy between the typefaces of the poem and the "themes" of a symphony. See pp. 24–27, 55–57, 94–95, 147.

31. "Page" numbers refer to the double pages, 1–11, which are the clearest subdivisions of the poem. The poem is printed on pp. 457–477 in *O.c.*

32. *O.c.,* 372. "Impersonnifié, le volume, autant qu'on s'en sépare comme auteur, ne réclame approche de lecteur. Tel, sache, entre les accessoires humains, il a lieu tout seul: fait, étant. Le sens enseveli se meut et dispose, en choeur, les feuillets."

33. The best studies of *Igitur* and of its relationship to *Un Coup de dés* appear in Maurice Blanchot, *L'Espace littéraire* (Paris: Gallimard, 1955), pp. 133–149; Gardner Davies, *Vers une explication rationelle du Coup de dés* (Paris: Librairie José Corti, 1953), and Paul de Man, "Mallarmé, Yeats and the Post-Romantic Predicament," Diss., Harvard, 1960, pp. 84–91.

34. Cf. Robert G. Cohn, *L'Oeuvre de Mallarmé: Un Coup de dés* (Paris: Librairie des lettres, 1951), pp. 250–253.

35. Cohn, *L'Oeuvre de Mallarmé,* pp. 251, 254–255. See also David Hayman, *Joyce et Mallarmé: stylistique de la suggestion* (Paris: Lettres modernes, 1956), pp. 110–112.

36. On the role of the white spaces in Mallarmé, see also Jacques Derrida, "La Double Séance," in *La Dissémination* (Paris: Editions du Seuil, 1972), pp. 201–317. Cf. p. 11 of the poem:

> *un roc*
>
> *faux manoir*
>> *tout de suite*
>>> *évaporé en brumes*
>>
>> *qui imposa*
>>> *une borne à l'infini*
>>>> (*O.c.,* p. 471)

37. Cf., in a slightly different context, de Man, p. 129.

38. Cohn, *L'Oeuvre de Mallarmé,* p. 408.

39. Cf. Bruns, p. 117; A. R. Chisholm, *Mallarmé's "Grand Oeuvre"* (Manchester: The University Press, 1962), p. 96; Cohn, *L'Oeuvre,* pp. 387–420 and *Mallarmé's Masterwork,* p. 18.

40. This is expressed in the "coda" of the poem on pp. 10 and 11, which reads "RIEN/N'AURA EU LIEU/QUE LE LIEU/EXCEPTE/PEUT-ETRE/UNE CONSTELLATION" (Literally: Nothing will have taken place but the place, except, perhaps, a constellation). See Cohn, *L'Oeuvre,* p. 389.

Tongued with Fire:
The Primitive Terror and The Word
in T. S. Eliot

Heather McClave

And what the dead had no speech for, when living,
They can tell you, being dead: the communication
Of the dead is tongued with fire beyond the language of the living.
("Little Gidding")[1]

In the poetry of T. S. Eliot, the ineffable remains a mystery of absolute being which both precedes and fulfills human speech. Intuited in terms of the cosmic perspective of *Four Quartets,* it is at once the "primitive terror" described in "The Dry Salvages"—the primal element behind all memory, all recorded history—and the Word beyond language that embodies ultimate meaning. What seems at first too sordid and dangerous to contemplate as an aspect of Prufrock's "overwhelming question" becomes, in Eliot's later, more orthodox view, an intimation of Grace: a revelation of Love and Truth; the beginning and the end; the source of Incarnation and the mode towards which all created forms evolve.

"It is impossible to say just what I mean!" Prufrock exclaims, introducing a particularly subjective version of ineffability that continues to be a major concern throughout Eliot's work. Initially, in an early poem such as this "Love Song," the failure of adequate speech may seem largely a matter of individual character and aesthetics, of a weak man in an ugly world. In "Gerontion," it may seem a matter of constricted experience. By the opening section of *The Waste Land,* however, where we see that essential responses to life are disen-gaged or frozen, as in the hyacinth garden ("I could not/Speak, and my eyes failed, I was neither/Living nor dead . . . "), the inability to speak and the depletion of common language become manifest limits of the human condition.

Throughout his career, Eliot struggles at length with both the content and the form of the ineffable, making a gradual transition from a subjective to a visionary point of view. His focus shifts from a moral horror at the nastiness

163

and futility of human desire to an awesome sense of a transcendent conver-
gence of temporal and eternal reality—a crucial movement from the unspeakable to the inexpressible.

II. The Primitive Terror

I have said before
That the past experience revived in the meaning
Is not the experience of one life only
But of many generations—not forgetting
Something that is probably quite ineffable:
The backward look behind the assurance
Of recorded history, the backward half-look
Over the shoulder, towards the primitive terror.
("The Dry Salvages")

Even in his late verse, as in the passage from "The Dry Salvages" cited
above, Eliot still associates the ineffable at least partly with inchoate origins,
though by then he has learned to link beginnings to ends, and to accustom
himself, as he says in his essay on Dante, "to find meaning in *final causes* rather
than in origins."[2] These final causes, to be sure, involve something equally
ineffable—the universal attraction towards God—but they depend on a different
perspective of life. Instead of taking their bearings from a time before the
creation of language, they emerge through the eternal Word of God as realized
in the Scriptures and in the Person of Christ. Yet until Eliot adopts this comprehensive view of final causes, he holds fast to an exceptionally grim and fatalistic
sense of origins.

The opening epigraph of the original *Waste Land* manuscript, featuring the
death of Kurtz in *Heart of Darkness,* ends with what in this context (as in Conrad)
seems to be a definitive apprehension of something appalling in the species:
"The horror! the horror!"[3] Eliot's major early poems, "The Love Song of J.
Alfred Prufrock," "Gerontion," and *The Waste Land,* proceed from a comparable judgment taken from a "backward half-look/ . . . towards the primitive
terror" while the terror still seems palpably close, chaotic, and private—not yet
incorporated into the larger scheme of shared experience and accessible meaning that he affirms in *Four Quartets.* The nameless retrospective horror that he
first presents, moderating hysterical fear through prim distaste, suggests the
reaction of a man who assumes that he has already seen or suspected too much,
and who dreads that he needs more than the world can provide—a man of
disappointed expectations, coming of age as his culture breaks down. The
studied desiccation of such figures as Prufrock, Gerontion, and Tiresias and
their haunted aspect of déjà vu carry the sense of those unspeakable dark
depths welling up to a fragile surface, the verge of expression.

Lyrically passive and insular in a manner reminiscent of Keats and Tenny-
son, the worlds of these poems reflect the conflicting needs that we associate

with personal and cultural adolescence. Here, the longing for continued dependence is coupled with the resentment of external control, while the desire for
adult prerogatives is infused with fear. These tensions, which are so sexually
charged, threaten disaster whether they are exposed or repressed. The uneasy
calm one may achieve by expressing feelings at a calculated distance—as
through personae, dogmatic satire, and indirect speech—is a self-imposed version of order, based on the sense (and the latent hope) that options have
narrowed and that choices are final. In a letter to Paul Elmer More dated
"Shrove Tuesday, 1928," shortly after his formal conversion to Anglo-Catholi-
cism in 1927, Eliot gives a particularly striking image of the abysmal depths that
seem to undermine his attempts to reach out beyond the self, pointing to

> the void that I find in the middle of all human happiness and all human relations,
> and which there is only one thing to fill. I am one whom this sense of void tends
> to drive toward asceticism or sensuality, and only Christianity helps to reconcile
> me to life, which is otherwise disgusting.[4]

This void, it would appear, is a personal rendering of the general primitive
terror—where *center* ("the void . . . in the middle") corresponds to original *source*
—and is equally ineffable. Like the great void in Genesis, it requires the action
of the Word to fill it, to make it substantial. Yet Eliot's categorical pronounce-
ment, that treats perceptions as though they were permanent facts, disguises
the driving force behind this experience of emptiness: a desperate hunger for
satisfying relationships that voids the heart of contact, a hunger that renounces
what it craves by insisting that life is both insufficient and tainted. Eliot's term,
"disgusting," recalls the fastidious hostility towards women so evident in "Prufrock," "Portrait of a Lady," and the puerile couplets on Fresca excised from
the *Waste Land* manuscript.[5] In these poems, where women serve as objects of
desire and thus as examples of what life affords, they, too, are characterized
as dangerous voids, somehow alluring but essentially sickening—even fatal, as
the detail of twisting the lilac stalks in "Portrait of a Lady" suggests.[6]

At this stage in Eliot's career, the void remains a fixed center of existence,
ominously compelling and in that sense empowering. However Christianity
may help "reconcile" the poet to what he sees, it does not seem either to reveal
that world more fully or to redeem it. What is missing so tangibly here, what
the poet fails to feel or imagine, is an available otherness he can touch and be
nourished by, an otherness he will later find provided by the Christian doctrine
of Incarnation. Being like ourselves but different, Christ offers an image of
relating to the world without losing a particular identity. To accept otherness
as part of ourselves—the difficult communion Eliot undertakes in "Ash-
Wednesday"—we must forgo our attempts to formulate reality on our own
terms; otherwise, we merely reproduce what we already know and are. This
process of disillusionment is hard enough. Beyond that, however, we must
actively seek a common language, as Eliot seeks the resonance of universal

images so as to have a sense of contact with the actual world. For the poet, this awareness of viable shared speech, strictly purified, leads to a belief in a further fusion with the Word. In this way, over time, the private void appears not only full but also integral as part of the cosmic "still point of the turning world."

Eliot's early intimations of negative ineffability, defined both as the basal "primitive terror" and as a central void, seem to necessitate a strategic distance from these primal sources. Instead of delving into the terror or the void, he focuses on what succeeds or surrounds them: "tradition" and its culminating "meaning"; the impersonality of the poet and "objective correlatives" for his feelings. In essence, he uses implicative language not only to describe, but also to contain and thus to overcome what seems unspeakable.

Characteristically, Eliot begins in the middle of history, presenting the self as an aspect of tradition—as a certain point of view, a voice, an impulse, an aggregate of experience in the midst of an established, informing vision and speech. Surveying the modern predicament, he combines a Puritan sense of the Fall with late Victorian fatigue, judging the time long past for simple innocence or spontaneous innovation. Tradition precedes us with the pressure of its lessons and obligations, its ways of rendering the world. Tradition overtakes us and all that we do, as the composite whole absorbs the part. Whatever we say draws on prior references and belongs to the larger speech of the tribe; and inevitably, we transmit more than we understand. Yet words themselves seem worn out, inadequate, showing through, at perilous moments, to an underlying void of meaninglessness.

However vulnerable they may appear as entities—indeed because of such vulnerability—self and tradition are treated as permanent facts of life. Until the *Ariel* poems, these givens seem both rigid and inscrutable, with personality fixed in the obsessively repetitive patterns of "Prufrock," "Gerontion," *The Waste Land,* and "The Hollow Men," while the past surfaces as a recital of echoes. Even such remnants of speech seem more real and recognizable than the disembodied personae that apply them, for we can identify a context of meaning in regard to Biblical citations, or Hamlet, or Mylae. By contrast, the speakers themselves, fleetingly evoked through literary pastiche, show little evidence of a depth of internal structure and direction which would qualify as character. Instead, they remain local figures, instances of human consciousness that fade, if not into a coherent body of literature tantamount to the Word, at least into some general system of reference.

The merging of these personae into world literature, which effects a kind of transcendence through connotation, parallels the role Eliot sets out for the artist in regard to tradition in a definitive essay of this period, "Tradition and the Individual Talent." What happens to the artist, he says, "is a continual surrender of himself as he is at the moment to something which is more valuable. The progress of an artist is a continual self-sacrifice, a continual extinction of personality."[7] Here, it seems, he restates his sense of a personal void and of relationships as being inherently annihilating in terms of an artistic imperative. An obvious comparison may be instructive: where Keats in his apposite remarks on "Negative Capability" and "the camelion Poet" praises the receptive freedom of "being in uncertainties" and the adaptive freedom of "filling some other Body,"[8] Eliot stresses the sacrificial duty of dying, again and again, not into the world at large, but rather into the discrete canon sanctioned by the past.

We must examine Eliot's cycle of surrender with special care. Although his apparent emphasis is on progressive self-effacement, moving from "surren-der" to "self-sacrifice" to "extinction," his latent reluctance to lose himself entirely becomes clear with his insistence on the momentary ("himself as he is *at the moment*") and recurrent ("continual") nature of this encounter with otherness.[9] Art, as well as any instinct for survival, requires a functioning separate self. The understated aspect of this drive towards self-destruction, which keeps the process "continual," is the vital rebound of a private identity affirmed as itself—perhaps even reconstituted—through its contact with tradi-tion. At some point, Eliot seems to resist his strategy to fill up the inner void so as to feel vicariously alive, whether through tradition or Christianity. Instead, he positions himself somewhere between these poles of subject and object, maintaining a separate speech, and perpetually dying in place.

Throughout the early poetry, the givens of self and tradition, identity and inheritance, are treated more like burdens pressed upon unwilling witnesses than like providential opportunities. It seems that everything that matters has happened irrevocably, but that no one can tell what it means. Everyone knows too much, and wishes it were otherwise—better to have been a "pair of ragged claws" as in "Prufrock," or "Dull roots" in "The Burial of the Dead," than to let the weight of unassimilated knowledge lead to the kind of "overwhelming question" that is prompted in "Prufrock" and posed in "Gerontion": "After such knowledge, what forgiveness?" Can we be relieved of our claustrophobic self-consciousness? In the face of a past that will incorporate all that we do, what purpose and what outcome can our efforts have? When the speech of the dead is pure fire, as the epigraph to "Prufrock" taken from the *Inferno* suggests and "Little Gidding" confirms, what muddy words can we use?

The fragmentary dramatic monologues that Eliot presents, however laden with references, force us to recognize the limits of world literature reduced to a single point of view or to a single poem. Indeed, though the poems reach out to the larger tradition, the self-conscious irony used in their approach makes the contrast disappointing, so that we often miss more than we find in the work at hand.

In "Prufrock" especially, the allusive language of the speaker seems more a diversion than a source, a refracting surface meant to conceal the pressure of the unsaid by camouflaging basic obsessions—a desperate yearning for contact thwarted by an equally desperate fear of being engulfed; a sense of worthlessness combined with a defensive fascination with the self as an object. Still, despite the decorous manner of the poem, strange and faintly ominous pockets of speech turn up in unexpected places like a running commentary on Prufrock's situation: streets that serve as "muttering retreats" and "that follow like a tedious argument"; an omnipresent "overwhelming question"; the women "Talking of Michelangelo"; those who "will say: 'How his hair is growing thin!'"; "the voices dying with a dying fall"; "The eyes that fix you in a formulated phrase"; "the mermaids singing, each to each"; the "human voices" that wake him at the end. Significantly, we never hear specific words unless the matter is trivial, for the content is suppressed while the process of speaking continues: "Oh, do not ask, 'What is it?'/Let us go and make our visit."

As far as we can gauge it, the ineffable in this case seems primarily an internal matter consisting of what Prufrock wants to avoid saying. The premise behind his chronic evasions, I think, belies his timid appearance: the sense that, if he were to speak, something absolute would happen—the word would be true, and he, by proclaiming it, would be powerful. This interpretation allows a different reading of what sounds at first like Prufrock's double frustration of feeling more than words can express and trying to use language precisely: "It is impossible to say just what I mean!" Taken literally, saying what one means would break down the careful division between inside and outside, between the self assumed to be real and the outer world depicted as a conditional projection—much like "death's dream kingdom" in "The Hollow Men." For Prufrock, clearly, this exposure would be too revealing—"as if a magic lantern threw the nerves in patterns on a screen"—because it would realize the self at the cost of relinquishing the dream.

While "Portrait of a Lady" resembles "Prufrock" in form and theme, it marks a crucial shift in attitude towards viewing the world external to the self as real and separate, and accepting a place in a process beyond one's control. The speaker, in short, joins life as it is, though at the safest possible distance: for while he evokes a much more fully realized other (the Lady) than Prufrock, he also takes a more conspicuously distinct refuge in his own mind. Closely observed for clues, life in these terms seems a journalistic narrative undercut at moments by the perceiver's self-awareness: "Inside my brain a dull tom-tom begins/Absurdly hammering a prelude of its own"; "I feel like one who smiles, and turning shall remark/Suddenly, his expression in a glass." *Expression,* certainly, is a crucial issue in the poem as the self-absorbed, nervously ironic young man listens to the orchestrated conversation of the Lady who embodies the tradition he must face. Soon he, too, must learn to speak, to give himself up to public custom and scrutiny, to take the chance of wanting to be understood. That prospect terrifies him, since such expansion depends on language, and the language adopted to describe life seems to belong to it, forcing him into a crude protean mimicry of what he sees:

And I must borrow every changing shape
To find expression . . . dance, dance
Like a dancing bear,
Cry like a parrot, chatter like an ape.[10]

In "Gerontion," however, the scale and import of expression radically enlarge as Eliot channels archetypal history, the objectivity we contrive by connecting multiple points of view, through the pure subjectivity of "a wilderness of mirrors." Instead of trying to suit expression either to personal phantasy, as in "Prufrock," or to life's appearances, as in "Portrait of a Lady," the speaker in this poem grounds his language in general experience where both aspects may coincide: "Here I am, an old man in a dry month,/Being read to by a boy, waiting for rain." There is a new quality in these lines, a sense of persistent concentration, as though life and thought had settled into their most elemental forms. Later, when applied to the spirit, this sense leads to the incantational clarity of "Ash-Wednesday." Both poems, in different ways, work through profound resignation towards what Eliot calls in "Little Gidding" "A condition of complete simplicity/(Costing not less than everything)"—a condition of absolute being.

The heightened objectivity apparent in the content of "Gerontion," which gives glimpses of human life throughout recorded history, uses words to represent *facts* as well as perceptions: "Rock, moss, stonecrop, iron, merds." The life accepted as fact becomes a matter of the larger history to be validated from without the self as part of a natural process. Questions still arise, as in "Prufrock" and "Portrait of a Lady," but here they are real, rather than rhetorical, forcing us to look outside ourselves for greater resources of meaning: "After such knowledge, what forgiveness?" And a related question, phrased as an anatomy of experience, details the personal cost of endurance:

I have lost my passion: why should I need to keep it
Since what is kept must be adulterated?
I have lost my sight, smell, hearing, taste and touch:
How should I use them for your closer contact?[11]

Once established, the world of fact and the language that describes it seem increasingly inconsequential. Given what we have seen and become, where we can no longer help ourselves and where we count our lives as losses, what remains?

With "Gerontion," Eliot brings in for the first time a reverent view of Incarnation as an intrinsic part of our history, so that factual speech partakes of certain truth even as the deteriorating cycle of nature partakes of eternal life:

The word within a word, unable to speak a word,
Swaddled with darkness. In the juvescence of the year
Came Christ the tiger[12]

Hidden yet implicit, the silent word suggests another dimension of ineffability
that redeems and contains the primitive terrors we struggle to conceal. In effect,
the generative Word replaces the degenerative void at the center of all expressive life, providing a new and fully integral focus of meaning. Language in
this context is no longer merely expressive or descriptive: it is an inspired sign,
the embodiment of mystery. Thus the ineffable we know from within gains
both a deeper source and an ultimate referent in God; and between that
beginning and that end, it also gains an articulate medium.

Eliot sets out the same issues in *The Waste Land* as in "Gerontion," but
bases the poem in a complex of anthropological and religious symbolism
instead of in an individual speaker. By converting the dramatic monologue to
a loose medley of voices, he breaks down both the authority of a single
perceiving consciousness and the generic forms—such as Culture, Society, and
History—it may presume to know. The question of meaning becomes all the
more pressing on this chaotic plane which resembles some pre-Apocalyptic
limbo outside natural time and thus removed from the possibilities of change.
Here again the inner Word is hidden, while ostensible language is scattered into
different voices, dialects, and codes. Elusive images, like the detritus of the
human race pictured in "East Coker" as "old stones that cannot be deci-
phered," point to once-valued instances and systems the significance of which
has been lost or forgotten: the natural cycle; the testimony of the prophets; a
private moment of passion; the historical past; soothsaying; literature and
myth; religion. Yet connections between these aspects seem, at most, arbitrarily
imposed.

The ineffable makes its presence felt throughout *The Waste Land* both in
terms of what is left unsaid and in terms of what remains inexplicable. Pressing
though still obscure, the source of the ineffable seems to hover precariously
between Word and void. Silent figures, such as Phlebas the Phoenician, and
speechless figures, such as the man in the hyacinth garden and the beleaguered
husband in "A Game of Chess" ("Speak to me. Why do you never speak.
Speak."), haunt the poem with a passivity that suggests a primary failure of
vitality and will. Like Prufrock and Gerontion, these figures stay self-absorbed
instead of looking for more compelling answers to their lives in the surrounding
world. Their failure to act manifests itself as a failure to speak where speech,
in the context of major religious traditions, has been valid and transforming.
In this lapse they seem allied to the Grail heroes examined by Jesse Weston
in *From Ritual to Romance,* who by neglecting to ask about the nature or purpose
of the Grail lose the opportunity to heal the ailing Fisher King and to restore
his ruined land:

If you had found the word to say,
The rich king who in distress does lay
Would of his wound be fully healed.
. . . .
Ladies sad will lose their mates,
The land in desolation lie . . .[13]

Ask at all, the moral plainly goes, and ye shall receive. Yet the situation implies
still more: say, and ye shall empower and create; say, and ye shall relate directly
to the world; say, and ye shall be fulfilled.

A variant of saying nothing that makes *The Waste Land* especially painful
to read is saying nothing worthwhile, not communicating, using a cryptic or
casual language that reflects the degradation of speech:

'What shall I do now? What shall I do?'
'I shall rush out as I am, and walk the street
'With my hair down, so. What shall we do tomorrow?
. . . .
You ought to be ashamed, I said, to look so antique.
(And her only thirty-one.)
I can't help it, she said, pulling a long face,
It's them pills I took, to bring it off, she said.[14]

As Sweeney aptly notes in "Fragment of Agon,"

I gotta use words when I talk to you
But if you understand or if you dont
That's nothing to me and nothing to you[15]

Despite the widespread dislocation of language in *The Waste Land,* the
potential for meaning inheres in the words themselves and in what they allu-
sively symbolize. Like the physical world and the people that Eliot depicts,
words seem dormant rather than dead, implicative yet opaque. The essentials
of life and myth remain even in this extremity of insular solipsism, waiting,
available for whatever renewed sense of purpose and vision we might have:

In this decayed hole among the mountains
In the faint moonlight, the grass is singing
Over the tumbled graves, about the chapel
There is the empty chapel, only the wind's home.[16]

These things, which are either rubble or the coordinates of vision—nothing or
everything in absolute terms—press us to consider as a possibility a traditional
view that Emerson, for one, declares to be the truth in his famous essay,
"Nature": that words are signs of natural facts, which themselves are signs of
spiritual facts. Words, then, through natural symbolism, can give us a lease on

a higher dimension of ineffability suggested in the lines above by "singing" and "the wind's home," examples of the act and source of ultimate inspiration. The attitude Eliot allows here, which he promotes more forcefully in the Ganga section that follows with its commandments of "Give," "Sympathize," "Control," sees a heightened significance in the world beyond what we need and use, and adopts a posture of responsible reverence.

To the eye of faith, the confusion of order and value apparent in the poem can have a different bearing. As Eliot remarks in a footnote to his essay of 1928, "Second Thoughts about Humanism," "to the Greek there was something inexplicable about (*logos*) so that it was a participation of man in the divine."[17] "Inexplicable," a word that seems logically this side of the ineffable while leading into it, appears earlier in a related context in *The Waste Land*:

> where the walls
> Of Magnus Martyr hold
> Inexplicable splendour of Ionian white and gold.[18]

Understood in this way, words are not merely a medium of human communication, but also an introduction to the ultimate mysteries prefigured by the Church. Against this background, the "inviolable voice" of Philomel—another martyr rarefied through her afflictions—carries further reverberations. Philomel, having had her tongue torn out to prevent her from speaking about her rape, represents most graphically the mutilated state of human expression that the poem both describes and protests. Yet there is hope as well as loss in her example, for her forced "change" from speaking to singing parallels the "sea-change" of Phlebas the Phoenician intimated in the line taken from Ariel's Song in *The Tempest*, "Those are pearls that were his eyes," which concludes,

> Nothing of him that doth fade
> But doth suffer a sea-change
> Into something rich and strange.[19]

Though *The Waste Land* points towards final things on many levels, its main concern is with a process of purgation that makes dying in some form a precondition to higher life—whether dying outwardly by fire or water, or dying inwardly by fear. Such lyrical descriptions as those of Philomel, Magnus Martyr, and Phlebas show us "something rich and strange," further incarnations of ourselves with otherness, that still lie ahead. The task set for the rest of us, however, is to prepare for the literal and metaphoric *conversion* of our very being by learning to understand meaningful speech; by speaking purposefully ("These fragments I have spelt into my ruins," the original manuscript reads)[20]; by acting on the authoritative words of the past—such as those of the thunder—that we receive; and by aspiring—as Eliot does in what he calls the only "good" lines in the poem, "the water-dripping song in the last part"[21]—to

incantation. *The Waste Land* ends at the beginning of this prospect, with fragments shored against ruins and with some hope of resolve; yet the fragments
massed together do not body forth the missing Word, and what hope there is
does not stare down the horror.

III. The Perfect Order of Speech

Out of the sea of sound the life of music,
Out of the slimy mud of words, out of the sleet and hail of
    verbal imprecisions,
Approximate thoughts and feelings, words that have taken
    the place of thoughts and feelings,
There spring the perfect order of speech, and the beauty
    of incantation.

("Choruses from the Rock")

The sense of the void never really leaves Eliot, whether he tries to fill it,
deny it, instruct it, incorporate it, or relinquish it to the offices of Grace. He will
continue to say in various ways what he states so fully in "The Dry Salvages":
"We had the experience but missed the meaning"; and he will continue to
search for the meaning. The quality and direction of that search change dramatically, however, as he commits himself to the Christian faith and appears at
once to embrace the world more intimately and to renounce some of his early
hopes for intense human contact and passion. Perhaps, as an older man, Eliot
grows into the persona he adopted while young (which was prematurely mid-
dle-aged), so that the facts of his life catch up with his projections of it. If this
is true, he then becomes real to himself and less subject to his assumptions; in
particular, he can justify his lingering sense of surviving after better times have
passed while subordinating it to his conviction that the Incarnation has transformed all time into Eternity.

With the *Ariel Poems* and "Ash-Wednesday," Eliot's poetry makes a definitive break with the static, claustrophobic atmosphere of subjective dependency
that seems so oppressive in such works as "Prufrock," "Gerontion," and *The
Waste Land*. It is as though the author has let go of the need to hold on to
everything at once, and can now allow more of life to flow through him. As
a consequence of this detachment, he can enjoy the world as a revelation in
its own terms and attend to the vividness and transience of particulars without
trying to contain them in a cumulative question or image. He can speak in his
own voice as a man of experience with a deeper tone (anticipated by "Pre-
ludes") of active suffering and compassion, not as one merely passing the time
in a local interlude, but as a vital part of an organic whole.

One of the most striking aspects of the shift in Eliot's sensibility is the
transition from what Northrop Frye calls disparagingly "the mythology of
decline" to the avowal of a creative process of general evolution that prompts
and completes the development of all things on a vertical plane.[22] As the

epigraph to this section shows, the articulated word, inspirited by "the life of music," gives form to human thoughts and feelings, and by embodying them as art replaces and improves them as "the perfect order of speech." Refined in a similar way because equally directed towards God, the instinctive "life of music" resolves into the conscious "beauty of incantation." Of course this perspective involves human evolution as well: for language and the self, fused in the literal Word, the Person of Christ, undergo a comparable purification as superficial traits, or "personality," recede into a progressive definition of eternal essence.

"The detail of the pattern is movement," Eliot tells us in "Burnt Norton," and for much of the time movement is his greatest concern—the spiritual vicissitudes of finding and keeping a viable Way; the instability of the expressive language that mediates between inchoate sound and devotional incantation. Cyclic patterns repeat insistently, providing a kind of continuity that approximates stillness—the seasons, for example, or the stars, or given groups of words and themes—but does not achieve it until the patterns, which are technically "imitations," resolve into the mystery figured most vividly here as "the still point of the turning world," the point of utmost concentration and simplicity.

The *Ariel Poems* chronicle early stages of spiritual awareness. The first two poems, "Journey of the Magi" and "A Song for Simeon," are set in the period between the Nativity and the Resurrection in which the old dispensation still holds emotional sway over the new. The Magi narrative lingers over sensuous particulars of the journey towards Bethlehem, but omits any substantive description of the arrival, only wondering later: "were we led all that way for/Birth or Death?" since the knowledge that this confrontation brings has changed life so dramatically that the past with all its assurances seems dead, irrelevant, while the present has no discernible boundaries. Simeon, too, seems largely retrospective, more eager to be released from a sordid world where the Infant is "the still unspeaking and unspoken Word" than to live on as a witness to the salvation that will come. The remaining poems in the group, "Animula" and "Marina," reflect on the one hand the need for the ministrations of Grace in a brutally destructive world, and on the other a vague intimation of a powerful but not clearly Christian "grace dissolved in place" operating in the prospect of a reunion with a lesser Messiah, a child thought lost.

"Ash-Wednesday" consolidates these spiritual soundings by assuming a Pascalian posture of faith as a willful act of hope and humility. In effect, the poem reformulates the essentially passive aspects of *The Waste Land* into active tests of faith in which a despairing sense of loss becomes a means of renunciation, while the accomplishment of shoring disparate fragments against ruins becomes the task of "having to construct something/Upon which to rejoice." Although the speaker, in a lyrical address to the Muse of the piece, a sovereign "Lady of silences," can imagine the ultimate resolution of language into purely ineffable "Speech without word and/Word of no speech," he is resigned to making a statement and a plea:

Lord, I am not worthy
Lord, I am not worthy

but speak the word only.[23]

In the source of these lines, Matthew 8:8, the second phrase reads as a declaration of faith when the centurion says to Jesus, "Lord, I am not worthy that thou
shouldst come under my roof: but speak the word only, and my servant shall
be healed." Here, however, it seems more qualified and self-limiting, as if to
say, "Lord, I am not worthy, but can only speak the word in hope of being
healed," as well as to cry for help: but speak the word only, Lord, and I shall
be healed.

The heart of "Ash-Wednesday" is its incantatory *credo* in part V, invoking
the still hidden Word, an artful balance of world-weariness and strenuous
affirmation:

If the lost word is lost, if the spent word is spent
If the unheard, unspoken
Word is unspoken, unheard;
Still is the unspoken word, the Word unheard,
The Word without a word, the Word within
The world and for the world;
And the light shone in darkness and
Against the Word the unstilled world still whirled
About the centre of the silent Word.[24]

Despite the erosion of used language and the literary tradition, and despite our
failure to receive or repeat properly the given Word that establishes forever the
meaning of all derivative life and speech, the Word remains: ineffable ("The
Word without a word"), incarnate ("the Word within/The world"), and redemptive ("and for the world"). Three sets of triplets, having at their center the
fundamental mystery of "The Word without a word, the Word within," extend
the "If . . . then" form of a causal hypothesis into an operative certainty within
and beyond temporal cause and effect, "If . . . Still . . . And." The simple, total
existence of the Word, which Eliot conveys by using "is" as the only verb in
the second triplet, contains and perfects the language we have spoken and lost,
and gives our muteness a higher reference in its resonant silence.

As Eliot asserts in "Burnt Norton," the language that we use and make into
art leads towards this absolute still point of the Word, but represents at best
an analogy of that unimaginable truth:

Words move, music moves
Only in time; but that which is only living
Can only die. Words, after speech, reach
Into the silence. Only by the form, the pattern,

> Can words or music reach
> The stillness, as a Chinese jar still
> Moves perpetually in its stillness.[25]

In these terms the given things that used to seem like burdens in the early poetry—the words and forms we inherit through the tradition, the identity Eliot portrays first as a mechanical pattern of the mind's obsessions and later as an integral point that reconciles its beginnings and ends cyclically within itself—become indications of Grace, parts of a universal motion towards God. The revelation of what this process finally means bursts in emphatically in "Little Gidding" as a continuous presence:

> The dove descending breaks the air
> With flame of incandescent terror
> Of which the tongues declare
> The one discharge from sin and error.
> The only hope, or else despair
>   Lies in the choice of pyre or pyre—
>   To be redeemed from fire by fire.[26]

Here the further Incarnation of the Pentecostal descent from the ineffable to human speech expresses and fulfills "the silent Word" of "Ash-Wednesday," while its "flame of incandescent terror" expresses and fulfills the poet's deepest soundings of tradition and the self—"the communication/Of the dead . . . tongued with fire beyond the language of the living" ("Little Gidding"), and the once unspeakable "primitive terror" ("The Dry Salvages") of our prehistoric origins.

With his insistence on the *choice* of pyre or pyre, Eliot moves from essentially passive modes of knowing ("Prufrock," "Gerontion," *The Waste Land,* "Journey of the Magi," "A Song for Simeon") and being (*The Waste Land,* "The Hollow Men," "Ash-Wednesday," "Animula," "Marina") to an active assertion of spiritual consciousness. The affirmation with which he concludes not only *Four Quartets* but also his own difficult search for the truth is that everything we have and are has a place and purpose in Divine Love, which calls us to itself, and which ultimately will resolve the world into a condition of being beyond silence and speech by redeeming it:

> When the tongues of flame are in-folded
> Into the crowned knot of fire
> And the fire and the rose are one.[27]

For Iva Dee Hiatt
you are the music
While the music lasts.

NOTES

1. Unless otherwise indicated, all quotations from Eliot's poetry will be taken from T. S. Eliot, *Collected Poems 1909–1962* (New York: Harcourt, Brace & World, Inc., 1963).
2. T. S. Eliot, *Selected Essays* (New York: Harcourt, Brace & World, Inc., 1960), p. 234.
3. T. S. Eliot, *The Waste Land,* edited by Valerie Eliot (New York: Harcourt Brace Jovanovich, Inc., 1971), p. 3.
4. Louis Simpson, *Three on the Tower: The Lives and Works of Ezra Pound, T. S. Eliot and William Carlos Williams* (New York: William Morrow & Co., Inc., 1975), pp. 160–161. Simpson suggests that the letter should be dated 1929.
5. See *Waste Land,* pp. 23, 27, 39, and 41, as well as the editorial note on p. 127 concerning p. 23.
6. See "Portrait of a Lady," *Collected Poems,* p. 9.
7. *Selected Essays,* pp. 6–7.
8. Hyder Edward Rollins, ed., *The Letters of John Keats* (Cambridge, MA: Harvard University Press, 1972), pp. 193 and 387.
9. The sexual quality of this description recalls the similar language used in the last section of *The Waste Land,* lines 401–405:

    > *Datta:* what have we given?
    > My friend, blood shaking my heart
    > The awful daring of a moment's surrender
    > Which an age of prudence can never retract
    > By this, and this only, we have existed

10. T. S. Eliot, *The Complete Poems and Plays* (New York: Harcourt, Brace & World, Inc., 1962), p. 11.
11. *Collected Poems,* p. 31.
12. *Ibid.,* p. 29.
13. Jessie L. Weston, *From Ritual to Romance* (Garden City, New York: Doubleday Anchor Books, 1957), pp. 15–16. See generally pp. 12–24, "The Task of the Hero."
14. *Collected Poems,* pp. 57–58.
15. *Ibid.,* p. 123.
16. *Ibid.,* p. 68.
17. *Selected Essays,* p. 433. My parenthetical rendering of Eliot's Greek.
18. *Collected Poems.,* p. 63.
19. William Allan Neilson and Charles Jarvis Hill, eds., *The Complete Plays and Poems of William Shakespeare* (Cambridge, MA: The Riverside Press, 1942), p. 546.
20. *Waste Land,* p. 81.
21. *Ibid.,* p. 129, note to p. 71, #2.
22. Northrop Frye, *T. S. Eliot* (New York: Capricorn Books, 1972), p. 24.
23. *Collected Poems,* p. 89.
24. *Ibid.,* p. 92.
25. *Ibid.,* p. 180.
26. *Ibid.,* p. 207.
27. *Ibid.,* p. 209.

Wallace Stevens
and the
Poetics of Ineffability

Alfred Corn

Wittgenstein enjoins us not to speak of those things that do not belong to discourse: "Whereof we cannot speak, we must remain silent." And yet wonderfully often speakers or writers manage to find ways of talking approximately or indirectly about experience that they actually hold to be outside or above the reach of words. Ways of overcoming the obstacles to speech vary; they are part of the set of stylistic and contextual qualities that confer identity and identifiability on a writer. Of course the unsayable or "ineffable" itself is not the same category for all potential speakers (few of whom, in any case, will be writers). In certain religious faiths, it is accounted a sin to make any mention of the name of God, or of the divine; thereof, the righteous will keep silent. In other instances, both religious and secular, verbal expression is not held to be sinful or contaminating but merely inadequate and paltry, compared to some areas of private experience. This group includes most of the writers thought of as being concerned with the ineffable. It includes, for example, the later Stevens; but the early Stevens is often best understood as belonging to yet another contingent. This third group includes the temperaments who find imaginative writing (in a non-trivial sense) impossible: because they see no transcendent sanctions that could be drawn on to form truthful statements in literature. For them, the universe is silent, and thus silence is truer than any utterance. To invent is to fabricate, to fabricate is base or invalid, and so there is truly nothing to write.

It is tempting to call this last obstacle to speech "negative ineffability"; and it is one that determines much of Stevens's early poetry. The negative mythological figure for the world of *Harmonium* is the Snow Man, who perceives "nothing that is not there, and the nothing that is." If there had been no other figures in the pantheon Stevens invented for his poetry, he could not have written many more poems. But Stevens began to imagine other altars, engaging

---

A version of this essay first appeared in the Winter 1981 issue of the *Yale Review*.

in an extended poetic pilgrimage and entertaining many ideas on the nature of truth, of the imagination, and the philosophical status of poetic utterance. Why Stevens did not from the start understand poems as "fictions," and statements in them as hypothetical, has to do both with his own skeptic's temperament—which must have been useful in his bond surety investigations for the Hartford Accident and Indemnity Company—and with modernist developments in American poetry during the first two decades of this century (which cannot be taken up here in detail). In any case, the notion that the poet "nothing affirmeth and therefore never lieth," clearly failed to satisfy Stevens: poems must be true, otherwise they are of no importance.

Poems must be true because, with the death of God, the arts must come to replace religion. In a letter to Barbara Church (which is dated August 12, 1947, but reflects beliefs he developed during his student days at Harvard fifty years earlier) Stevens said: "As scepticism becomes both complete and profound, we face either a true civilization or a blank; and literature ought to be one of the factors to determine the choice. Certainly, if civilization is to consist only of man himself, and it is, the arts must take the place of divinity, at least as a stage in whatever general principle or progress is involved." What did living in a universe empty of deity mean for Stevens? The blankness, cold, and misery mentioned in "The Snow Man" are metaphoric ways of conveying it, and a more succinct formulation is found in his *Adagia*: "Reality is a vacuum."[1] Against human mortality, suffering, and meaninglessness, Stevens proposes the imagination as a redemptive force, to push back (here he inverts the metaphor) against the "pressure of reality." The imagination is also the psychological faculty that allows poems to be written; indeed, the proportional equation "silence is to speech as death is to life" stands at the center of Stevens's poetic vocation. If one can write poems, one may find a sanction for human existence, and so may live.

Stevens's view of the "imagination as value," a conviction he repeats in many prose contexts and draws on as the emotional substance for so many poems, could be seen as absolute, no less comprehensive than a belief in the divine. Just as frequently, however, he expressed an opposing view: "The ultimate value is reality."[2] When poetry fails to reflect reality, it presents merely a "dead romantic," a "falsification." Stevens is never clear and precise as to how the false imagination is to be distinguished from the true, the dead romanticism from the live; but, in general, he seems to look for a marriage, a mystic union between the imagination and reality, without explaining how wedlock is to be effected. (Readers will recall, in this connection, the fable of the "mystic marriage" between the captain and the maiden Bawda in *Notes Toward a Supreme Fiction*.)

It is apparent that, although Stevens was drawn to philosophical issues and discourse, he did not demand of himself the development of a system organized and expressed with philosophical rigor: "What you don't allow for," he wrote to one of his correspondents (*Letters,* p. 300), "is the fact that one moves in many directions at once. No man of imagination is prim: the thing is a contra-diction in terms." This is as much a program as a description: Stevens wishes to *postpone* the hasty formulation of a system, to forestall final conclusions. He wishes to rest neither in the imagination nor in reality because rest is undesir-able; it is hard to distinguish from philosophical or psychological stasis or perhaps paralysis; and life is supremely a question of movement and change. In a letter to Sister Bernetta Quinn (April 7, 1948) he says: "I don't want to turn to stone under your very eyes by saying 'This is the centre that I seek and this alone.' Your mind is too much like my own for it to seem to be an evasion on my part to say merely that I do seek a centre and expect to go on seeking it. I don't say that I do not expect to find it. It is the great necessity even without specific identification."

Even if philosophical or religious finality were attainable, Stevens recog-nizes that the "never-resting mind" would not accept any such finality: "Again, it would be the merest improvisation to say of any image of the world, even though it was an image with which a vast acccumulation of imaginations had been content, that it was the chief image. The imagination itself would not remain content with it nor allow us to do so. It is the irrepressible revolution-ist."[3] The view of truth (and life) that emerges from these statements is one shared by many modern philosophers of mind: truth is not a set of propositions but is a psychological process. For Stevens, there is (and should be) a constant oscillation between the categories reason/fact and imagination/fable. A poetry or a life content with either of these opposing terms will not constitute fulfill-ment. Poets (considered exemplary for all of us) will always be seeking, voyag-ing, and questing, so long as they are alive.

This summary of philosophic and poetic ideas, though it is partial and perhaps supererogatory for the Stevens scholar, may retrace for nonspecialists the steps taken during Stevens's long career. In early Stevens, the ground is, generally, bare reality, the wintry landscape of nothingness seen by the Snow Man; the *figure* is the imagination that comes to free the mind from its subjec-tion to reality. In the later Stevens it is more often the imagination that is the ground, all-pervasive and easily available.[4] Reality then seems to become the figure brought in as a contrast, a "refreshment," a cleansing away of the dull fictional film habitually covering our view of things. The emblematic figure typically summoned by Stevens in 1922 is the "One of Fictive Music"; for the later Stevens, it is the "Necessary Angel" of reality. But, more and more often, Stevens begins to call for a fusion of reality and imagination into one entity, variously referred to as the Grand Poem, the Supreme Fiction, the Central Mind, or the Central Imagination. This hypothetical category seems to become in some sense possible to Stevens, even though it always remains a projection. There is a constant future-tenseness to Stevens's visionary insight; he gives notes *toward* the Supreme Fiction, *prologues* "to what is possible." A title Stevens considered for his first book was *The Grand Poem: Preliminary Minutiae*; and the early Stevens could say, "The book of moonlight is not written yet nor half begun," and, "Music is not yet written but is to be."

The implication is that Stevens believes the great book can be written and that he will do it. By 1943 and the writing of *Notes*, it is apparent that the projective character of his vision has crystallized as doctrine. In an essay com-posed that same year he says, "The incredible is not a part of poetic truth. On the contrary, what concerns us in poetry, as in everything else, is the be-lief of credible people in credible things. It follows that poetic truth is the truth of credible things, not so much that it is actually so, as that it might be so."[5] A few years later, in *The Auroras of Autumn*, he would put the matter this way:

> There is or may be a time of innocence
> As pure principle. Its nature is its end,
> That it should be, and yet not be . . . .

Although Stevens's *summum bonum* belongs to futurity, his adumbrations of it remind one of other poets' efforts to recount mystic experiences actually undergone, remembered wordlessly, and termed ineffable in the usual sense. Here it will be useful to consider some of Stevens's reflections on ultimate value, which, in this instance, he terms "nobility":

> I mean that nobility which is our spiritual height and depth; and while I know how difficult it is to express it, nevertheless I am bound to give a sense of it. Nothing could be more evasive and inaccessible. Nothing distorts itself and seeks disguise more quickly. There is a shame of disclosing it and in its definite presenta-tions, a horror of it. But there it is. The fact that it is there is what makes it possible to invite to the reading and writing of poetry men of intelligence and desire for life. I am not thinking of the ethical or the sonorous or at all of the manner of it. The manner of it is, in fact, its difficulty, which each man must feel each day differently for himself. I am not thinking of the solemn, the portentous or demoded. On the other hand, I am evading the definition. If it is defined, it will be fixed and it must not be fixed. As in the case of an external thing, nobility resolves itself into an enormous number of vibrations, movements, changes. To fix it is to put an end to it.[6]

"Vibrations, movements, changes": much of Stevens's poetic style is cov-ered by these terms, and they constitute part of the difficulty of his "manner." The whole passage, with its strenuous effort to get at the inexpressible, suggests that Stevens's first intuitions concerning the nature of a supreme and always future fiction may have come to him out of his struggle with style and expres-sion itself. The title of the essay from which this passage is drawn (see the footnote) refers not only to nobility, but also to "the sound of words." Consider then another passage, one where Stevens discusses our feeling for words themselves.

The deepening need for words to express our thoughts and feelings which, we are sure, are all the truth that we shall ever experience, having no illusions, makes us listen to words when we hear them, loving them and feeling them, makes us search the sound of them, for a finality, a perfection, an unalterable vibration, which it is only within the power of the acutest poet to give them.[7]

A paradox present in the apologia for words and their sounds, words at their most *physical*, in short, is that the principal result is immaterial and non-verbal. Stevens says as much in another essay ("Effects of Analogy"): "There is always an analogy between nature and the imagination, and possibly poetry is merely the strange rhetoric of that parallel: a rhetoric in which the feeling of one man is communicated to another in words of the exquisite appositeness that takes away all their verbality."

The inference, then, is that our surest clue, our only available insight, into the nature of the "central imagination" are words and their sound. Unlike most poets of mystic insight, Stevens does not deplore the inadequacies of his medium; he celebrates it and becomes its hierophant. Is it appropriate to call this a "verbal sublime"? There is at least one major precedent for it in literature— the poetry of Mallarmé. Other affinities between the two poets have been noted: the view of the poet as a sacramental figure; the recourse to music as the best analogy for poetry; and the belief (Mallarmé's belief) in a final Book that the world was meant to become, a Book not yet written. (This must be one of the sources of Stevens's Supreme Fiction.) In actual fact, the French poet Stevens most often mentions is not Mallarmé, but Paul Valéry, who, however, belongs to the same tradition: Stevens wrote prefaces for two of Valéry's dialogues, *Eupalinos* and *Dance and the Soul,* when these were translated and published in the Bollingen series. This view of the sacramental role of the poet, whose poems may be considered incantations or prayers, is not foreign to Valéry's own poetics and fits well with something he once said about prayer and unknown tongues. (His prototype, obviously, was Roman Catholic liturgical Latin): "C'est pourquoi il ne faut prier qu'en paroles inconnues. Rendez l'énigme à l'énigme, énigme pour énigme. Elevez ce qui est mystère en vous à ce qui est mystère en soi. Il y a en vous quelque chose d'égal à ce qui vous passe."[8] For his part, Stevens said (in the *Adagia*), "Poetry is a search for the inexplicable," and "it is necessary to propose an enigma to the mind." Although he did not write his poems in Latin, no small number of the incantations Stevens proposed to his mind (and ours) employ French words; and much of his vocabulary (in the poems) is composed of archaism, coinages, and sound-words either onomatopoeic in nature, or modeled on Elizabethan singing syllables ("hey-derry-derry-down," etc.), or similar to scat-singing in jazz ("shoo-shoo-shoo," and "ric-a-nic," for example). The point is, no doubt, to invent that "imagination's Latin" Stevens speaks of in *Notes Toward a Supreme Fiction.* It is in this sense, perhaps, that he wished to be understood when he said, "Personally, I like words to sound wrong."[9] An overstatement; but it is certainly true that

Stevens has one of the most noticeable styles in our poetry; and it could be said that he wrote an English that often sounds as if it were another language. How is the poet to overcome universal silence? One way is to make a joyful noise.

In view of his high claims for poetry, it appears that nothing can be more serious than poetic style. In his essay "Two or Three Ideas," he proposes that, as poems and their style are one, so men and their style are one; the same may be said of "the gods." Then why not interchange *all* the terms? The style of men, and their poems, and their gods, are one; thus, style is an index of the divine. The task, as Stevens saw it, was to discover and compose a style that would serve as just such an index. Already noted is Stevens's reliance on a special diction to give the effect of "otherness," of enigmatic mystery, an effect appropriate to a supreme, future fulfillment. Beyond that, the poet must in-clude in his repertoire accents of grandeur and nobility. Stevens draws on several sources for these. Anyone who has heard him read, or recordings of his reading, will have immediately noted the resemblance of his elocutionary style to that of the Protestant minister—the intonations of prayer, the accents of exhortation. By the same token, the language of Stevens's poems is often Christian in flavor: "Sister and mother, and diviner love. . . . "; "Whose spirit is this? we said, because we knew/It was the spirit that we sought and knew/That we should ask this often as she sang." Stevens is like other Romantic poets in adapting Christian rhetoric to his purposes, and, of course, he borrows directly from Wordsworth, Shelley, Keats, and Whitman themselves. More surprising, however, is his enormous reliance on Shakespeare, and not merely for personae like Peter Quince and Marina. Stevens tends to draw on Shake-speare's high rhetoric for certain moments of large, visionary utterance. When, in "Final Soliloquy of the Interior Paramour," he writes, "We say God and the imagination are one . . . /How high that highest candle lights the dark," it is impossible not to think of Portia's lines in Act V of *The Merchant of Venice*: "How far that little candle throws his beams!/So shines a good deed in a naughty world." Stevens's recasting is no disgrace to its source; and part of the power of these lines lies in the connection the reader makes between the sense of Shakespeare's greatness and the philosophical amplitude of the issues being treated in the poem.

Stevens has come so far from "the nothing that is" as to speak of deity, God, with a capital letter.[10] The gradual pilgrimage from Nothing to Something recapitulated in his career as poet is a process enacted constantly (though on a much smaller scale) in his later poems. The typical embodiment of the change is metaphor, which he describes variously as "metamorphosis," "transmuta-tion," and even "apotheosis." Metaphor is the agency by which a real but empty thing is imaginatively transformed into something "unreal" and fulfilling. The poem as a whole is to be taken as an extended metaphor. Two passages from Stevens's essays point to this process:

The way a poet feels when he is writing, or after he has written, a poem that completely accomplishes his purpose is evidence of the personal nature of his activity. To describe it by exaggerating it, he shares the transformation, not to say apotheosis, accomplished by the poem. It must be this experience that makes him think of poetry as possibly a phase of metaphysics; and it must be this experience that teases him with that sense of the possibility of a remote, a mystical *vis* or *noeud vital* to which reference has already been made.[11]

Certainly a sense of the infinity of the world is a sense of something cosmic. It is cosmic poetry because it makes us realize that we are creatures, not of a part, which is our everyday limitation, but of a whole for which, for the most part, we have as yet no language. This sudden change of a lesser life for a greater one is like a change of winter for spring or any other transmutation of poetry.[12]

The metaphor of the passage from winter to spring as representing the shift from one ontology to another is very frequent in Stevens, and, in fact, is the basis for the final poem in the 1954 edition of the *Collected Poems,* "Not Ideas About the Thing, But the Thing Itself." Recalling that "metaphor," by its etymology can suggest the notion of "transport,"[13] (itself a term with several possible meanings), one is given a clue to part of the intention in a volume like *Transport to Summer* (1947), which may be understood as a book-length embodiment of the central doctrine of metaphysical transformation. The volume opens with a summer poem, "God Is Good. It is a Beautiful Summer Night" (to be read, "God=Good=Summer), but, not resting with that, goes on to include poems oscillating back and forth between summer and winter settings, and ends with *Notes,* which includes the same constant pendulum swing, beginning with autumn and ending with the "Fat girl, terrestrial, my summer, my night." If it is desirable to isolate a central controlling "structure" in the Stevensian imagination, no doubt it is the idea of metaphoric transformation that must be proposed. At the lower end of the scale, this provides the endless variety of tropes invented by Stevens in the poems; at the next level, it presents the poem under the aspect of transfiguration or apotheosis; and then, the volume of poems as a change from the wintry mind to the *summum bonum* of summer. It is fair to say, too, that Stevens's long poetic career moves generally from a predominantly "wintry" metaphysics to a more positive and reassuring stance. And, if seasonal change is the most frequent *temporal* metapor for revelation in Stevens, the most frequent *spatial* one is "pilgrimage":

The number of ways of passing between the traditional two fixed point of a man's life, that is to say of passing from the self to God, is fixed only by the limitations of space, which is limitless. The eternal philosopher is the eternal pilgrim on that road.[14]

The metaphorical transformation of reality, then, was actually a kind of religious pilgrimage for Stevens. And its completion he viewed as an apotheosis, but one that must be undertaken again and again—it is never final. The exact nature of deity is not to be stated; Stevens is content with formulae such as the "central imagination" or the "central poem." The act of writing offers the only clue Stevens has to the nature of the divine, and the intuitions of poetry all have to do with a directional transformation, from thing to figure, from fact to fable. A poem such as "A Primitive Like an Orb," which touches on all these ideas, can be read almost as a catechism for Stevens's beliefs about poetry and its relationship to the divine. This meditation on "the essential poem at the centre of things" is a fine sample, too, of Stevensian rhetoric at its most expansive and harmonious, a rhetoric developed from Christian, idealist-philosophical, and Shakespearean language. Three stanzas from the poem:

II

We do not prove the existence of the poem.
It is something seen and known in lesser poems.
It is the huge, high harmony that sounds
A little and a little, suddenly,
By means of a separate sense. It is and it
Is not, and, therefore is. In the instant of speech,
The breadth of an accelerando moves,
Captives the being, widens—and was there.

IV

One poem proves another and the whole,
For the clairvoyant men that need no proof:
The lover, the believer and the poet.
Their words are chosen out of their desire,
The joy of language, when it is themselves.
With these they celebrate the central poem.
The fulfillment of fulfillments, in opulent,
Last terms, the largest, bulging still with more,

V

Until the used-to earth and sky, and the tree
And cloud, the used-to tree and used-to cloud,
Lose the old uses that they made of them,
And they: these men, and earth and sky, inform
Each other by sharp informations, sharp,
Free knowledges, secreted until then,
Breaches of that which held them fast. It is
As if the central poem became the world. . . .

The central poem of the world is clearly not, here, a nothingness. The universal vacancy so apparent to Stevens in the first phase of his career has come to be replaced by a sense and a rhetoric of fullness. A primary source of his conviction as to the certitude of that fullness is the feeling emanating from that very rhetoric, in poems lesser than the "essential poem." The obstacle to utterance is removed, for Stevens, by the transforming power and cosmic harmony manifest in *poesis* itself.

NOTES

1. *Opus Posthumous,* ed. Samuel French Morse (London: Faber & Faber, 1966), p. 168.
2. *Ibid.,* p. 166.
3. "Imagination as Value," *The Necessary Angel, Essays on Reality and Imagination* (New York: Vintage Press, 1968), p. 151. Cited hereafter as *NA.*
4. "Yet the absence of the imagination had/ Itself to be imagined," he says in "The Plain Sense of Things." All poetry not specifically cited as from *OP* is taken from *The Collected Poems of Wallace Stevens* (New York: Knopf, 1954; rpt. 1965).
5. "The Figure of the Youth as Virile Poet," *NA,* p. 53.
6. "The Noble Rider and the Sound of Words," *NA,* p. 33.
7. *Ibid.,* p. 32.
8. "Comme le temps est calme," *Morceaux choisis, prose et poesie* (Paris: Gallimard, 1930), p. 56. "That is why one should pray only in unknown words. Return the enigma to the enigma, enigma for enigma. Lift up what is mystery in you to what is mystery in itself. There is in you something equal to what goes beyond you." (translation mine.)
9. *Letters of Wallace Stevens,* ed. Holly Stevens (London: Faber & Faber, 1966), p. 340. Cited hereafter as *Letters.*
10. The question of the precise nature of Stevens's religious beliefs, or hypotheses about the divine, is an interesting one. To be considered are statements as various as: "Proposita: 1. God and the imagination are one. 2. The thing imagined is the imaginer . . . . Hence, I suppose, the imaginer is God." (*Adagia, OP,* p. 178.) "It is the belief and not the god that counts." (*Adagia, OP,* p. 162.) "God is a postulate of the ego." (*Adagia, OP,* p. 171.) "God is in me or else is not at all (does not exist)." (*Adagia, OP,* p. 172.) "I am not an atheist although I do not believe today in the same God in whom I believed when I was a boy." (Letter to Sister Bernetta Quinn, 21 December, 1951.) "At my age it would be nice to be able to read more and think more and be myself more and to make up my mind about God, say, before it is too late, or at least before he makes up his mind about me." (Letter to Thomas Mc Greevy, 24 October, 1952.)
11. *NA,* p. 50.
12. *OP,* p. 189.
13. It is probably this valence of meaning that suggested to I. A. Richards his meta-phorical terminology of "tenor-vehicle-ground."
14. *OP,* p. 193.

On Not Having the Last Word: Beckett, Wittgenstein, and the Limits of Language

Bruce Kawin

I

> You must go on, I can't go on, you must go on,
> I'll go on.
>
> Samuel Beckett, *The Unnamable*

Samuel Beckett's novels could be considered the "final" step in the devel-opment of self-conscious fiction. The narrative structures begun in *Watt* and continued in *Molloy* and *Malone Dies* are frought to completion in the last volume of the Trilogy, *The Unnamable,* which constitutes the very limit of the novel. The Unnamable is a consciousness. It is hard to say whether he can express himself only in words, or whether he *is* only words, for we encounter him in a book made up entirely of his monologue and he continually discredits any process but that of his own speaking. The problem is the same, of course, whether he is a thinking book or a mind that can only speak: that is the essence of systemic self-consciousness here. He has to be content with the word "I" when he wants to refer to himself, but he senses that his identity can be found only beyond the reach of words and that even the referentiality of "I" is a self-declaring failure. He expects to find timelessness and silence and himself all at once, and his fate is to speak until words evoke that silence. Unlike Malone, he does not have the relatively easy solution of being able to die, since his *only* mortality is textuality and since he may even be a postincarnate Malone, the inhabitant of fiction's Purgatory. He must speak until there is no need to speak; he must say "I" until he has defined himself. Restricted to language, he has no way of going beyond "I" to what it represents; restricted to his own consciousness in a Cartesian nightmare, he has no way of establishing anything about himself except that he *is* conscious. So in this novel, the tension of an unnamable speaker exactly overlaps the tension of ineffable subject matter. *The Unnamable,* as a limit of the novel, is an extraordinary resource for the future of fiction. It is the Logos that reanimates the genre.

The Unnamable has no discernible plot, no namable character, no describable setting, no clockable time. All it has is a voice, or mind, speaking in the
continuous present. Three-fourths of its length is occupied by a single paragraph. Its stream of sentences and fragments, separated more often by commas
than by periods, exactly expresses the movements of the narrator's mind and
records his every thought. He does not think his sentences out in advance: he
is unable to silence himself long enough to compose. Something compels him
to speak and prevents him from doing anything else, so that it is as true to call
him a verbal consciousness as to call him language made self-conscious. The
progress of his self-awareness is worth describing.

   The narrator labels himself "I," immediately putting that sign under erasure: "Where now? Who now? When now? Unquestioning. I, say I. Unbeliev-
ing. Questions, hypotheses, call them that. Keep going, going on, call that
going, call that on."[1] He is awakened from sleep or death or blank paper, but
in any case from silence. He is Beckett's archetypal character, a life force that
had underlain such heroes of the earlier fictions as Belacqua, Watt, Murphy,
Molloy, Moran, and Malone (who all resemble him) and that is now being
forced to awaken into a new but more accurate manifestation. The karma of
his failures at self-description is inseparably that of Beckett, who has in all those
novels failed to describe him; reincarnation, so to speak, is mandated. The
narrator seems to be asking the forces that have animated him, "What situation
am I in now? Who am I supposed to be this time? What time is it?" When he
gets no answers, he gives in, takes a deep breath, and makes the old inevitable
definition: I will call myself I, without believing it. He feels commanded to
"keep going on" but makes it clear that he is only settling for the terms "going"
and "on." He makes the reader aware that every word in this book is in
quotation marks or under erasure, that each is a little wrong. Not even
his speaking is free of *différence*: "I seem to speak, it is not I, about me, it is not
about me."

   The narrator has a collective name for his fictional alternates or pseudo-
selves: Mahood. At first he feels he has two alternatives to the articulate
darkness in which he appears to be. He can be a name, Mahood, and be the
subject of more stories, or he can be Worm, an unspeakable negative. (He is
never called "the Unnamable" except in the book's title, but many critics have
found it convenient to call him that.) These alternates represent poles of language. If he were Worm, he would not speak at all, even to try to name himself:
he would just be Worm, the existential equivalent of a Black Hole. When words
try to deal with Worm, they address not the silence, in which there may be
some kind of Being, but absolute negation. When they handle Mahood, they
are on holiday, spinning stories, their nouns and verbs apparently applying to
real things and actions in a welcome escape from self-consciousness. The Unnamable occupies a middle ground. It is difficult for words to find something
to say about him because he has no story, but relatively easier and more

valuable than to surrender to Worm, the antithesis of being. When the Unnamable rejects both Worm and Mahood and decides to seek the silence on his own,
to talk not about them but about "I," the history of fiction enters a climactic
phase—or perhaps a better term for this stage would be "peripeteia." It is as
if *The Unnamable* were the novel (as a genre) awakened into self-consciousness,
just as its narrator is roused from a dream of Malloy and Malone. Groping
through its new awareness, the novel nearly succumbs to the temptations of
Mahood—nearly constructs characters so that it can discuss itself in more
familiar terms. (And most of the criticism of this novel has fallen for the game,
insisting that Malone is orbiting or that there is a jar outside a restaurant,
whereas all of these are irrefutably dispensed with in the course of the book.)
But it sees that such a solution is evasive, that the quietus at which it arrives
is only the blank space between novels, between new and compulsory dreams.
If language is ever to know itself, if the novel is ever to learn to speak on its
own, *The Unnamable* must pursue its self-consciousness to the root and speak
from that base.

Until he can arrive at the door that he imagines opening on himself and
the silence, the Unnamable is doomed to keep talking, like a man whose one
necessary task is to drill a well but whose only tool is a paintbrush. Language
always has these problems but tends to ignore them: Beckett is neither obscur-
ing the function of literature nor spinning death dirges, as many critics have
suggested (Wylie Sypher, for instance, considers *The Unnamable* an extreme case
of "loss of the self," an anonymous complaint against life[2]). On the contrary,
he is awakening language from a drugged sleep, infusing it with new potential—and in these early stages, the oversleeper may be forgiven some groggi-
ness. Literature is addicted to Mahood, and the doctor who attempts to introduce
it cold turkey into the real world is liable to encounter the most resistance from
the patient. This new art must begin by talking about itself in order to be
itself—to come to terms with the self-consciousness that allows it to be both
abstract and factual, even if those terms are under erasure.

All the terms of the Unnamable's compulsion are arrived at instantly, just
as the life-functions of a child are breathed into motion at birth. Within fifteen
pages of beginning, he abandons his "puppets":

> All these Murphys, Molloys and Malones do not fool me. They have made me
> waste my time, suffer for nothing, speak of them when, in order to stop speaking,
> I should have spoken of me and of me alone. . . . They never suffered my pains,
> their pains are nothing, compared to mine, a mere tittle of mine, the tittle I
> thought I could put from me, in order to witness it.[3]

So he begins the attempt again: "I, of whom I know nothing."[4] He knows that
his use of words makes him appear to be like them and subject to their limits,
but he is contemptuous of that assumption: "It's a poor trick that consists in
ramming a set of words down your gullet on the principle that you can't bring

them up without being branded as belonging to their breed."[5] His salvation is that he fails to understand or remember most of the words he uses, so that his processes are able to function in an ever-renewed present tense, not bound by previous identities or assertions, or by the lies and evasions that come from speaking an inadequate language. He is constantly free to experiment, to seek that impossible point where the closed system comes to terms with the animating metaconsciousness.

Somehow, between the words, the Unnamable finds that point. The novel ends with a four-page sentence in which he starts his attempt all over again, defining the place of his confinement as the inside of his head and allowing the words to tell him what to do. What he encounters is a manifestation that releases him from his task and appears to proceed from outside him. His attempt brings him to the edge of silence, where he is up against the same limits but where he feels something outside the closed system taking place—something that has slipped between the lines and brought him to an intuition.

The novel reaches its climax not in an impossible statement but in the narrator's sense that he is at the door that leads to his true self, that he is waiting for himself in the silence, that his true self will speak itself by speaking silence. In great excitement, the narrator feels himself waiting for an ineffable language to manifest itself so that he can be done with his saying and join what his saying has continuously shown:

> he is made of silence, there's a pretty analysis, he's in the silence, he's the one to be sought, the one to be, the one to be spoken of, the one to speak, but he can't speak, then I could stop, I'd be he, I'd be the silence, I'd be back in the silence, we'd be reunited, his story the story to be told, but he has no story, he hasn't been in story, it's not certain, he's in his own story, unimaginable, unspeakable, that doesn't matter, the attempt must be made, in the old stories incomprehensibly mine, to find his, it must be there somewhere, it must have been mine, before being his, I'll recognize it, in the end I'll recognize it, the story of the silence that he never left, that I should have never have left, that I may never find again, that I may find again, then it will be he, it will be I, it will be the place, the silence. . . .[6]

He was booted out of the silence by an author who made him speak, by an author who woke him from the blank pages that followed *Malone Dies*—or perhaps by an incomprehensible birth that filled him with words and made him subject to the compulsions of the murmuring voices. There is no way he can speak the "I" of the metaphysical self (both "he" and "I," and of course, beyond either term), but he can bring himself to a point where he will be ready for that self to accept him into its totality. Of course, that self, incomprehensibly his, has manifested itself throughout the work, but the words have not been able to declare it (the self is a limit of the world).

Arriving at an intuition that cannot be included in the text, the Unnamable finds himself suddenly at "the door." He feels the words giving out and the silence coming over him, but the words—necessarily unable to attain silence—declare up to the very last their compulsion to "go on." Up to the final printed moment, he remains verbally conscious; thus he never has an overview, never knows whether the silence that may be coming will be "the one that lasts" or only the space between literary incarnations. In the extraordinary moment that ends the novel, he accepts this compulsion as his own:

> you must go on, I can't go on, you must go on, I'll go on, you must say words, as long as there are any, until they find me, until they say me, strange pain, strange sin, you must go on, perhaps it's done already, perhaps they have said me already, perhaps they have carried me to the threshold of my story, before the door that opens on my story, that would surprise me, if it opens, it will be I, it will be the silence, where I am, I don't know, I'll never know, in the silence you don't know, you must go on, I can't go on, I'll go on.[7]

He accepts his vocation, and the pseudoexternal command, "you must go on," ceases. He has apparently discovered that the voices that force his expression are his own, that he is the entire narrating system and not just its mouthpiece. This instant of absolute systemic self-consciousness is not described in the text but is shown by the disappearance of "you must go on"; it is prompted by his intuition of being at the door, to which he has been brought by sheer persistence; and it immediately yields to the silence that may show his perfect integration (there is no way, of course, to know exactly what that silence "means").

The Unnamable is a record of turmoil, the birth-pang of the mind of the text, which occurs as the conscious self beats at the limits of apprehension that divide it from the metaphysical self. Beckett does not invent a silent language here, but he brilliantly dramatizes the limits of self-consciousness. In so doing, he creates a new character—the 'I' that attempts to speak itself—and summons the "I" in common usage to an awareness of its possibilities. This self-conscious pronoun can prove the basis of a revolution in literature. "I" is not only the manifestation of human consciousness in language; it can now be seen or employed as language's attempt at self-consciousness. Written by Beckett, The Unnamable is a work that speaks itself, all the internal filters and presenters of earlier self-conscious fiction having been dispensed with; all that remains is the fact of language, interposed between the will to expression and the metaphysical self, and now allowing "I" to be recognized as a direct manifestation of the presence of being, relentlessly unnamable and ubiquitous. What this revolution in fiction implicitly accomplishes, then, is to put the mind of the text on much the same level as human consciousness. The work remains able to speak in fictions; it does not have to be simply the factual record of its author's speech or the gropings of its narrator to apply words to his situation. But in an important sense, it can never again be innocently regarded as fiction, for it has become autobiography.

Systemically self-conscious fiction is a different category of expression from first-person narration. Goaded by many challenges—in particular, the problem of dealing with the ineffable and the related problem of dramatizing personal identity—the self-conscious novel has developed a means of dramatizing its own limits. Thus *The Unnamable* appears consumed in self-analysis and preoccupied by failure—an analysis and a failure that are inseparable from its awareness of the limits of language and from its awareness that the only alternatives it has to its current paradoxical state of being are to achieve silence or to lapse into conventional fiction.

II

There are, indeed, things that cannot be put into words. They make themselves manifest. They are what is mystical.

Ludwig Wittgenstein
Tractatus Logico-Philosophicus

Any question that can be formulated is one that obeys the rules, or conforms to the structure, of logic; any such question can have a logical answer. A metaphysical question, on the other hand, cannot be formulated because it would have to be answered in alogical terms—which, as Wittgenstein points out in the *Tractatus,* do not exist. "It is impossible to represent in language anything that 'contradicts logic' as it is in geometry to represent by its co-ordinates a figure that contradicts the laws of space, or to give the co-ordinates of a point that does not exist."[8] It is possible to speak nonsense but not to mean anything by it; it is possible to stimulate the hearer's imagination with metaphor and paradox (the sound of one hand clapping, for instance) so long as one realizes that one is not really saying anything—that some term in the statement is inadequately defined or misused (clapping requires two hands). It is impossible to think illogically. It is impossible to make a meaningful statement about the ineffable.

This does not imply that there is no such province as the ineffable, but simply "defines" that area by exclusion. The ineffable is not in the "world," not knowable, not a matter of "facts in logical space."[9] Both the world so defined, and language, share the same limits—in fact, determine each other's limits.[10] What Wittgenstein does in the *Tractatus* is to "signify what cannot be said, by presenting clearly what can be said."[11]

The structure of the *Tractatus* is a great poetic achievement, and it has a good deal more humor and simplicity than is usually acknowledged. One might say that Wittgenstein creates the world in six major propositions, then declares the sabbath in his seventh proposition and closing sentence: "What we cannot speak about we must pass over in silence." Another is to say that he organizes the formal logic of everything that can be known, leaving "in the silence," as Beckett would say, that which cannot be thought about and which is outside the "limited whole" of the world. When he declares that "propositions *show* the logical form of reality. They display it,"[12] he implies that the knowable, as a category, manifests something undiscussable and mandates a mystical perspective: the system can be seen whole only from the outside. Wittgenstein discredits metaphysical *statement* while providing mystics with a logical justification for their insistence on the ineffability of certain holistic intuitions.

Logic is a limited system. What the correspondence between language and the world indicates is simply that they share a structure. The totality of facts in logical space, like the language that can discuss it, is a set of terms that reflect "termness" and describe the terminological. The logical form of a proposition is, from this perspective, a manifestation of something inaccessible to logic:

> Everything that can be thought at all can be thought clearly. Everything that can be put into words can be put clearly.
>   Propositions can represent the whole of reality, but they cannot represent what they must have in common with reality in order to be able to represent it—logical form.
>   In order to be able to represent logical form, we should have to be able to station ourselves with propositions somewhere outside logic, that is to say outside the world.
>   Propositions cannot represent logical form: it is mirrored in them.
>   What finds its reflection in language, language cannot represent.
>   What expresses *itself* in language, *we* cannot express by means of language. . . .
>   What *can* be shown, *cannot* be said.[13]

Language and logic amount to a point of view. A point of view cannot observe itself. This is one reason that absolute self-knowledge cannot be discussed: it involves a point of view outside the knowing self, which is, of course, a contradiction in terms.

The self is relevant to this discussion, in fact crucial to it, since from *The Cloud of Unknowing* to *The Unnamable* it has been affirmed that the experience of self-realization is ineffable. The self is a limited whole, and to "know" it fully is to transcend the phenomenal world, to become the "knower" on another level. For some people this is described as discovering that one is divine, or as becoming one with the Higher Self; it is an essential element of what William James called the "conversion experience."[14] The self so contacted cannot be described as an element of personality; the Hindus came closest by arguing that Atman (the Higher Self) and Brahman (the Self of the Universe) are identical; the great Hindu philosopher Shankara defined Atman as Brahman-within-the-creature. The self *shows* and cannot *say* what it has in common with the nature of Being. This philosophical paradox is relevant to the structure of self-conscious or reflexive texts, many of which attempt to describe their own awareness of being limited systems. Not surprisingly, many such texts—like *The Unnamable*—are organized around the attempts of a first-person narrator to define his own processes and end in a silence that cannot be analyzed. It can never be established whether Beckett's narrator lapses into silence from exhaustion or joins the transcendent self whose story is on the other side of the "door" of textuality; one knows only that when he says 'I" he does so without considering the term adequate—and that he does *finally* stop talking. The special brilliance of *The Unnamable* lies in Beckett's keeping rigorously coterminous the limits of textuality and the limits of the verbal consciousness of the narrator. The self is the most present manifestation of the ineffable with which any human being can deal. Because the mind (or at least the left hemisphere of the brain[15]) is accustomed to expressing its processes in words, many religious exercises—from silent meditations to language-defying koans—lead the initiate through a process of seeing past the mind to a point where instantaneous, metaphysical, holistic intuitions can take place and where the compulsion to explain Vision not only drops away but even appears rather perverse.

Everything within the logic/language system—the totality of facts in logical space, which is the world—can be expressed. To see the system whole, one would have to be outside the system. That is a functional description of transcendence. Reflexivity climaxes in the experience of absolute self-knowledge, a system's observing itself. What it observes, it cannot say. *The Unnamable* shows that it is a text; what it *says* is that it is having trouble naming itself and has to wait for some kind of door to open from the other side of what it cannot identify as textuality, or even as the limits of logical space. The conversion experience involves sudden access to the whole self, and therefore suggests to the convert such terms as "higher control," because the experience can "make sense" only in terms of a system higher than the personal. The experience might well be one of systemic self-knowledge, but that does not make *sense,* and it is easier to conceptualize this wholeness as proceeding from the "Other" of God and then to ascribe to God that radiant completeness. Some critics miss the point of *The Unnamable* by identifying the "Other" as Beckett, rather than as the narrator's projection of his own intuited wholeness. By doing so they also miss the *positive* implications of Beckett's presentation of a limited whole which is embattled with the failure of language. It should be clear that Beckett is presenting the human condition at the edge of silence, that his "failures" are comical, necessary, and charged with the energy of what cannot be said. Unlike the majority of writers who have dealt with these problems, he simply does not cheat: the visions remain extra-textual. This is precisely what John Barth in his influential essay on "The Literature of Exhaustion" fails to see: systemic self-consciousness is a breakthrough, not a breakdown.

One way of understanding silence is as a category outside language, not simply as an intermission within language. Silence can indicate that language has been stymied and can thus point past itself to another aspect of experience.

The ineffable is the All both of holistic intuition and of the Universe—an All that is regularly identified as God, but that can as easily be considered an irreducible Oneness. When God defined himself to Moses, he said, "I AM THAT I AM," and in that tautology mirrored the self-evident and nonsensical quality of metaphysical statement just as he identified the gist of the conversion experience. Offering the same words men similarly enlightened would use, God implicitly linked his own self-knowledge with that of man—who is made in God's image, just as reflexive texts are made in man's, all of us sharing the same quality of systemic completeness that is the absolute and prime characteristic of the Universe.

The upshot of all this is that language and its world are in their own way ineffable; they have meaning only intra-referentially, and even that meaning can vanish when seen in perspective. All the propositions of logic, Wittgenstein argues, "say nothing."[16] The entire *Tractatus* turns out to be "nonsensical," but only once it has "been understood"; its propositions have to be transcended if the world is to be seen correctly.[17] It is, to borrow Stanley Fish's term, a "self-consuming artifact." Wittgenstein climbs the "ladder" so it can be thrown away; he articulates the inside boundary of silence, leaving the silence its integrity and the mind its job.

To climb the ladder, in this sense, means to gain access to a view some-where outside the world. Wittgenstein's propositions do not appear "nonsensi-cal" to the logical mind engaged in reading his book; rather, they show how things are. Their limitation is that they too belong to the logical world and therefore cannot say anything about the system that contains them and whose form they mirror. The *Tractatus* is an internal view of the interior. In other words, because these propositions are propositions, they can make only logical statements; one must see the system they describe from the outside of that system—make an imaginative leap. To consider what it means to say "the whole of logical space" or "the totality of propositions" is to begin to feel "the world as a limited whole," which Wittgenstein identifies as the mystical per-spective.[18]

From that perspective Wittgenstein's propositions simply manifest their limits; they are not so much nonsensical as they are tautological, asserting $x = x$. They show that they say nothing, like all tautologies. One has the illusion that $x = 2$ really *says* something, represents an advance in scientific knowledge or whatever, so long as one forgets to notice that it is the form of the state-ment—that it is an equation—that determines the statement. It is instantly reducible to $x = x$, and is thus self-evident and ineffable. Tautologies are not pictures of reality, Wittgenstein asserts, because they "admit all possible situa-tions"; they "do not stand in any representational relation to reality"; they are "unconditionally true." They are nonsensical, he argues, but are "part of the symbolism," like the 0 in Mathematics.[19]

The problem here is that a tautology is an excellent description of reality, whether or not Wittgenstein chooses to call it a "picture of reality." Reality is what exists, and we have no way of knowing whether reality admits "all possible situations." The mystical insight consists primarily in seeing that although logical statements operate logically on the logical world, there is more going on. Wonderful equations are written on the blackboard, but the black-board vanishes—or better, the equals signs reveal the equality of signs. This is comparable to the Hindu observation that the Universe is equal to itself, a statement that says "nothing" but opens the possibility of everything. One way to get to this insight is to answer "all possible scientific questions" or to describe the inevitable form of all meaningful statements—the project of the *Tractatus*:

> Scepticism is *not* irrefutable, but obviously nonsensical, when it tries to raise doubts where no questions can be asked.
> For doubt can exist only where a question exists, a question only where an answer exists, and an answer only where something *can be said.*
> We feel that even when *all possible* scientific questions have been answered, the problems of life remain completely untouched. Of course there are then no questions left, and this itself is the answer.
> The solution of the problem of life is seen in the vanishing of the problem.
> (Is this not the reason why those who have found after a long period of doubt that the sense of life became clear to them have been unable to say what constituted that sense?)
> There are, indeed, things that cannot be put into words. They *make themselves manifest.* They are what is mystical.[20]

Eliot had a related insight in the *Four Quartets:* it is "Only by the form, the pattern" that words can "reach / The stillness."[21] Meaning is made manifest in form, the way something looks from the outside and the way it feels itself from the inside. In the terms of the *Tractatus,* the form of the whole shows the reader that it is limited but makes no mystical or exterior-viewpoint statements. The same is true of each of its propositions, whose "nonsense" or tautology factor is manifest, but which makes sense when one enters it (i.e., reads it with the intention of understanding, thinks with it, shares its limits). These propositions manifest logical form but cannot describe, discuss, or represent it; logical form is self-evident in them, and therefore ineffable. Here we arrive at the crux of the problem.

As Eliot says, words "reach into the silence" only "after speech." Words move "only in time," but they have an atemporal dimension as well, one in which they are not moving and cannot die. The quality of that non-movement, he insists, is not "fixity,"[22] but rather a gathering together of all time into an eternity that is necessarily present, a stillness around which movement and time are organized and from which they proceed. This still point makes itself manifest in the dance, for instance, which cannot represent it, but which also could not exist without it. Its verbal counterpart is silence, the timeless gathering together of the inexpressibly unified Universe, the water of which we notice the wave-forms, the space where there are no paradoxes because there are no limited terms to be tricked into apparent self-contradiction. A paradox appears contradictory in terms of normal logic and the normal world, but may be self-evidently accurate in an alogical context, as when one is in the grip of a transcendental insight or conversion experience. A paradox has one kind of meaning in the logical world, which Eliot calls the world of time, and another kind based not on what is said but on what is, in the world of the still point. In the logical world, a paradox is a tension between what is said and what is trying to be said; the former is usually a contradiction, the latter a transcendental insight or the destroyer of categories.

Words reach into the silence only after being spoken—"after," not in the sense of temporal sequence, but of overtone, vibration, additional function. Their sound may still be going on, but their form addresses the silence, manifests the still point, on another level than that of logical meaning. Wittgenstein explains that process as one of formal complementarity, the fact that propositions share logical form with reality and make it manifest. One might say that they vibrate at the same frequency, that there is a tuning-fork relationship between propositions and reality.

There are many ways to deal with the ineffable, but two suggest themselves in this context. One is simply to *be*. In that condition there is no need for language and in fact no language. Everything exists; nothing requires expression. The problem, as Wittgenstein says, has vanished, and its absence may amount to beatitude. The other way is to enter time, to enter the diachronic succession of moments and then to accept its conditions: partial expression and the illusions of separate personal identity, death, history, etc. Fragmentary expression involves dividing the Universe up into separate terms and then putting them one after the other, like frames in a movie projector, in order to form in the mind of the audience a more unified image or concept. In this condition, the way to deal with the ineffable is to *speak*. Often one proceeds by using language against itself, making it aware of its boundaries, spinning paradoxes, metaphors, myths, and reflexive structures, setting images before or between mirrors, trying to get the words to see past themselves so that reader or listener can join their battle, until he too can jump levels, climb Wittgenstein's ladder and see the world. This is what Eliot means when he says that one enters time in order to conquer time. Such a notion can be related to Shankara's view of the Universe as a game whose object is to understand itself as such, that is, as a game whose point is that everything is One, differentiation and sequence being totally illusory.[23] God creates or enters time in order to discover Himself behind all the masks, and thus to return to atemporal Oneness. Language behaves the same way and has a complementary structure— except that it cannot achieve insights or return to its original nature. One might say that language needs man in order to discover itself and that reflexive fiction is one place where the masks are nearly allowed to fall. We may use language

as a mirror for ourselves and our role in the game, seeing it in relation both
to the ineffable and to silence, watching it enter the category of expression and
manifest the category of logical form, even while it points past itself to the
undifferentiated, the whole, the silence.

The ineffable is so only from the point of view of language and the logical
mind. That which is ineffable, however indescribable, is self-evident. It makes
itself manifest; it is a property of the system. A conversion experience involves
discovering the obvious. It transcends not terms but "termness"; it is universal
but incommunicable. This accounts for the gulf between the convert and the
skeptic. The skeptic can always say, "If it is so obvious and present and simple,
why can't you tell me what it is?" and the convert can always say, "You have
to discover it for yourself, but it would help if you adopted a perspective above
this level." To this the skeptic can of course reply, "That makes no sense." It
is easy to get lost in terms and to feel that they account for everything, but with
a shift in perspective it is simple to see that terms are one system and that they
are barred from representing the aterminological.

Later, in his *Philosophical Investigations,* Wittgenstein shows a concern not
so much with "the limits of language" as with "the limits of a language"—a
particular language game with its own rules and frame of reference. Many
philosophers embraced the *Investigations* as a refutation of the *Tractatus,* taking
their cue from Wittgenstein himself. It seems to me, however, that the issue of
the ineffable was not at all dismissed by Wittgenstein's change in attitude. What
he did was to complicate the presentation of what goes on within logical space,
introducing a relativist perspective in which language games have meaning in
relation to one another.

There may well be more than one kind of meaning and more than one
way of expression. Each particular language game will limit its world. Each
game plays by various internally consistent rules, and these rule-systems vali-
date each other within the totality of games. What I am suggesting here is that
the final sentence of the *Tractatus* remains valid. It is clear that from the
perspective of, say, language game 5, the statements that are sensible in language game 7 might not make sense. The ineffable can never make sense. The
many language games outlined in the *Investigations,* and the others that follow
from those, operate within logical space because they are languages, have rules,
make particular statements. They may well be illogical in relation to one
another. But there is still no language that is silent, that *has* to be silent—no
language that can dispense with fragmentation and sequence, or that can allow
a point of view to observe itself. The ineffable remains outside all language
games, unless a single syllable like *Om* is defined as a complete language. In
such a case *Om* would have to *be* the sound that is the Universe, and not be just
a reference to it; a basic assumption underlying that game would be that
something like the Hindu cosmology was correct. There would be no way of
making any other statement (there would be no otherness) and certainly no way

of writing fiction (there would be no fictions and no way of making discrimina-
tions or recombinations). Another necessary property of this language game
would be that signifier and signified are identical. The literature of the ineffable,
in contrast to the language game of *Om,* accepts the conditions of time and
fragmentation; it turns the necessary failure of its means of expression into a
way of goading and guiding the audience to an intuition of that Something
whose perfection lies partly in its inexplicability.

NOTES

1. Samuel Beckett, *The Unnamable,* in *Three Novels by Samuel Beckett* (New York: Grove Press, 1965), p. 291.
2. Wylie Sypher, *Loss of the Self in Modern Literature and Art* (New York: Random House, Vintage Books, 1962), pp. 147–158.
3. Beckett, *Three Novels,* pp. 303–304.
4. Ibid., p. 304.
5. Ibid., p. 324.
6. Ibid., p. 413.
7. Ibid., p. 414.
8. Ludwig Wittgenstein, *Tractatus Logico-Philosophicus,* trans. D. F. Pears and B. F. McGuinness (London: Routledge and Kegan Paul, 1961), 3.032.
9. *Tractatus,* 1–1.13.
10. *Tractatus,* 5.6–5.61.
11. *Tractatus,* 4.115.
12. *Tractatus,* 4.121.
13. *Tractatus,* 4.116–4.1212.
14. William James, *The Varieties of Religious Experience: A Study in Human Nature* (London: Collins, 1960), pp. 219–57.
15. We are assuming a population of right-handed subjects, for whom the left hemi-sphere is normally dominant in linguistic and sequential processing, while the right hemisphere is normally dominant in spatial and holistic processing. See S. J. Dimond and J. G. Beaumont, eds., *Hemispheric Function in the Human Brain* (London: Eleck Science, Ltd.; and New York: Wiley, 1974) for an introduction to the relevant research. For up-to-date developments in the field, see *Brain/Mind Bulletin* (bi-weekly; P.O. Box 42211, Los Angeles, CA 90042).
16. *Tractatus,* 5.43.
17. *Tractatus,* 6.54.
18. *Tractatus,* 6.45.
19. *Tractatus,* 4.461–4.464.
20. *Tractatus,* 6.51–6.522.
21. T. S. Eliot, "Burnt Norton" V, in *Collected Poems 1909–1962* (New York: Harcourt, Brace, and World, 1963), p. 180.
22. "Burnt Norton" II, *Collected Poems,* p. 177.
23. See *Shankara's Crest-Jewel of Discrimination,* ed. Swami Prabhavananda and Christo-pher Isherwood (New York: Mentor Books, 1970) for the title piece, a clear intro-

duction to Shankara's philosophy, and "A Hymn." See also Alan Watts's paraphrase in *The Book: On the Taboo Against Knowing Who You Are* (New York: Macmillan, 1967), pp. 11–14, and Shankara's other major work, the *Commentary* on the *Vedanta Sutras of Bādarāyana,* trans. George Thibaut, 2 vols. (New York: Dover, 1962).

Portions of the material in this essay appear in the author's *The Mind of the Novel: Reflexive Fiction and the Ineffable* (Princeton University Press, 1982). Reprinted with permission.